AT
THE
Sands

The Casino That Shaped Classic Las Vegas, Brought
the Rat Pack Together, and Went Out With a Bang

DAVID G. SCHWARTZ

WINCHESTER BOOKS

WINCHESTER BOOKS
Las Vegas, Nevada

At the Sands:
The Casino That Shaped Classic Las Vegas, Brought the
Rat Pack Together, and Went Out With a Bang

Cover design by Asya Blue
Layout by David G. Schwartz
Text set in Adobe Caslon Pro
Chapter titles set in Dancing Script

In memory of

Sheldon Smith
and
Alan Reed

Their love for Las Vegas and history continues to inspire.

$\mathcal{C}$ontents

AT THE *Sands*

*F*ools Rush In

The gambler was in the air, coming back to Las Vegas.

The newspapers called him a publisher and café owner. The gossip columnists called him only by his name, which in Hollywood was enough. But his friends—and his enemies—knew him for what he really was. A gambler.

Billy Wilkerson couldn't remember a time when he wasn't gambling. His dad, Big Dick Wilkerson, was a legendary gambler in his native Tennessee. In 1902, the elder Wilkerson won the rights to bottle Coca-Cola across the South in a poker game. He flipped that concession for a movie theater, which he sold for $4,000, which he promptly lost in another poker game. Big Dick, unsurprisingly, died penniless. Wilkerson had to drop out of medical school, thwarting his dreams of becoming a doctor, which had replaced his earlier dream of becoming a priest.

Wilkerson the younger was already, by this time, a confirmed, if not degenerate, gambler. Betting on ball games, card games, horses—it was Wilkerson's greatest pleasure and only real escape. Gambling also gave him a very real lifeline after his father died. A friend from medical school won a New Jersey movie theater, thanks to a World Series bet, and asked Wilkerson to manage it in exchange for half of the profits.

That break, in 1916, led to a series of jobs in and around New York's film industry (and a stint running a speakeasy) before, in 1929, Wilkerson bought a share of a Manhattan-based film trade paper. Hoping to hit a big score to finance a daily version of the paper in California, Wilkerson chose to play the markets—on October 29, 1929. Cleaned out completely, he did not give up on his dream. After relocating to California, he published the first edition of the *Hollywood*

Daily Reporter less than a year later.

This was the life of a gambler: from the top to the bottom and back again, all on the flip of a card or a horse's gallop.

Hollywood, when you thought about it, was a big poker table: A nice bankroll might get you in the game, some skill could keep you there, but it almost always came down to luck. What Hollywood sold—fame, wealth, power—could only be purchased with the currency of luck. That was just as true for a studio boss as it was for an aspiring starlet. Or a publisher.

As he looked out the window of his chartered airplane—he could still travel in style, even with five alimonies—Wilkerson thought about luck. Lately, most of it had been bad. Four hundred dollars a month, Vivian had stuck him for. Bad luck, but at least Bautzer spared him a trial with that settlement.

Then there was good luck. Like that January morning when he'd walked down to the Top Hat Café for a Coke. (He loved his Cokes. Sometimes twenty a day.) Then she walked in—the most sensual, innocent girl he'd ever seen, and he'd seen plenty. She was one of a bunch of kids from Hollywood High School across the street, cutting class and, like Wilkerson, drinking Cokes.

"Who's that?" he asked the manager.

"Her name's Judy, Mr. Wilkerson."

"Can you make an introduction?"

The manager went over and, after some hesitation, walked Wilkerson down the counter.

"How would you like to be in pictures?" the 46-year-old publisher asked the teenager.

"I don't know," Judy said coyly. "I'll have to ask my mother." Wilkerson gave her his card.

A few days later, mother and daughter walked into the *Hollywood Reporter* office, just down the block from the Top Hat. An introduction to talent agent Zeppo Marx, a word to director Mervyn LeRoy, who signed the 16-year-old to a contract, and Judy, now Lana Turner, was on her way to stardom. Not that she forgot Wilkerson or vice versa; he was the best man at her third wedding eleven years after that fateful afternoon at the Top Hat.

Some said it was a real-life Cinderella story, but Wilkerson knew it was just luck. Maybe Judy decides to stay in class that day. Maybe he's more interested in his racing form and doesn't look up at just that moment.

Luck.

Wilkerson had enough of it to make him a man to be reckoned with, which gave him entrée into private poker games, like the one at MGM production head Irving Thalberg's Santa Monica mansion, in which players could win or lose tens of thousands of dollars. It also gave him a view into what made Hollywood tick. Something, he was convinced, was missing from the town: real glamor.

And, if he was honest, Wilkerson didn't want to just be the ink-stained publisher cataloging Hollywood's deeds and silencing, for his friends, its misdeeds. He wanted to be the one throwing the party, making the connections. And what better way to do that than by opening a restaurant?

He started with Vendome, a lunch joint, but really hit his stride with the Café Trocadero, a slice of Parisian style that opened on the Sunset Strip in 1934. Thanks to publicity from the *Reporter*, the Troc became *the* place to be seen in Hollywood. Tuxedoed and evening-gowned film stars danced and gossiped, while the general public came, in hopes of seeing a slice of the cinema and maybe, just maybe, being discovered. If it could happen at a soda fountain, why not at the Troc? Sunday night "Amateur Hour" launched more than a few stars, including Phil Silvers, Jackie Gleason, and Judy Garland.

Luck.

Wilkerson chased luck in the Saturday night poker game in the Trocadero's back room. Only the biggest names were invited, and they played for only the highest stakes. Sometimes luck was with him, sometimes it wasn't. Wilkerson sold the Trocadero in 1937 after having remodeled it three times in as many years, but extracted from the new owner the concession that he and his family would be able to dine at the Trocadero for free in perpetuity.

Next was Ciro's, another nightclub, and the LaRue, a restaurant that, within weeks of its 1944 opening, became a Tinseltown institution and nationally famous. *Time* magazine ran a story on the restaurant in which its owner noted that LaRue, which had cost $44,000 to open, had earned more than $100,000 over its first ten weeks.

The money Wilkerson earned that wasn't spent on alimony (though he only had four ex-wives by this point) fueled his gambling addiction. By the fall of 1944, he was out nearly a million dollars for the year. His good friend, Twentieth Century Fox production head Joseph Schenk, sat him down for a man-to-man talk.

"If you can't stop," he advised, "get on the other side of the table. Build a casino."

Wilkerson had a vision of doing for gambling in Nevada what he had done for nightlife on the Sunset Strip. The resort he imagined, the Flamingo, would be a black-tie, glamor-filled casino that would put the existing hotels of Highway 91, that stretch of roadway south of Las Vegas that wasn't yet called the Strip, to shame, the way the Trocadero had eclipsed the roadhouses of Sunset.

Building a casino was expensive, and Wilkerson's hopes of boosting his capital at the craps tables of Las Vegas failed. So he turned to backers who brought an infusion of capital—and a new partner, Benjamin "Bugsy" Siegel. Over the next two years, Siegel pushed him out of the Flamingo. When it opened, on December 26, 1946, the "sportsman" had even crossed Wilkerson's name off the matchbooks. Wilkerson had been dealing with gamblers, racketeers, and tough guys since his speakeasy days, but no one he'd done business with matched Siegel's temper. Even Siegel's murder in June 1947 couldn't persuade him to return to the Flamingo.

But now, three years later, Wilkerson couldn't help but return to Las Vegas for a second chance. He had already sold his interest in LaRue and was ready to open a Las Vegas version of the restaurant with Nola Hahn, a notorious Los Angeles gambling operator and longtime friend. They both thought it was a can't-miss opportunity. LaRue was already famous worldwide, and there wasn't anything like it in Las Vegas. They wouldn't corner the market on a high-class dinner/late night supper place in town—they would create it.

As the plane began its descent, Wilkerson looked forward to closing the deal that would let him build a Mojave outpost of Hollywood's Parisian chic. But his fingers were itching at the thought of the city's craps tables.

***

Las Vegas in 1950 was already a far cry from Las Vegas in 1944, when Wilkerson had first envisioned the Flamingo. Only six years had passed, but much had changed. Maybe the city hadn't become a little piece of Paris in the desert, but it had grown. With the opening of Wilbur Clark's Desert Inn that spring, Highway 91 had come into its own. Joining the El Rancho Vegas and Last Frontier, which had preceded the Flamingo, and the unpretentious Thunderbird, which opened in 1948, the Desert Inn was the brainchild of Clark, a well-traveled casino dealer and operator who usually had a smile on his face.

The amiable Clark was perfectly cast as the Desert Inn's public face. The casino, though, was actually run by Moe Dalitz, who, with his associates in Cleveland's Mayfield Road Gang, had thrived as bootleggers during Prohibition before diversifying into a range of quasi-legal and flat-out illegal hustles. The Desert Inn would become, for Dalitz and those in his orbit, a chance at middle-aged respectability, a chance for him and his partners to remake themselves as builders, philanthropists, and even pillars of the small community of Las Vegas. For now, though, that was in the future. All that mattered was that this fusion of back-east chutzpah and out-west hospitality was prospering. Which itself made people take notice.

Las Vegas itself had just a shade under 25,000 people, a far cry from the 8,422 who had called it home a decade earlier. But it still retained the feel of a small town. The leading item of *Fabulous Las Vegas*, the city's fledgling entertainment magazine, might be a successful campaign by the local Red Cross or a casino cashier's Florida vacation. Flipping through the pages, you got the feeling that everyone in town was personal friends—but also the distinct impression that anyone bringing to the small town their own gifts, including that most precious of gifts, money, would quickly become a friend as well.

And there was, for a man like Wilkerson, still plenty of work to be done in rough-and-tumble Las Vegas. Sure, you might see Liberace at the Last Frontier or Peggy Lee at the Thunderbird, but more often than not it was lesser-known acts, like singer Rosalind Courtright at the Desert Inn, comedian Hank Henry at the Golden Slipper (soon to be renamed the Silver Slipper) or singing comedian Mary McCarty at the El Rancho Vegas. Food tended to be filling rather than delectable. There was no place anyone with class wouldn't be a little embarrassed to be seen. Gambling was one thing—you'd go anywhere for that, it was understood—but for a real night out, Las Vegas was sorely lacking.

Just like Hollywood had been. Until Wilkerson had changed it. Now there were a half-dozen quality joints in Los Angeles.

I should know, Wilkerson thought ruefully. *I used to own most of them.*

***

Nola Hahn had sat across the table from Billy Wilkerson more times than he could count, both playing poker and doing business. He'd bought the Trocadero from him over a decade before, and the bath he'd ended up taking on that one hadn't made him like Billy any less. But it did make him somewhat more cautious than usual.

"This place?" Hahn asked Wilkerson, not believing his eyes. "We're supposed to make this place into LaRue?"

"This place," Wilkerson reassured him.

"But...look at it." There wasn't much to look at. A card table, a dice table, a few slot machines. Sawdust on the floor. This wasn't even on the level of the Fremont Street clubs, and they would have to go to finishing school to qualify as dives.

"With enough money and Tom's help, we can make this place look like a carbon copy of LaRue." This was Tom Douglas, Wilkerson's interior designer of choice, who had worked his magic in his Hollywood clubs and, while he was still in charge, the Flamingo. "Some paint, some silk drapes—they'll think they're back on the Sunset Strip."

Wilkerson convinced Hahn they could make a go of the place. They bought the dilapidated Kit Carson club and started renovating, but brought in two other partners to spread the risk. They were Steve Pappas, a 34 year-old oilman from Missouri by way of Texas, and Bill Good, owner of Wofford Press in Los Angeles. They each had multiple interests; Pappas, for example, owned a bowling alley in Joplin, Missouri.

As opening day got closer, Wilkerson wanted less to do with LaRue Las Vegas. With perpetual money problems because of his gambling, he was realizing that, even with Ben Siegel dead and buried, Las Vegas was not a good place for him. Wilkerson focused solely on the restaurant, while Hahn took point on the casino side. They weren't looking to compete with the Flamingo or Last Frontier—just offer a few good games for the right clientele.

Hahn found himself pulled away from Las Vegas as well. His nine-year-old son and 13-year-old daughter were suddenly stricken with polio. Unable to breathe without artificial respiration, they were fighting for their lives in a Los Angeles hospital. Hahn still commuted to Las Vegas, supervising the renovation and hiring the casino staff.

Meanwhile, architect Stanley Harris and designer Douglas succeeded at turning the sawdust joint into a model of Parisian sophistication. After four months, LaRue was ready to open. The décor, naturally, was as completely and authentically French as was possible in Nevada. Shortly before the New Year, Wilkerson, Hahn, Good, and Pappas were ready to open the doors. Las Vegas was finally going to get a taste of France.

With any luck, the town would love it.

***

LaRue officially opened on Saturday, December 23. This was not the best time to open.

Still, LaRue was as authentically French as Wilkerson had hoped. The two doormen were dressed in uniforms that were duplicates of those worn by the *gendarmes*, down to the buttons.

"Where'd you get the idea for those?" a reporter interrupted Wilkerson as he was explaining about the doormen, gesturing at a nearby cocktail waitress. Their uniforms, truth to be told, showed a little more skin than was usual in Las Vegas.

As a strolling band of five troubadours serenaded the diners, Wilkerson looked over the restaurant. Tom Douglas hadn't let him down: The place looked as fine as anything he had seen in Paris. The chefs had been imported directly from France. And the casino, from the croupiers' uniforms to the selection of games, rivaled Monte Carlo.

And the place was packed—with starstruck locals, though, not well-off Angelenos. "It's the most beautiful restaurant on earth," Wilkerson heard a Las Vegan gush.

But once the locals figured out that they weren't going to be dining next to Gregory Peck or Lana Turner, they stopped coming. Within three weeks, Wilkerson and Hahn instituted conflicting changes intended to lure diners back. On one hand, they offered a $3 dinner. That wasn't exactly cheap—the El Rancho Vegas had its famous $1 all-you-can-eat buffet, and the Silver Slipper offered a five-course meal for $2.50—but it was approachable for residents who might otherwise be intimidated by French cuisine. On the other, they doubled down on the French atmosphere. Wilkerson brought in Jack Scholl and the Gypsies, whose European pedigree was sealed by the Magyar/Gallic piano and accordion stylings of the Hungarian-born Paul Gardos. Nola Han added chemin de fer in the casino. A player-banked version of baccarat popular in French casinos, it was a bit of a novelty in Las Vegas, the game made all the more exotic because of the set of mother-of-pearl gaming chips Hahn had imported from Europe at a price of $10,000.

Perhaps because of these mixed signals, LaRue struggled. Good, cheap food could be had at so many places in town, and gambling was everywhere. Getting dressed up to go out to eat exquisitely prepared French food just didn't have much appeal.

Wilkerson was around less and less. Partly it was LaRue's moribund performance, partly his continued losses at the tables, but partly it was because, even when he was winning, he didn't want to be away from Los Angeles. He started wooing Beatrice "Tichi" Noble, his maid's daughter. It didn't matter that he was 61 and she was 25. He wasn't lucky in Las Vegas…maybe he would be lucky in love. He was. They married in February.

The Saturday before he tied the knot with Tichi, Wilkerson formally sold his interest in LaRue to Steve Pappas, who, with Hahn, served as on-the-ground host and manager for the restaurant and casino, respectively.

Pappas introduced some more changes. LaRue now advertised "superb food at sensible prices" in a place "where continental charm prevails." By mid-March the mononymous Emile had replaced Wilkerson's hand-picked maître d', Richard Hubert. And Jack Scholl's Gypsy Ensemble was replaced by the band of Sunset Strip veteran Frankie Ortega, who played instrumental versions of popular songs.

None of this was enough to change LaRue's luck. The atmosphere was sophisticated, the food second-to-none, and the tables empty. In April, a new maître d', Johnny Saranto, arrived. He was renowned for his table-side-prepared Roquefort dressing, famous for its "suspicion" of garlic.

Pappas and Hahn, unfortunately, couldn't get even a suspicion of profits. Shortly after hiring Saranto, they were no longer buying advertising. As Wilbur Clark and Moe Dalitz toasted the one-year anniversary of the Desert Inn, LaRue's owners simply hoped to last another week. Things looked grim.

But this was Las Vegas, where luck gives anyone hope.

***

It's a misconception, maybe from watching too many movies, that the last bet is dramatic. We're conditioned to accept a certain pace to a desperate gamble, with stakes escalating in a climactic showdown. A royal flush beats aces full.

That's not how it usually ends up. Gamblers just keep plugging away until their bankroll is depleted. It might be that final chip, swept by the dealer when you bust after hitting a 13, or those last few cents played in a slot machine. It's the sound of a penny dropping.

Thus it ended with LaRue. Pappas and Hahn kept up the good fight as long as they could. By May 1951, it was obvious that LaRue was not catching on with locals or visitors. When Hahn couldn't make payroll and Pappas and Good were no longer willing to throw good money after bad, it ended.

A few weeks later, the partners were liquidating the fixtures. Even the walk-in refrigerator. "Like new," the classified ad read. "Used only six months. See at LaRue restaurant, on the Strip." Another Las Vegas dream, ended.

Billy Wilkerson found something more fulfilling than a lucky streak that October, when Tichi gave birth to a baby boy. In his sixties, Wilkerson knew for the first time the joys of fatherhood. Holding Willie junior in his arms for the first time did something that more bad beats than anyone could count, five divorces, and a death threat from Ben Siegel could not. The gambler stopped gambling, cold turkey. He wasn't counting on luck anymore. He just wanted to be happy.

Nola Hahn didn't have such a happy ending. He was never quite able to get back on his feet after washing out with LaRue. In 1954, he bought a share of the Rosarita Beach Hotel, a seaside resort not too far south of Tijuana. His wife Ruth died two years later.

The following year, he drove back up to Los Angeles, checked into the Beverly Hilton Hotel, and overdosed on barbiturates. A maid discovered his body, sprawled across the bed, next to a sheet of paper with only three words.

"Nobody to blame."

It was the stoicism of the true gambler who knew that the wheel of fortune never stopped spinning. Life had given him money, success, love, then taken it away. These things happened—nobody to blame. And it might have been the epitaph for LaRue's as well. Wilkerson and Hahn thought that visitors to Las Vegas—and locals too, for that matter—were starved for sophistication, for elegance.

They were wrong. People coming to Las Vegas in 1950 didn't want a place to see and be seen. They wanted a place to relax, a place that felt like home, if they treated you like a winner at home.

Winner might be a loaded term. Las Vegas, as has been said, isn't built on winners. The whole concept of a gambling casino is predicated on the fact that patrons will lose money playing negative expectation games. Casinos today report their "win," which is, more accurately, the money lost by gamblers. Higher win is seen as a good thing, boosting company profits and bringing money into state tax coffers. The less successful visitors are, the better Las Vegas does. So in Las Vegas, a real winner isn't someone who bets big and beats the house; instead, it is someone who is successful enough that they can afford to brush off big losses.

So it might be fitting that a big winner would eventually get involved with the now-shuttered LaRue and open a hotel over its bones that would give not just Las Vegas, but America a place where they could, if only for the weekend, feel like winners.

Anyone With a Million Dollars

In Las Vegas, a good idea and a decent bankroll can get you far, but having the right friends is more important. Or, in some cases, not having the wrong friends.

Case in point: Mack Kufferman. He was the sort of man who Las Vegas, circa 1951, should have loved, with the indistinct background that seemed tailor-made for investing in a casino: He was variously described as a "New Jersey liquor kingpin" and "Palm Springs millionaire." Kufferman established himself in Southern California in the 1940s and by 1950 was a fixture on the Palm Springs social scene, with his family written up in the society columns and his house's landscaping featured in newspaper spreads on xeriscape gardening.

In general, though, Kufferman had mastered an art dear to Las Vegas casinos owners of that era—the art of being as unobtrusive as possible. Even his appearance seemed calculated to avoid scrutiny. He was tall but not too tall, stocky but certainly not fat, his hair receding but not enough to say he was a bald man, or even balding. He had the broad, doughy face that would have perfectly fit a deliberately bland character actor of the era. You've seen this guy, but you can never remember him.

Being unmemorable was a virtue in Las Vegas during those years because for casino owners, most press tended to be bad press. For that matter, as far back as Prohibition, any news about gamblers was, by definition, bad news. In matters outside of officially sanctioned public relations, Las Vegas adopted this same attitude since national news about Nevada gambling was rarely positive.

The powers that be in Nevada—in those days a mixture of state legislators, Clark County commissioners, and the Tax Commission, which licensed gaming operators and ostensibly policed the industry—

were particularly leery of media attention in late 1951. The previous year, an ambitious junior senator from Tennessee, Estes Kefauver, had focused the nation's eyes on what he believed was a growing problem that deserved the kind of serious inquiry that could force changes in public policy or, at the least, get him into the White House. The United States Senate's Special Committee to Investigate Organized Crime in Interstate Commerce, which met from May 1950 to September 1951, indeed delivered publicity to its chairman. Around the nation, Americans huddled around television sets and even crowded into movie theaters to watch the Kefauver Committee, as it was popularly known (no doubt to the delight of its attention-seeking chair).

In its open sessions, the committee's modus operandi was to elicit testimony from a range of witnesses, from police officers to reputed mob chieftains like Frank Costello, who famously refused to allow his face to be broadcast on television. That the cameramen focused instead on his hands somehow made his testimony all the more menacing. One year later, the committee could be said to have accomplished its goals: The public knew more about organized crime, and Estes Kefauver was named by his countrymen as one of the ten most admired men in the world, putting him alongside Albert Einstein, the pope, and General Douglas MacArthur.

By the time the committee had called the last of its more than 800 witnesses, a picture had emerged of a country whose domestic prosperity and tranquility were being threatened by a nationwide criminal conspiracy called the Mafia. This group was far more dangerous than could be imagined. Fueled chiefly by money gambled illicitly by otherwise law-abiding citizens, the Mafia, which was also a major narcotics trafficker, fostered political corruption in cities across America, and, what's worse, had begun to infiltrate legitimate businesses. Even though they might not be bootlegging liquor or gunning down rivals as in the Prohibition days, the Mafia was deadly.

Las Vegas did not emerge unscathed. Kefauver conducted one day of closed hearings in the post office building (today the Mob Museum), during which his committee solicited testimony from a handful of witnesses, some forthcoming, some exasperatingly vague, and held three press conferences. Given that the committee's starting point was the harmful effects of gambling on society, it took a dim view of Nevada's curious experiment with legalizing and taxing gambling. In the press conferences that preceded and followed the day's closed testimony, committee members expressed their dismay that Nevada had given criminals the cover of respectability. It was no surprise, then, that when the committee issued its report on the Nevada hearings, it concluded, "As a case history of legalized gambling, Nevada speaks eloquently in the negative."

Ironically, Kefauver helped Las Vegas more than anyone else. The spotlight his committee focused on illicit gambling forced the closure of many illegal operations around the country, which was a boon for Las Vegas: Those who had worked and invested in those operations brought their talents and checkbooks to the desert. Their players were not long in following. But still, the threat of Congressional action that could throttle Nevada's gaming industry was very real. State officials kept this in mind as they reviewed applications for new casino investors.

***

So, needless to say, everyone in Nevada was eager to avoid any further scrutiny, and being adept at not being noticed was good if you wanted a casino license. On the surface, this boded well for Mack Kufferman who had not only no police record, but not much of a public history at all. So it was with some confidence that Kufferman bought the closed LaRue and began a substantial renovation of the property. Kufferman planned an enlarged casino and a new showroom, with an adjacent apartment complex to be built by Californian Paul Truesdale.

There was just one problem. Kufferman had, in some quarters, a lingering odor on him. He might effortlessly charm the local power brokers at the Palm Springs Racquet Club, but no one in Nevada wanted to read headlines about a former Garden State liquor magnate buying into the casino industry. The state's official policy was that past association with alleged mobsters was not an inherently disqualifiable act; gambling-based offenses were considered especially innocuous. Even convictions for having masterminded illegal gambling operations could be hand-waved away.

"The man gambles. That is no sign he shouldn't have a license in a state where it is legal." Last Frontier owner and Tax Commission member Bill Moore told the Kefauver committee in reference to Detroit's Mert Wertheimer, who had been granted a Nevada gaming license despite his notoriety elsewhere. This was, he said, the "basic policy" of the state, much to the consternation of the committee.

A bit of notoriety for having run a craps game or ten was one thing, but being tarred with the brush of "undesirable associations" was another. Joseph "Doc" Stacher learned this even before Kefauver shined the light of national attention on Nevada gaming. He was denied, in 1950, a license to buy a Reno gambling hall because, as Moore explained to the Kefauver Committee, he had questionable "associates in New Jersey." To openly say so would be the height of indiscretion, but Moore plainly meant Stacher had mob ties.

Indeed, Stacher had, since the Prohibition days, been not only an accomplished rumrunner and gambling operator but an intimate of Meyer Lansky. Lansky, dubbed "the chairman of the board of organized crime" by the *Miami Herald*, was indeed a figure whose power, like his wealth, could only be estimated and never directly measured.

Stacher himself, however, was no slouch. Nicknamed "the Professor," "the Judge," and "the Brain," his counsel was widely sought by a range of underworld movers and shakers. And, unlike Lansky, he generally succeeded in keeping himself out of the papers.

"Go ahead—hold another press conference," he would tease his lifelong friend and business partner.

But Stacher couldn't make himself completely invisible. So, when it came out that he and Kufferman were friends, all bets were off. The Tax Commission, which licensed all gaming operators, demanded to know just who was really behind Kufferman's ambitious plans when he applied for a license in December 1951.

"I'm the sole owner," he insisted. "Stacher has no interest at all. Yes, I know him, but he's not involved in LaRue at all."

This wasn't at all what the commissioners wanted to hear. Moore, still smarting from his grilling by the committee a year earlier, wanted nothing to do with anyone who even knew Doc Stacher's name. On the other hand, the possibility of someone opening LaRue, putting Nevadans back to work, was inviting. The commission didn't outright deny Kufferman a license; it simply deferred action on his application, with a message—which its members thought was crystal clear—that he would have to find a way to distance himself, and Stacher, from the project.

Kufferman, confident he had done nothing wrong (after all, he was a respected citizen in Palm Springs), reapplied the next month. The commission, almost without comment, again deferred the application— ironically, on the same day that a "Kefauver for President" club was announced in Las Vegas. Kufferman threatened to sue if he was denied a license without cause.

In April, after what it called a thorough investigation, the Tax Commission formally denied Kufferman a license, just as Kefauver was beginning a West Coast swing to wrap up primary votes ahead of the summer's Democratic National Convention. As was usual, the commission made no public explanation of its denial. Kufferman continued to insist that he would ultimately be vindicated and pledged to continue work on LaRue, which he had enlarged from a $500,000 remodel of Wilkerson's original restaurant to a $2 million resort-casino.

Kufferman's struggles with the local authorities grew as quickly as his budget. Only three days after he announced his attention to appeal the Tax Commission's denial, the Clark County Planning Board denied his request for a 10-foot variance that would have better aligned his "club," as the project was now described, with the Los Angeles Highway.

"I'm the one who's hurt in all this," a crestfallen Kufferman told the board. "It's going to cost me $20,000 to change the plans." In proportion to the $2 million project cost, that might not seem like a deal-breaker, but for Kufferman, it was just another slap in the face.

"That's tough," is all he could say when the board turned him down. The following day, he pledged to appeal this decision as well.

"I don't get it," Kufferman groused to his attorney, Cal Cory. "Moe Dalitz got a license here, and plenty others. I've never done anything wrong."

***

In truth, it wasn't anything Kufferman had done that squashed his chances in Las Vegas. It was where he was from. The powers-that-be, who affected cowboy dress and mannerisms even when they had never actually roped cattle for a living, didn't want the stench of New Jersey hanging over their state. It's not that they minded East Coast money. But, with the new attention brought by Kefauver, a former liquor dealer from New Jersey wasn't the best face to put on a substantial new development.

"And bosom buddies with Stacher, for crying out loud," Moore fumed to his fellow Tax Commission members. "Frankly, there's no way that fellow can get a license. Not with Kefauver running for President."

Kufferman was further hobbled by his choice of local representation.

Cal Cory was a well-liked local attorney who would rise to the position of general attorney for Nevada for the Union Pacific Railroad, a major employer. But he wasn't connected to the real power elite, the cowboys who decided who could do business with them and who couldn't.

As Ben Siegel, Moe Dalitz, and several others had learned, there was a right way to approach the cowboys. First, you made it clear that you would be far in the background—there was a reason that Wilbur Clark's name was on the Desert Inn and not Moe Dalitz's. Second, before you started building, you reached out to the right people. Clifford Jones, for instance, was an essential man to befriend. When Kufferman applied for his license, Jones was both the sitting lieutenant governor and a part-owner of the Thunderbird casino hotel. He earned the nickname "Big Juice" because of his connections. If you wanted to enter the Las Vegas gaming fraternity, to do so without Jones's approval was foolhardy.

The real money behind the LaRue project, however, which came not from Palm Springs or even New Jersey but from New York and Florida, was not to be denied. Meyer Lansky, a major part of the coalition that was coming together to fund the new casino, had, after all, consented to take on Jones as a partner in the Thunderbird, which he secretly had a major interest in.

"Too many New Yorkers," Lansky said. "We've got to give them a cowboy." The problem was, he needed someone they could trust, both to properly run a multimillion-dollar casino and not to get any ideas about who was really in charge.

Luckily, a man who fit that Stetson, was an adept gambler, and no stranger to Lansky and his associates could be found: Jake Freedman.

Freedman was an improbable cowboy. Born in Odessa, Russia, he emigrated to the United States with his family as a teenager, settling in Texas. Not happy as a street corner banana vendor, Freedman gravitated toward gambling as both a pastime and a profession. He first worked with a group of operators on Galveston Island, Texas, which was at the time notorious for its gambling. Freedman then shifted his focus to Houston.

As a bellhop at Houston's Rice Hotel, Freedman did more than tote luggage: He organized a sophisticated array of ostensibly illegal games, developing a client base that appreciated both his discretion and his eagerness to both take and place bets on just about anything. When one of his customers, news publisher William Hobby, ran for governor in

1918, Freedman helpfully organized the city's bellhops in his support. Hobby's victory certainly didn't hurt Freedman's prospects.

Freedman, who became a citizen after serving in World War I, prospered in Houston despite his propensity for gambling, partially by taking advantage of investment tips shared by his customers, which included advice about oil wells. Thus the diminutive gambler added "oilman" to his resume. By the 1930s, Freedman was nationally known for owning a stable of racehorses that competed across the country. He was esteemed as "the prince of Houston gamblers," with such influence that by not withdrawing his funds from Judge James Elkins' First National Bank during the Great Depression, he was credited with saving it.

The wealthy, politically connected Freedman reached his zenith with the Domain Privee. Opened in 1940, the Domain was an illegal casino housed in a Southern colonial mansion on a section of Main Street just outside Houston's city limits. Surrounded by a high fence and landscaped series of gardens and lawns, the Domain—which doubled as Freedman's home—had a strict admissions policy: Only the richest and best regarded members of Houston society were allowed entrance, and never more than 50 at a time.

Columnist George Fuermann described "Little Jakie" as walking around with as much as $100,000 in his pockets, using thousand-dollar bills as his "calling card."

"To say that Jakie's place is first class," the columnist wrote in his 1951 book *Houston: The Land of the Big Rich*, "is practically embarrassing to Jakie." His casino was on par with those in Monte Carlo, Paris, and Palm Springs. "Far less than a tenth of one percent of all Houstonians have ever been inside the Domain Privee. Almost the only way to get in is to have so much money that you have to weigh it. A poor man simply cannot get in Jakie's place. Not even a middling rich one. Just the Big Rich."

"Mr. Freedman is not home," visitors were politely told if they did not pass muster. The half-dozen armed guards known to be on the premises ensured their exit would be quiet.

And yet not even Freedman's formidable position in Houston's elite could protect the Domain Privee from the crackdown that followed the Kefauver Committee. So, when he heard that there might be opportunities in Las Vegas, he was all ears. Indeed, he had been coming to Las Vegas for years, but started raising his profile. In April,

1952, *Fabulous Las Vegas* reported that Freedman, an "oilionaire and sportsman" from Texas, had checked into the Desert Inn.

"There's one man who has achieved many friends from his personality alone," publisher Jack Cortez rhapsodized. "We hope he will someday settle here and become a staunch localite."

At the same time, the Tax Commission became increasingly insistent that it wouldn't license Kufferman.

"I own 13 corporations," he complained to anyone who would listen. "Who are they to do this to me? I've got a Dun and Bradstreet rating of $8 million. I could buy and sell this whole town."

Initially, Kufferman proposed hiring Freedman to run the casino. That, however, was not satisfactory to the cowboys. He then offered to sublet LaRue's gambling operations to Freedman. Still not good enough. Meanwhile, work on the project not just continued, but expanded. It was now not just a casino and restaurant, but a full-fledged hotel, and it had a name: The Sands.

In June, Freedman officially applied for a license to run the Sands. He sat for a 90-minute interview by the Tax Commission in which he sketched out his history at the Rice Hotel and in Galveston, as well as his major horseracing stable and his ownership of several oil wells.

"The Domain Privee," he explained, in his Yiddish-accented Texas drawl, "was a country club. Oilmen, cattle millionaires. Only the best."

When asked why he had sold such a thriving concern, Freedman blamed the weather.

"The wind began to change," he said. "There has been trouble at Ft. Worth and Galveston and I didn't want to get in trouble at my stage in life so I sold out."

The Tax Commission certainly appreciated Freedman's honesty. Instead of Kufferman's vague assurances that he was "only friends" with Stacher, Freedman was willing to name names and come clean about his partners. He was helped, too, by his choice of local attorney. The Arkansas-born Harry Claiborne had first come to Las Vegas as a military policeman at the gunnery range. Following the war, he became first a police officer and then deputy district attorney. He was only a few years into a private practice that would see him represent a range of high-profile clients, from Benny Binion to Frank Sinatra.

"This fella's a thoroughbred," Claiborne told the commission. "Nearly forty years a gambler, and not arrested once." The seven commissioners agreed that this was their kind of man.

But neither Claiborne's Arkansas drawl nor Freedman's volubility got him a license—at least not yet. His application was deferred, the Tax Commission explained, because they hadn't had time to conduct a thorough investigation. This would take some time. Even though Freedman had pledged to keep Kufferman completely at arm's length—he proposed leasing the property from him and not involving him at all in operations—this wasn't necessarily going to be good enough.

At its August meeting, the Tax Commission, almost reluctantly, denied Freedman's license application.

"We can't," commission member Robert Allen told Freedman and Claiborne, "approve any license for this hotel as long as Kufferman is involved in any way." The intimation was that Freedman would be merely a front for Kufferman and, by extension, Stacher.

"I've been a star all my life," Freedman protested, though he was too much a gambler to lose his composure when the stakes were so high. "And I'm not going to be a stooge for anyone at this late date.

"I'll tell you exactly who's going to be working for me: Eddie Levinson, Ballard Barron, Sid Wyman, Jack Entratter. You say no at any of them, they never set foot in the place."

Again, not good enough.

But that didn't mean it couldn't be made good. Freedman wrapped up negotiations to buy Kufferman out completely in September. The $789,850 purchase price allowed the millionaire a $70,000 profit, free and clear, after all of his expenses. And so he went back to Palm Springs, shaking his head at the unfairness of it all.

That month, the Tax Commission met once again to consider Freedman's application. This time, they said yes—with two provisions. Freedman had to swear not to engage in gambling in any other state and not hire or accept investment from anyone the commission found undesirable. This was codifying Freedman's earlier offer to vet all key employees with the state.

He (or Stacher) chose those employees wisely. Ballard Barron had come to Las Vegas in 1941 from Seal Beach, California, to run the gambling at R.E. Griffith's under-construction Last Frontier. The Texas-born Barron prospered in Las Vegas, becoming a known and respected member of the community. He was always helping out, serving on the wartime Red Cross fundraising committee, buying a block of tickets to a Damon Runyon Cancer Fund benefit, throwing dinner parties along with his wife, Beatrice. Barron had left Las Vegas for Long Beach the previous year, but associating him with the project brought a measure of goodwill. Barron did not ultimately take a position with the Sands, but remained close enough friends with Freedman that, after Barron's 1954 death, Freedman organized a memorial fund.

Ed Levinson was a veteran gambler, who had run gambling operations in Michigan, Florida, and a few other states, but had not even crossed paths with anyone involved with organized crime—at least on paper.

"I never got involved with any syndicates," he insisted, and his lack of a rap sheet was all the proof the Tax Commission would ask for.

The Tax Commission duly licensed Levinson in December to own a nine percent share of the property. He would remain involved with the Sands until his departure to run the Fremont Hotel.

Sid Wyman, too, had an extensive gambling background. Considered the premier bookie in the St. Louis area, he had decided, in the aftermath of the Kefauver Committee, to move to Las Vegas, where he could pursue his trade without restriction. Wyman, a lifelong tennis player and sports enthusiast, was only briefly involved at the Sands. After getting his gaming license there, he held shares and management responsibilities at the Royal Nevada and Riviera before buying a major share of the Dunes, which he controlled for 17 years.

Barron, Levinson, and Wyman were all good hands. But none of them could run a showroom or build the kind of excitement needed to stand out in an increasingly crowded town.

Jack Entratter, at 6'4," 240-plus pounds, stood out most places he went. Born in New York in 1914, he started in show business as a theater usher before working at the French Casino nightclub in Miami Beach. He then returned to New York, where he worked as a bouncer at the New York branch of the French Casino, then as a host at Sherman Billingsley's acclaimed Stork Club before, in 1940, joining nightlife impresario Monte Proser as a part-owner of the Copacabana. Entratter soon became the club's general manager, in charge of everything from hiring the entertainers to making sure the liquor was stocked.

Also a part-owner of the Manhattan nightspot was Frank Costello, the reputed boss of all bosses of the New York mob. While Costello's interest wasn't publicized, it was not unknown. Certainly, having Costello as a partner helped prepare Entratter for his career in Las Vegas, where silent partners often had major influence.

His twelve years at the Copa made Entratter a well-known show business figure, with connections that would be the envy of any theatrical producer. Certainly he was a man, like Jake Freedman, who was not stingy with favors, who knew the value of cultivating friends in high places, be they booking agents, police captains, or state senators.

But there was something else about Entratter that made him perfect for the Sands. On paper, a nightclub manager, dealing with prima donna entertainers and catering to the tipsy revelers, might seem like an effete, almost unmanly occupation in rough-hewn Las Vegas, especially to the cowboys, real and wannabe, who granted gaming licenses. What could a man who "worked" in a showroom have in common with men who sweated and labored in the brutal Mojave heat? In Entratter's case, everything. His flat feet, for which he had special prosthetics made, betrayed the years he'd spent hustling his ample physique from table to table, making sure everything was just so. He had a warm smile, a firm handshake, and the solid bulk that quietly said that if things somehow got less than polite, he was perfectly capable of taking you into a back room and beating the ever-loving shit out of you himself. Not that it would ever come to that: This was a man who lived to see his fellow man happy. But Entratter's physical prowess earned him, whether they realized it or not, the respect of the cowboys.

So, to run the restaurants and fill the showroom, Jack Entratter was a wise choice.

License in hand, Freedman could steer the project toward its opening. He promised a mid-November opening, although Stacher continued to call most of the shots, far out of earshot of the authorities. Costello, "Jimmy Blue Eyes" Alo, and other figures in the underworld also had interests in the project.

But, as far as the newspapers and tax commissioners were concerned, Jake Freedman was in charge. That was fine for all concerned. It was time to make money for everyone.

You and the Night and the Music

Meyer Lansky and Doc Stacher, with others, saw that the Sands had real potential. It could be more than the Flamingo, more than the Thunderbird. New York money and know-how, Texas gambling bonhomie, Hollywood glamor: The Sands could be something else entirely. The time was right, and, as Lansky knew from experience, timing was everything.

For a while, it looked like Estes Kefauver might ruin everything, but the cowboys came through. Thanks to the vigorous opposition of Nevada's Congressional delegation, Kefauver's proposals were blunted. The only anti-gambling laws that passed, an excise tax on sports wagering and restrictions on the interstate shipment of slot machines, were an inconvenience. Las Vegas had faced the worst and survived. If Estes Kefauver hadn't stopped the dice from rolling on Highway 91, no one could.

So by early 1952, it made sense to build a casino in Las Vegas that could show the country just what the boys could do, given enough open space. That meant not just a casino for serious gambling but also top-notch entertainment. By fusing underground capital, Texas gambling hospitality, and Manhattan nightlife, the Sands could demonstrate the possibilities of this stretch of desert road.

The Tax Commission's spring 1952 balkiness over licensing first Kufferman, then Freedman, obscured the real story—just how confident the real money was in the concept of the Sands. From the time that Kufferman first applied for a license to the September day when Freedman officially took possession of the Sands, the project expanded from a simple remodel and expansion of Wilkerson's LaRue to a full-fledged resort and casino, which meant enough of the right people were sufficiently convinced that the Sands could be profitable.

One of the best qualities of Lansky and Stacher—and their friends—was that they knew what they didn't know and didn't pretend otherwise. When they wanted something built, they hired an architect, hired a contractor, and left it at that. Sure, they might get creative with financing or procuring materials, but when it came to the nuts and bolts of design, they were content to let the experts draft plans and pour concrete. These weren't dilettantes who fussed over the drapery or demanded change orders. You hired people you could trust and trusted them to do their job.

In this case, Kufferman did exactly that, bringing on Wayne McAllister as soon as he closed on LaRue. McAllister was a known quantity, arguably the best in the nation at building the kind of place Kufferman's associates envisioned. Since designing Agua Caliente, a Mexican gambling resort, as a teenager in 1928, he had become a specialist in restaurants and casinos despite a lack of formal training or credentials. He had several hotel, nightclub, and restaurant commissions in Southern California, running the gamut from drive-ins to exclusive nightspots. He was also no stranger to Las Vegas, having designed the El Rancho Vegas, which, in 1941, was the first resort built on Highway 91, a stretch of road that by the time he came back to work on LaRue was already being called the "Las Vegas Strip." Interestingly, McAllister assisted Ben Siegel and his associates (which included, at a distance, Meyer Lansky) in remodeling the El Cortez on Fremont Street and declined a commission—his first—to take over the under-construction Flamingo after Siegel pushed Wilkerson aside. Reportedly, Kufferman had been Siegel's envoy. Then, McAllister had said no, but this time, he said yes. In the interim, he had designed the first plan for the Desert Inn for Wilbur Clark, before the project stalled and was taken over by Moe Dalitz and his Cleveland associates.

Neither Kufferman, Freedman, nor Entratter offered much input into the design process. They didn't much care about aesthetics. So long as the architect kept within his budget, McAllister had carte blanche. The designer conceived a look along the lines of his Los Angeles restaurants—modern, car friendly, and sophisticated.

Initially, the project was small. As of July, LaRue was a single structure with a square restaurant space called the Garden Room adjoining a cocktail lounge with a small stage. Beyond the lounge was the casino, which boasted only a dozen table games and 74 slot machines distributed in rows to the right and left of the tables.

By the time Jake Freedman and Jack Entratter came aboard, the project was unrecognizable. It now was a complete resort, albeit a rather modestly sized one. From the Strip, the most visible element of the design was the sign. Along the low-rise Highway 91, signs were the most distinguishable element of most resorts. The El Rancho Vegas was known for its rooftop neon-outlined windmill. The Thunderbird sported, in multicolored neon, its eponymous avian. Wilbur Clark's Desert Inn had a massive kidney-shaped installation next to its third-story Skyroom, in 1952 still the highest point on the Strip. To stand out, McAllister knew he had to create something distinctive, something that would fit with the prevailing desert modern aesthetic without blending into the background.

McAllister's solution was a 56-foot-tall monument to modern simplicity. A rectangular pylon anchored an eggcrate grill, over which was placed the word "Sands" with an oversize "S," with "A PLACE IN THE SUN" below it. During the day, the eggcrate grill gave the sign a feeling of being there and yet not there, with the script appearing to float in the desert sky. At night, red neon and white incandescent bulbs continuously traced the "Sands" letters. At any time, the sign gave the Sands the feel of a resort that was relaxed, fanciful, and fully modern—everything that a Las Vegas hotel wanted to project. This was not a stuffy European-style gambling salon or a grubby backroom dice den. Rather, it was an elegant, contemporary, and most of all fun resort. A place in the sun, indeed.

That phrase was tied to the Sands from its inception. It was a curious choice, given that the 1951 movie by that name was based on Theodore Dreiser's 1925 novel *An American Tragedy*, hardly the prospectus for a vacation getaway. Indeed, the film ends with one member of its love triangle dead and the other plodding to his execution, a distinct downer. Divorced of its cinematic context, though, "A Place in the Sun" perfectly described just what the Sands was to be: an oasis of relaxation, entertainment, and gambling, in the exotic desert. And for years, it was an important part of the name, featured in every advertisement and many news stories. Whatever else you might find at the Sands, you would never forget that it was your place in the sun.

The Sands' main entrance made a similar impression at street level. A narrow roof jutted out over the porte cochere, providing a measure of protection from the blazing sun to arriving guests. More striking were the three dogleg pylons that protruded from the main structure. The entrance bore more than a passing resemblance to Lawry's, a Beverly Hills prime rib restaurant that McAllister had designed five years earlier, which had four doglegs. The entryway was clad in textured green Italian marble, left unfinished to better weather the harsh desert environment.

The complex was executed in a style called "Bermuda modern," a fusion of sleek lines and tropical sensibilities. The vermiculite tile used for the hotel wings' roofing was lauded for its cooling characteristics, which reportedly earned it heavy usage in Bermuda and elsewhere.

McAllister more than doubled the main building in size. The core of the old LaRue remained, with the Garden Room on the building's north side, next to the Silver Queen cocktail lounge and small snack bar. The inside of the Sands wasn't all plain lines and bold geometry. Behind the bar of the Silver Queen stood a piece of art that would only make sense in Las Vegas in the 1950s. Muralist Albert Stewart depicted a saguaro cactus, a Joshua tree, a bucking bronco and rider, and, in the distance, the mushroom cloud of an atomic blast. The lounge itself curved 108 feet along two walls of the casino. With the capacity to serve over 500 customers at a time, it had a stage that would feature, for the price of a drink, a range of singers and comedians.

The casino had been enlarged from the original plan and a lobby with a reception desk added. The biggest change, however, was the 395-seat nightclub added to the rear of the building. This, by the opening date, would be named the Copa Room. A deliberate homage to Entratter's former club, the Copa Room had what was described as a "Brazilian Carnival" motif. Recessed, nearly flush chandeliers provided light from within cutouts in the room's light green ceiling. Along the sides of the room, quasi-abstract sculptures depicting the riotous revelry of Carnival provided the atmosphere.

Behind the Copa Room were storage and mechanical facilities, whose two wings enclosed a service yard. Sunrise Terrace, a glass-enclosed area for light dining, was south of the Copa Room. Named for Sunrise Mountain, which it faced, it was easily accessible from the Paradise pool, which was named for Paradise Valley. Beyond the pool were the resort's rooms, 200 of them in five buildings, named, with deference to Freedman's history as a horseman, after famous racetracks: Arlington Park, Belmont Park, Hialeah, Rockingham Park, and Santa Anita.

Touring the property with McAllister one last time before opening, Freedman and Entratter were satisfied. He had built them a resort worthy of the trust that Lansky and his associates had placed in them. The next step was to get it open.

***

By 1952, Las Vegas casino openings had come a long way. At the 1941 opening of Thomas Hull's El Rancho Vegas, the big attraction was the roast beef, coated in two inches of rock salt and slowly cooked over charcoal. Colonel Bob Russell led a cowboy singalong at the sneak-peek preview, while Hull brought out what were no doubt to him the big guns for the grand opening, a smorgasbord of talent that included the resident El Rancho Orchestra, Pierre Carta and his Desert Caballeros, singer Lorraine de Wood, and dancers Dan Hoctor and Petite Chiquita. Five years earlier, the Flamingo had boasted Jimmy Durante and Xavier Cugat as its debut stars. In 1950, the Desert Inn opened its doors with ventriloquist Edgar Bergen supported by future *Guys and Dolls* star Vivian Blaine and comic duo Abbott and Costello. That was the bar that Freedman and Entratter had to, at bare minimum, meet.

Onstage performances were only part of the opening, though. They were important in establishing the casino as a glamorous, prestigious place for the tourists, but this was arguably the least important group that owners courted at the opening. They worried far more about making a good impression on the national media. Favorable press notices were vital to building a name for the Sands in an era when casinos did not advertise much.

The press junket would be one of the most potent tools in publicist Al Freeman's arsenal over the years. It was a self-evident business expense to fly 146 radio, television, magazine, and newspaper personalities into Las Vegas for the opening, with accommodations, food, and drinks all on the house, as well as 25 silver dollars, to gamble as they wished—or not. Needless to say, the opening would get national publicity far in excess of its actual newsworthiness.

The most important group that the opening was designed to lure, however, was significantly more discriminating than the eating press.

They also had the potential to make or break a new casino far beyond that of the kinds of people who got their news from newspapers. These were the *gamblers*. The word, as men like Freedman and Entratter would use it, didn't mean simply one who wagers on a game of chance. A hotel guest betting a dollar on roulette or his wife putting a nickel in a slot machine was not, in their minds, a gambler; they were mere tourists, to be tolerated and even humored, but never truly respected.

A gambler, to them, was someone who bet enough to hurt the house. Today, they might be called a high roller or even a whale, but back then, just "gambler," spoken with the right inflection, did the job. It was a term of respect: Being called a gambler meant you had not just the means and the fortitude to bet big, but also the confidence that, if you lost big, you were good for it. A gambler was only as good as his reputation, and in those days, a gambler would protect his reputation with his life. Being discovered as a cheat might fog that reputation, more for the clumsiness of being caught than any ethical concerns over the purity of the game. Not paying an honestly incurred debt would destroy it. For men of certain aspirations, being known as a gambler was more precious than any material wealth.

Though the law of averages said they must, in the end, lose, these men (and, in 1952, "gamblers" were exclusively male, though a not insignificant number of women gambled) could make or break a casino with their play. First, they could drop enough money to make a significant dent in the casino's significant overhead. Second, their visible presence would give the place legitimacy. Gamblers of this magnitude were known and respected by the savvier tourists, and even if they couldn't approach a professional's bankroll, being able to say that you gambled alongside Nick the Greek, or at least in the same room as him, was a hell of a story to tell back in Winnetka.

All the theatrics around Ben Siegel aside, Meyer Lansky and his partners approached their business rationally and systematically. No need to shout or threaten when the right look would do. And it bears saying that Lansky might have been the guy who put the "organized" in organized crime. Since that impromptu conference in an Atlantic City hotel back in 1929, with a few exceptions like the case of Siegel, reason had ruled the day. That meant everyone had a crystal-clear idea of what they were doing, and what their partners were doing.

The Sands, therefore, had a clearly demarcated division of labor. Jack Entratter had final responsibility for entertainment, food, drinks, and publicity—all the things that could attract and keep happy the tourists and media. Jake Freedman had a less well-defined but no less important remit: to serve as ambassador both to the gamblers and the cowboys who dominated Nevada politics. Entratter was Broadway and Hollywood, Freedman Houston, Dallas, and Carson City. Finally, Ed Levinson was casino manager, keeping the gamblers coming. No one cared much who grabbed which headline, who schmoozed which Hollywood star. All that mattered was money in the drop boxes—and that enough of it found its way back to New York, Miami, and parts unknown.

With so much money poured into the Sands, Freedman and Entratter were careful to accommodate the cowboys. They hired longtime local Matt Howard, who was also a member of the state boxing commission and a member of the Sheriff's Mounted Posse, to oversee the bar. That gave Howard power to hire two dozen bartenders and a smaller number of bar backs and porters. Making sure some of those jobs were reserved for the sons, sons-in-law, and nephews of well-connected power brokers would go a long way to keeping the cowboys on the Sands' side.

In that cooperative spirit, Freedman was perfectly happy to cede booking of the opening to Entratter, who in turn was equally sanguine when Freedman strode through the casino, tossing out thousand-dollar bills to wide-eyed tourists.

The important thing, Entratter knew, was to begin building anticipation. At the end of the night, the business was always the same: people dressed in their finest, they drank, they ate. Entertainers entertained. Then the lights went up and everyone went home. To make a night out really magical, you had to build anticipation. The Sands' opening didn't just mean there would be a seventh major resort on what was sometimes called the Las Vegas Strip, but was usually still known as the Los Angeles Highway: it was going to be the greatest event in the history of entertainment.

In Entratter's hands, even mundane human resources matters became newsworthy. In late November, from California to Georgia, papers devoted a few column inches to a simple fact: Jack Entratter was hiring dancers. The set formula for shows in Las Vegas those days was a headliner and a few complementary supporting acts: a singer with a comedy trio, a pianist, maybe a juggler. And a line of dancing women—the legendary Las Vegas showgirls—was essential. Entratter dubbed the Sands' chorus line the Copa Girls. They would be advertised alternately as "the most beautiful women in the world," and "the most beautiful women in the West." And the fact that 415 dazzling young women had descended on the under-construction Sands to audition for the 14 spots on the line became national news, thanks in part to the pouting, hopeful photo of Lorraine Carol, the first in line for the interview, circulated by publicist Al Freeman.

Similarly, Entratter turned a series of construction slowdowns that had pushed the opening back from mid-November to December to his advantage. Days before the December 15 preview opening, both the *New York News* and *Hollywood Reporter* (in what was no doubt a bitter pill for Wilkerson to swallow) made it known that the former Copacabana boss was paying 115 construction workers $15,000 a day in overtime to get the resort ready on time. An event worth that kind of investment couldn't be missed.

Demand indeed outstripped supply. In November, Entratter announced that he had already had to turn down hundreds of requests for New Year's. By the time the casino was actually open, he was able to say that he and Freedman were deep into plans to double the hotel's capacity to 400 rooms. Anticipation was that high.

***

At last, construction was complete, $75,000 worth of liquor stocked, and the gamblers en route.

The opening would unfold over three days. On Monday, December 15, the Sands would open to locals, who would be treated to a full run-through of the casino's amenities and given the chance to play. The following night, the general public would be allowed in; this included both tourists and gamblers. On Wednesday, an official ceremony would mark the resort's debut.

For the opening, Entratter had booked Danny Thomas, a veteran nightclub comic, singer, and radio star. Thomas was at the height of his powers, fresh off starring in a remake of Al Jolson's *The Jazz Singer*. Also on the bill were singer Connie Russell, making her Las Vegas debut, and dancer Lew Wills, Jr. Music was provided by Ray Sinatra and an orchestra comprised of local musicians. Sinatra, who had gained national renown as Mario Lanza's band leader, was second cousins with Frank.

The day of the opening, Entratter chartered planes that flew in press and celebrity guests from Esther Williams to Fernando Lamas for the event. Howard Hughes lent his personal Constellation, which was used to ferry a group of New Yorkers, including columnists Earl Wilson and Hy Gardner. A flotilla of planes reportedly brought in $10,000 worth of Dutch asparagus, Italian chestnuts, and Brazilian palm hearts, which would be complimentary hors d'oeuvres not just for the big bash, but for years at the Sands. All in all, the preparations cost $35,000, exclusive of entertainment costs.

The first night's festivities went off almost without a hitch, though there was one heart-stopping moment. A rare December storm downed electrical wires, plunging the Sands into darkness just as Thomas was about to take the stage. An automatic backup generator clicked on, lighting the casino as bright as midday, before even one throw of the dice was missed.

The following morning, with the help of a "miniature atomic bomb," the doors were open to the public, never to be closed, publicist Freeman promised, except by a real atomic blast. A slightly less explosive catastrophe had the potential to mar the big night, though: Danny Thomas found himself afflicted with "Vegas throat," the bane of many a singer in that dry, smoky town. He couldn't speak, much less sing. Luckily, there were a few entertainers in the house. After getting clearance from the powerful union leader James Petrillo and the American Guild of Variety Artists, an all-star troupe took the stage: Jimmy Durante, Frankie Laine, Jane Powell, Ray Anthony, the Ritz Brothers, Denise Darcel, and Eddie Jackson. With that impromptu bill, Entratter turned a potential liability into an asset, underscoring for the public first, the caliber of patron that the Sands would attract, and second, that even if the announced talent couldn't perform, they would get a night to remember.

Entertainment was, indeed, going to be the Sands' calling card. Before the opening, Entratter made public that he had spent $250,000 on entertainment for the property's first ten weeks. He had inked Thomas for three weeks at $15,000 per; Lena Horne, also for three weeks, at $13,000 per; Edith Piaf at $10,000 per week for two weeks; and Billy Eckstine also at that rate, also for two weeks. This totaled $124,000, with a similar amount spent on supporting acts, musicians, and the Copa Girls. The announcement not only let the public know that the Sands was sparing no expense to keep them entertained; it informed artists and booking agents that the Sands was in the game.

In the excitement of the opening, there was even a publicity-conscious effort at historic preservation. At the opening festivities, a few items were placed in a nine-foot aluminum time capsule: microfilms of the year's trade papers and gossip columns; a gold-plated auto jack, a reference to a signature Danny Thomas routine; Jimmy Durante's hat and a copy of his life story; a Frankie Laine record; Bing Crosby's pipe; Arthur Godfrey's ukulele; and the autobiography of Tallulah Bankhead. Throughout the coming year, more visiting celebrities would contribute items. The capsule would be buried December 17, 1953, to be unearthed in 2052.

One final point was repeated in newspapers across America: The Sands was giving money away. The day after its formal December 17 opening, newspapers reported that the Sands had lost $285,000 in its first six official hours of business. An estimated 12,000 visitors swarmed the casino throughout the day. In the first few hours, luck ran against the house. The most improbable bettors were taking the brand-new Sands to the cleaners.

"Just a bunch of nice, average people, many of them locals, wearing jeans and shorts," is how Al Freeman described the winners. "Mostly at the slot machines."

Most new businesses would hardly advertise their losses, but news of the Sands' "too loose" slot machines was calculated to drive the small stakes players who could keep the casino filled, keep the atmosphere right, into a frenzy. Even if the players had kept the entire $285,000 (they didn't), those losses were worth their weight in newsprint. The Sands would never have trouble drawing tourists.

The gamblers came, too. Syndicated Broadway gossip columnist Earl Wilson dutifully wrote that he saw, in the shade of 90 slot machines, "Gambling Society" in its glory: Ray Ryan of Texas, reputed to be the fastest gambler west or east of the Mississippi; Nick the Greek; Al Levy of San Francisco; and a host of celebrities like Jimmy Durante, Frankie Laine, Terry Moore, and Spike Jones. Some of the stars were serious gamblers; others were not, but the public was hungry for news of each.

"Miss Moore said that she had lost $20," Wilson wrote. "The report was that Ray Ryan had lost $20,000—not a large sum to him."

Freeman, dashing around the casino in his Western finery, was, by the end of the opening, positively jovial.

"We were a $200,000 loser for a while," he told Wilson. "But we overcame it." The intimation—that the casino's big wins were at the expense of heavy plungers who could afford to lose so much, underwriting cheap vacations for the tourists—would become a mainstay of Las Vegas promotion for years. Wilson claimed to be a little ashamed to have only lost $2 in the face of such gambling nobility. The mere presence of a Nick the Greek or Ray Ryan encouraged the tourists to open their wallets.

"All the loose money in America seems to be here," Wilson concluded.

Jimmy Durante summed up the mood when he shouted, "It cost $5.5 million to build this place and the bosses are burned up! It took 'em four hours to get even!"

*O*n the Sunny Side of the Street

By bringing Jack Entratter on board, the owners of the Sands were making a statement: This casino would live and die by its entertainment.

Six nights a week, Entratter would stage two shows a night, at 8 p.m. and midnight. Until 1955, entertainment was offered for no cover charge and no minimum. The showroom wasn't expected to make money, just to fill the Sands with gamblers and their friends. Entratter installed his right hand from the Copacabana, Nick Kelly (born Nicolas Fiore), as showroom reservations manager. This was the man who decided if the Copa would accommodate you. For each performance, Kelly would give maître d' Emilio Muscelli a seating chart. Emilio would be sure to direct his ushers to seat the high and mighty appropriately. While a generous tip could secure common weekenders a better view, it was only the people the Sands was really designed to please—high rollers, movie stars, and the quietly wealthy—who would be seated on King's Row, down by the stage.

After the Danny Thomas/Lena Horne/Edith Piaf/Billy Eckstine series got the Sands established, Entratter began really stretching his wings as a booker. He decided he could turn movie star Van Johnson, who had risen to stardom chiefly playing everyman soldiers, into a nightclub act. Johnson begged to differ.

"Jack," the actor said, "I don't have the right material, and I don't have the money to buy it."

"Don't worry about it," was Entratter's response. He advanced him $10,000 toward his salary, which Johnson used to hire writers to put together a passable set. Putting Johnson onstage was not actually as much as stretch as some might think; before his movie career, he had played cafés and theaters as a dancer and singer.

When Johnson opened in April, he walked on stage wearing a conservatively tailored blue suit with flaming red socks. When he danced, the audience caught glimpses of the socks, which drew laughs. With well-written comedy and a few song and dance numbers that harked back to his film career, Johnson made the audience feel that, for 30 minutes, he was a true star. Though he didn't have the sterling voice of opera singer Ezio Pinza, who had preceded him at the Copa, or the nimble feet of Gene Kelly, the audience was won over, according to a *Billboard* review, by his charm and humility. Johnson went over so well that several hotel employees took to wearing bright red socks—for a few days, at least.

Johnson made his set look so easy that two other movie people, Peter Lawford and former Copa Girl June Allyson, each decided they wanted a turn onstage as well. The night that Johnson debuted, Lawford signed a contract with Entratter.

Entratter secured another early triumph with his booking of Tallulah Bankhead. The stage, radio, and occasionally screen star might seem an odd fit for the Copa. After all, she had never performed in a nightclub before. But she was a longtime personal friend of Entratter—godmother to his daughter Carol.

"Tallulah just offered her talent as a token of friendship—am I supposed to say no?" Entratter asked. He did not add that he was paying her $20,000 a week, an increase over the then-stratospheric $15,000 Danny Thomas had received to open the hotel, and an indication of how rapidly headliner salaries were escalating. Entratter began promoting Bankhead's May debut in February, promising that when she was performing, switchboard operators would greet callers by saying, "Howdy dahleeng, Sands Hotel," a riff on her most famous catchphrase.

"Entratter's going to fall flat on his face with that booking," Broadway insiders insisted. Yet Entratter, who possibly understood Las Vegas audiences better than his critics, extended her set from one week to three.

"Dahlings," Bankhead finally said when she walked on stage, "I never thought I'd be shilling for a gambler's joint." She started with a monologue on gambling, did a five-minute version of Dorothy Parker's "Telephone Call" sketch, and sang two songs. Her singing wasn't technically outstanding, but her between-numbers patter endeared her. Audiences couldn't get enough of her, with *Variety* columnist Joe

Schoenfeld declaring, "Bankhead was banknite for the Sands Hotel."

Bankhead apparently found the nightclub stint enjoyable enough that she returned for another string of performances the following year.

The big gamble on high-priced headliners at the Sands paid off. Each new star's two- to four-week run gave tourists and gamblers alike another excuse to visit the Sands. The Copa's ambitious booking forced the other six Strip resorts to bring in their own big names. This quickly gave Las Vegas a critical mass that Palm Beach, Miami, and even Manhattan could not match. With big gamblers dropping six figures on a good weekend, casinos could afford the stars. Seven hotels with seven floor shows that rivaled anything on Broadway, plus free drinks, as much gambling as your bankroll could handle, and the occasional pre-dawn atomic fireworks—what more could anyone ask?

By the Sands' six-month mark, columnist Earl Wilson (whose syndicated column was now being published in the *Review-Journal*) reported that Las Vegas was becoming more than just a vacation spot; it was the talk of Broadway. Who was going to play where, the gossips wanted to know, and how much were they getting? Did Tallulah Bankhead have a facelift before her Sands engagement?

The Sands changed the dynamics of show business not just in Las Vegas, but nationwide. The typical nightclub had a weekly entertainment budget of $1,000, $2,000, or perhaps, $5,000. Entratter's paychecks made Las Vegas a booking agent's dream—if you could get your client into Las Vegas, you not only got them a great payday, but achieved a bump in prestige that boosted their value across the country. Closer to home, Entratter's aggressive signings kicked off a bidding war with the Sahara, which had opened a few months before the Sands in 1952 and was equally eager to establish itself. With Entratter quite publicly paying top dollar for top acts (the salaries of headliners were shared with reporters and liberally printed in stories about the Sands), anyone was fair game. In 1954, Noel Coward's agent turned down a $37,500 offer to play the Sands; the following year, he would debut at the Desert Inn.

In one case, a star priced himself out of the Sands, but found a home nonetheless. Entratter initially booked Johnnie Ray at $8,500 a week. When the opening of the hotel was pushed back to December, Ray was forced to postpone the booking. Once news of higher paydays started to circulate, however, Ray wanted more.

"I'll be happy to sing," the "Cry" singer told Entratter when asked to play the Sands in early 1953, "for $20,000."

"You're going to have to go somewhere else," was Entratter's response. Some stars might be worth that much, but Ray wasn't one of them.

Frank Sennes at the Desert Inn thought differently, paying Ray his requested $20,000. Publicists, who had once trumpeted the big bucks they were doling out, now, with more a mind on booking agents and rival entertainment directors, were forced to issue retractions: Milton Berle had not, it was reported, been getting $37,500 a week to bring his act to the desert.

Not every bet paid off for Entratter, though. The Desert Inn had done well with package shows like Sennes' Minsky's Follies, which featured mostly dancing women and no star headliner. In December 1953, Entratter brought in "The Student Prince," a package put together by Paul Small (who, incidentally, had booked Van Johnson into the Copa back in April). "The Student Prince" was a shortened "tab show" version of a 1924 Sigmund Romberg operetta that had been well received on Broadway.

Planned since June as the first of a series of tab shows that would include "Gentlemen Prefer Blondes" and a revival of the Ziegfeld Follies, "The Student Prince" starred Jan Kiepura and Marta Eggerth, who had shined as the leads 25 years earlier. With such a diverse string of successes behind him, Entratter might have thought that Copa audiences were ravenous for anything he put onstage.

This was not the case, as "The Student Prince" bombed so spectacularly that its planned three-week run ended after six nights. The leads might have once been famous in their roles, but that, as a *Billboard* reviewer's acid pen wrote, "was 25 years ago." Their voices were no longer up to the challenge. Floated as a trial balloon, "The Student Prince" was savagely punctured. Billy Eckstine was hurriedly brought on to fill the sudden vacancy. Plans for future tab shows were put on hold, although the revived Ziegfeld Follies was eventually staged.

The real reasons for the "Student Prince" debacle went deeper than Jan Kiepura's rendition of "In Heidelberg Fair" not being up to snuff. The gamblers just didn't go for that kind of stuff, Once Eckstine took over, though, the gamblers returned, and so did singers.

The tab show failure marred an otherwise magnificent first year of operation for the Copa and the Sands and proved that one fact of the gambling tables carried over to show business: No matter how lucky you had been in the past, you were only worth as much as your last throw of the dice.

***

Seventeen-year-old Judy Lee Johnson was going to the audition. End of conversation.

She had graduated high school earlier that year and was in the middle of a babysitting job when her mother, who had been a dancer and musician herself, called her.

"Come on down here," she said. "We're going to the Shamrock Hotel, and you're going to be in a contest."

"I don't want to be in a contest, Mom."

"Yes, you do. This could be a big break for you."

Johnson showed up, with her mother. She filled out an application and sat down to wait with the other two dozen hopefuls. Charlie Evans, a local gossip columnist and sometimes-publicity agent for the Sands, was in charge of the proceedings. Finally, Evans asked the girls—in small groups—to stand up, turn around, smile, and sit down. Then do it again. Then do it again. In between, the contestants chatted awkwardly and worked on their make-up.

Then, Evans called her up.

"Congratulations," he said. "You just won the Texas Copa Girl contest."

Johnson had arrived around 11 a.m. By 2:30 that afternoon, she had signed an AGVA contract and had her tickets (round-trip, Continental Airlines) for Las Vegas. She was going to be a Copa Girl.

"At the Sands, we have the girls wear only the nicest costumes," Evans told Mrs. Johnson. "You won't have to worry about your daughter. Mr. Entratter insists on a show that he wouldn't be ashamed to bring his mother to."

Nice costumes or not, this was no bit part. The headlining stars and opening acts cycled through the Copa room every two to four weeks. From the start, there was one constant in the showroom: the Copa Girls.

The institution of the chorus line migrated from London and Paris musical theater to the United States in the early 20th century. Florenz Ziegfeld, via his Ziegfeld Follies revue, was its chief popularizer. The show, which he ran from 1907 to 1931, featured star singers and dancers set against the backdrop of 120 Ziegfeld Girls, chosen more for their beauty than their terpsichorean talents. Soon, any vaudeville theater worth its salt had its own chorus line. Individually anonymous but collectively famous dancing girls became a *sine qua non* of nightclub entertainment.

Upon helping to open the Copacabana in 1940, Jack Entratter decided to distinguish the new club by creating a signature line, called the "Copa Girls." It was a group with a single qualification.

"All you need," Entratter said repeatedly, "is to be beautiful." Dancing talent could be minimal, but physical beauty was non-negotiable. With such simple prerequisites, casting calls were rarely short of volunteers. In 1957, Entratter estimated that, over the years, he had screened 48,000 applicants for a total of 4,125 jobs on the line, and paid out a total of $1,000,000.

"Any girl who is truly beautiful has a $10,000 a year job awaiting her here, and it entails just 12 minutes of work six nights a week," he said.

By that point, the Copa Girls were featured in a lavish opening number that kicked off the night's entertainment. There were other duties, too, such as taking part in promotional shoots and "decorating" the casino after shows.

For all the glamor Entratter created around the Copa Girls, recruiting and hiring them was an efficient, almost impersonal process. It started with an open casting call, sometimes in Las Vegas, but often in New York or Los Angeles. Jake Freedman's Texas roots opened up another source: Copa Girl contests in Houston, Dallas, and El Paso, like the one that Judy Johnson entered. Usually, a local affiliate—it could be a columnist like Evans or a local television station—held a preliminary screening interview. A few days later, Entratter himself would arrive, briefly talk with the remaining candidates, and choose one, a few, or no winners.

Women selected as Copa Girls signed a standard contract that specified their workload (two shows a night, with three on Saturday, between 8 p.m. and 2:30 a.m.) their pay ($150 a week, later $175, plus round-trip air transportation), and the length of their job (two weeks of rehearsals at half salary followed by six weeks onstage). Once they arrived in Las Vegas, new showgirls were housed at the Sans Souci motel across the street before they chose a roommate or two and got an apartment. Those who liked the lifestyle could sign on for another stint; those who didn't, moved on.

Entratter had no shortage of applicants because working as a Copa Girl could lead to bigger things—a function of the close relationship

Entratter had with the William Morris Agency. Over the years, several dancers had made the jump to Hollywood, and Entratter was proud to point out that June Allyson, Olga San Juan, and Lucille Bremer had gotten their starts in his line. In 1957, Entratter reported that 72 out of the 382 dancers he had hired in Las Vegas had subsequently gotten paying work in television or movies.

Entratter hired to a very specific standard of feminine beauty. The average Copa Girl, according to a 1957 *Esquire* article, was 5'4", 116 pounds, with a 32- or 34-inch bustline, 24-inch waist, and 34-inch hips. Entratter preferred a face with "small features, the American girl look, oval rather than round," framed by black hair, that the auditioner would pull away from her head to give him a better look at her face.

Such beauty was not easy to find; Entratter recalled having auditioned 500 women at one session and hiring one. Indeed, he frequently complained about the passing of "the American girl," and suggested publicly that he might be forced to start scouting for talent overseas. When he reportedly received a flood of angry letters from beautiful American girls, he split the country into ten regions, set up a national talent search, and offered lucky winners $5,000, six-month contracts as Copa Girls.

And yet times changed. By the 1960s, Entratter was even more convinced that the American girl was a disappearing species.

"There don't seem to be many beautiful girls with a burning desire to work in a nightclub anymore," he complained. "Once, it was comparatively easy to find dozens of girls who were not only gorgeous but felt that a chorus job was a wonderful way to get started in show business. Today, the girls are waiting for a break in TV or movies, and the sad thing is that the majority will wait their lives away for something that isn't going to happen." Yet he refused to compromise his principles, insisted that any girl he hire not just be beautiful, but be a "lady" as well.

Entratter's idea of ladyship was as exacting as his beauty standards. Even as other casinos from the Tropicana to the El Rancho Vegas brought on topless dancers, Entratter strenuously insisted that his dancers would never be underdressed.

"Nudity wouldn't add anything to our production," he said. "We keep our beautiful girls dressed in beautiful gowns. They feel pretty, and the audience appreciates the total effect."

Nor did Entratter like excessive makeup.

"All that eye stuff is terrible," he said. "I just won't tolerate that kind of exaggeration."

The girls were encouraged to "decorate," as they called it, the casino on worknights. Some played nickel slot machines or blackjack, others had a drink in the Silver Queen lounge or sat in the Garden Room. While it didn't matter so much what exactly they did at the Sands, the girls were strongly discouraged from being seen in any other casinos.

Sometimes, there was a bit of a disconnect between the glamorous girls onstage and the women who played slots and ate pie between shows. Once, Entratter called backstage for Judy Johnson.

"There are some men out here who would like you to sit with them," he said. "This isn't part of the job—you don't have to if you don't want to."

Johnson came out wearing a plain pleated brown dress and granny shoes. She could see by the look on her "date's" face that this wasn't what he was expecting.

Such pairings often led to real dates, and sometimes longer-term relationships. This was not discouraged, nor was the attention of the "stage door Johnnies" who would send long-stemmed roses, sometimes with pieces of jewelry, to the back. If a Copa Girl wanted to respond, to encourage a romance, there was nothing wrong with that. But Entratter drew a firm line: There was never, ever to be an exchange of cash for companionship. Any girl caught hooking was immediately fired and told to never reapply.

The Copa Girls exemplified everything about the Sands, good and bad, over its first decade and a half. It was a world of mystique, of allure, where anything could—and often did—happen. The commonplace was elevated into the legendary. And, while there was amazing freedom, there were rules that had to be followed. Six weeks at a time, the Copa Girls were living the dream—just like the gamblers at the tables, and the bosses in the back.

***

He's coming.

And that was all you needed to say, to get people excited. They knew who you were talking about, what he was going to do.

It was far from Las Vegas, in Atlantic City, a town whose best days were behind it. Every year, fewer people were making the trip "down the shore." The city was crumbling. Stars were staying away.

And yet, when Skinny D'Amato posted those billboards near his 500 Club, people walked faster, they smiled more brightly. There was hope again. They just needed to know, he was coming.

By the time D'Amato changed the billboards to read "He's here," the whole city was along for the ride, even though only a few could make it into "the Five" to hear him sing. And, when the billboards finally changed to "He's gone," the city was a little duller, even if it was the middle of the summer.

That was the power of Frank Sinatra.

Sinatra grew into something greater than a man by the sheer artistry of his singing and the power of his personality.

"Naked in the steam room," Sands casino manager Ed Walters remembered, "he was 5'7", 5'8". With lifts in his shoes, 5'9", 5'10". But when he walked on stage, he was ten feet tall."

Before he was Chairman of the Board, he was simply "the Voice," a testament to more than his exquisite tone. It was his phrasing, which borrowed equally from the jazz and saloon songbooks. Example: how his "when I propose" in the final verse of "Anything Goes" on *Songs for Swingin' Lovers* takes the song out of the exceptional and into the sublime. He didn't just know the lyrics. The Voice convinced you, this was a man who knew *life*.

On up-tempo numbers, he sang smooth, bright, playfully, like a champion boxer toying with a sparring partner in training camp. It was a joy to hear the fluidity, the technique, even though you knew something was held back. Swagger.

But, on a record like *Frank Sinatra Plays for Only the Lonely*, all of the sadness, all of the pain, all of the vulnerability was right there. Listen to "Angel Eyes" and try to deny it. This was a man who had been knocked down, and yet had, as another song went, not merely survived, but lived.

Sinatra didn't sing for the winners. He sang for the losers. Guys who had been punched in the face, kicked to the curb. They'd been hurt, but at least they had the satisfaction of having tried. He gave voice to the passed-over, the downtrodden, the busted-out. And they loved him for it.

And, by its very design, a casino, any casino, was a place for the busted out. Whatever one's accomplishments in the world, one's pedigree, one's sense of self, there was a single truth inside the casino:

The wheel must spin, the cards must turn, the dice must fall, and you must lose. A man could defy the odds, curse the heavens, flout good taste, but he could never, ever beat the house advantage. The powerful, the weak, the fearless, the timid: All were destined to lose.

So when Sinatra strode upon a casino stage, ten feet tall, he was giving strength to his people. Hearing him sing his pain and hurt made losing more than you felt comfortable talking about something noble. You were not squandering money at the craps table: you were joining Frank in his pain. It was a sacrament played across the green felt, closing the circle that had begun on stage. If dropping a few hundred, or a few thousand was all it took to feel some kinship with the man, it was, no matter what your credit report said in the morning, a bargain indeed.

But for Frank Sinatra to be the Chairman, to be the essence of cool, he needed the right stage. The Sands provided that stage. The partnership between Old Blue Eyes and the Place in the Sun would last 14 years, and it would leave both better off than they would have been without each other.

When Sinatra first played the Sands in October 1953, he was considered something of a project for Jack Entratter. Frank had attracted the gamblers in an earlier run at the Desert Inn, but his attitude had rubbed some the wrong way. Though even (most of) his detractors admitted he was a talented singer, his devotion to perfection struck some as the mark of a prima donna, and his naturally combustible temper, when mixed with his wealth and celebrity, was a cocktail best enjoyed in small doses. And that was when he was in a good mood. And, as the 1940s turned into the 1950s, he was not often in a good mood.

After shooting to fame as the idol of bobby-soxers in early 1940s, he hit a rough patch late in the decade, as his teen fans grew into adulthood and tastes changed. Frankie Laine and other "belters," who employed a more muscular vocal technique than Sinatra's "crooning," came to the fore, as did a country influence that was alien to the Hoboken-born Sinatra. The embarrassing failure of *The Miracle of the Bells*, a 1948 RKO film starring Sinatra as a priest, was a further sign that the singer was slipping from grace. Late that year, Sammy Davis, Jr. spied Sinatra, with no hat, walking down Broadway completely unnoticed. He once would have been mobbed by adoring fans.

Over the ensuing four years, the dissolution of his first marriage, the death of his beloved publicist George B. Evans, and the revelation that he owed $200,000 in taxes to the IRS, Sinatra became even more a man in eclipse. The media gloried in Sinatra's woes. Even before he threw a punch at Lee Mortimer after the columnist had alleged in print Sinatra was a mob bagman, delivering $2 million in small bills to deported mafioso Lucky Luciano, Sinatra was not a darling of the press.

To be fair, Mortimer had been prodding Sinatra for years. "His voice is all right if you don't like singing," he once wrote. The lanky singer only sold records, Mortimer wrote on another occasion, because his fans were "imbecilic, moronic, screemie-meemie autograph kids." Still, the punch ended in a trial that resulted in Sinatra having to publicly apologize to the columnist he had once called a "degenerate." If his previous antics had not, this assault on a member of the Fourth Estate earned Sinatra the enmity of Mortimer's employer, the not insignificant Hearst newspaper chain.

After all the bad years, Sinatra was, in the fall of 1953, in the midst of a personal and professional renaissance. He was beginning to find a style that fit the new decade, both on stage and on screen.

First, Sinatra moved from Columbia to Capitol Records, where he would record a series of albums that would enshrine him as perhaps the definitive vocal artist of the 20th century. Second, his film career turned around dramatically with his casting as Private Angelo Maggio in *From Here to Eternity*. Sinatra, desperate to redeem himself, threw himself into the part so completely that crew members, at some point, stopped calling him "Frank" and began referring to him as "Maggio." Ultimately, Sinatra would win an Oscar for Best Supporting Actor for the role.

Sinatra had sung for Entratter at the Copacabana in New York, and naturally planned to perform in the Copa Room. As early as May, he was at the Sands, ostensibly to chat with his cousin Ray, leader of the house band; he had already filed an application to buy a percentage of the casino. He was finally booked into the Copa Room in early October 1953. By then, the Sands was hitting on all cylinders, a stage worthy of his talents. And Sinatra's own star had begun to rise again.

Entratter had opened the checkbook for previous entertainers. But the Sands offered something to Sinatra that, on paper, was an even greater prize: a piece of the action. After months with little forward movement, Harry Claiborne, who had successfully pled Jake Freedman's case before the Tax Commission, began pushing in front of the Tax Commission Sinatra's request to buy a two percent interest in the casino.

Federal authorities long assumed that Sinatra was merely holding his ownership shares in the Sands—which eventually grew to nine percent, making him the largest single owner after Freedman, Entratter, and casino manager Carl Cohen—for a mob investor, possibly Doc Stacher, Frank Costello, Gerardo Catena of Newark, New Jersey, or Meyer Lansky—perhaps even some combination of them all. Still, Sinatra was proud to be an owner of the Sands, and grew to consider the hotel's success a sign of his own prowess as a businessman, even though he had little to do with casino operations. Dean Martin, who bought ten shares in 1961, was the only other entertainer afforded this privilege.

And yet, Sinatra was willing to let the Sands wait. Only two weeks before he was scheduled to begin his Copa engagement, he announced that he was going to cancel it if his deal to play Terry Malloy in *On the Waterfront* went through. Although Sinatra was eager for the role—the movie would be filmed in his native Hoboken—director Elia Kazan preferred Marlon Brando, whom he ultimately persuaded to take the part. This freed Sinatra to debut on schedule at the Sands, but he was undoubtedly resentful of Brando, as the film went on to win eight Oscars—including one for Brando himself as Best Actor.

Entratter may have helped Sinatra get over the sting of rejection by making him feel not just welcome, but essential, at the Sands. Sinatra got the run of a three-bedroom suite in the Churchill Downs building, then the resort's finest. If anything could be done to make the singer feel at home, Entratter did it.

Still, Sinatra's opening night was rocky: Some in Las Vegas took exception to his "rough treatment" of his backing band on opening night. The show was unusual for Las Vegas in that the opening acts, which typically numbered three, were reduced to one, the tap-dancing Nicholas Brothers, to give Sinatra an entire hour, rather than the 30 to 40 minutes most headliners enjoyed.

Sinatra, backed not by Ray Sinatra's orchestra but by an eight-piece band with Bill Miller, his lifelong accompanist, on piano, performed mostly old favorites: "I Get a Kick Out of You," "You Go to My Head," "They Can't Take That Away from Me," "This Can't Be Love," "It All Depends on You," "All of Me," "I've Got the World on a String," and "Night and Day," which he had sung on his first solo recording session 11 years earlier. The crowd loved each one, but absolutely bonded with Sinatra during his rendition of another tune that would become a signature, "One for My Baby."

Sinatra had played some major venues since the August release of *From Here to Eternity*, including Bill Miller's Riviera in North Jersey, but the proximity of Las Vegas to Los Angeles-based entertainment columnists meant this was the stage that mattered. Some of the press refused to forgive Sinatra for his past indiscretions. *Billboard's* reviewer groused that cutting out the opening acts was appreciated by his fans but "politely endured" by others, who would presumably have rather watched the Y-Knot Twirlers, a square dance octet, or pianist/tap dancer John Bachemin than have had another half-hour of the headliner.

Going further, Sean Flannelly declared that the gig was a failure: "He is a warmed-over has-been." Bill Willard of *Variety* started his review by noting that though Frank had always appealed to gamblers, "his vocals and attitude have left much to be desired among discriminating customers." While "the stamp of quality" was evident on all of the songs, Willard regretted Sinatra's "tendencies to insert dubious gags or parody lines in great established melody, and mechanically phrased offerings of humility." And there were too many slow-tempo songs, selected, Willard thought, to appeal to Sinatra's new audience.

"As he meanders down memory lane, Sinatra slams the door on his former worshippers to please an older and less exuberant set of applauders," Willard noted. But the new approach pleased the audience, as Sinatra never failed to exit to "king-size mitts."

The Hollywood Reporter's Bob Clemens offered an unqualified endorsement, saying the singer had come into his own, "with all the old feeling and new found poise." This was the consensus around Las Vegas, after the opening jitters had passed. More importantly, the gamblers adored Sinatra. The casino was packed like never before, and these audiences bet big. And in Las Vegas, you couldn't argue with that.

Following the triumph of his first stand, Sinatra had one more hurdle to face: the Nevada Tax Commission. Just after he closed his first stand at the Sands, the Commission was ready to publicly rule on his license application. This was not a done deal—the allegations that Sinatra fraternized with organized figures were serious, particularly as the state looked to avoid scrutiny post-Kefauver.

Meeting on October 30, the Commission approved Sinatra to take a two percent share of the hotel for $54,000. Interestingly, this valued the Sands at $2.7 million, even though the casino had cost $5.5 million to build and had been smashingly successful. The approval was not unanimous, though: Member Robert Allen didn't think it was appropriate to extend the privilege of casino ownership to a known tax scofflaw.

"I move that he take the $54,000 and give it to Uncle Sam," Allen said when the matter came up to a vote.

In Nevada, though, deference to the federal government carried little weight.

"I say, let the government collect its own money," responded another member, to a round of affirmations and a smile from Claiborne. Sinatra further explained that, under an IRS-approved payment plan, he was contributing $1,000 of his salary each week toward his tax debt, and had already reduced it to $90,000. That was good enough for the Tax Commission, who approved, with Allen's dissent, Sinatra's application. The kid from Hoboken was now a casino owner.

*N*ice *Work if You Can Get It*

In the early 1950s, the casino manager was the most important man (because, in those days in Las Vegas, women were not permitted to deal, much less supervise men who dealt) in the house. Like a Roman patriarch, the casino manager had the power of life and death over his dealers. There was no human resources department, no law in the casino outside of that laid down by the casino manager. If he said you stayed, you stayed. If he said you went, you went quietly, praying that you had not fucked up so badly that he put the word out.

The Sands opened with a good casino manager—Eddie Levinson, who came to Las Vegas by way of Chicago, Detroit, Covington, Kentucky, and Miami, where he ran illegal gambling, from clandestine casinos to bookmaking. This was a good choice to open the Sands. Once the casino was prospering, though, it was clear to Meyer Lansky, Doc Stacher, and their partners that it needed a manager who was better than good: Carl Cohen.

It is impossible to overstate the respect gamblers, dealers, and owners had for Carl Cohen. He was a casino manager, as Duke Ellington might say, beyond category. The best, with no qualifiers.

Cohen understood that, like water seeking its own level, money must find its way from the gamblers' pockets to the casino's drop boxes, from there to the count room, and from there to the pockets of the owners, licensed and not. His job was to make sure that happened.

When a tourist gingerly laid his ten dollars on the craps table, the house edge was all the casino needed. But the Sands was not built on tourists. The special people—its most important customers—weren't awed by the green felt or perplexed by the dealers' patter. Such special people needed special consideration, special treatment, which had to walk a razor-thin line. One couldn't be too lenient—let one gambler not pay a rightfully incurred debt, and word would spread more quickly than light—but one also couldn't be too efficient. After all, gamblers had plenty of choices, and to run off a player worth tens of thousands of dollars over a hundred-dollar dispute was foolhardy.

So casino managers must heed advice as old as Daedalus: Do not soar too high over the customers and dealers, demanding strict adherence to every rule at every time, lest they go elsewhere, but do not allow yourself to be drawn into the morass of calculated shot-taking, convenient mishearing, and deliberate stupidity that would drag you down as surely as it sank the casino's win.

Carl Cohen, above all others, was the master of walking that line. He not only accepted that money could bend reality on its way to the count room, he facilitated that journey, sometimes accelerating it, sometimes delaying it, but always with an eye to the two principles that guided him, and any other sensible casino manager.

Keep the customer happy. Protect the house.

It's easy to see how those two edicts could conflict. Countless lesser managers have been broken on this central paradox, compromising when they should have held firm, taking the hard line when they should have conciliated. But not Cohen. Even if, in the heat of the moment, the gambler didn't like his decision, he had to admit it was impossible to disagree with it.

Cohen was a bulldog of a man—over six feet tall, about 280 pounds. But his pale blue eyes betrayed a true sensitivity. Dressed in his suit, which was usually slightly too tight (he constantly struggled with his weight, usually losing), he was charm personified. Usually, Cohen did not walk, so much as float on a bubble across the floor, smiling, shaking hands, gliding from table to table by the mere power of his grace and goodwill toward all mankind.

But when something was wrong, and simple goodwill couldn't set it right, it was another story. "The deadly walk," Ed Walters, who went to work for Cohen in 1959, called it. "The walk of the man who is going to decide if you live or die."

An illustration: Don Adams parlayed his success as Maxwell Smart on *Get Smart* into a series of engagements at the Sands. At first, everything went swimmingly. Adams even celebrated his birthday at the hotel, posing for publicity pictures as he cut a *Get Smart*-themed cake with his wife and young daughter. A notorious gambler, Adams was in heaven while he played at the Sands. The laughs from the Copa crowd were all the proof he needed that he was golden.

But Jack Entratter wasn't happy that Adams wasn't working new material into his act. The Sands, after all, was the showplace of the nation, and to put over the same gags that you did in Chicago and Miami…it wasn't what Copa audiences expected.

"I know the crowd," Adams told him when Entratter suggested that some new material might freshen things up. "They laugh every time. I don't need to change."

Entratter had a word with Cohen. That night, Cohen walked toward Adams, who was playing blackjack, with deadly intent. The dealers and boxmen almost felt sorry for Adams as Cohen walked up behind him, clapped him on the back, and ushered him to a dead blackjack table where they could speak.

"Don," Cohen started, "we love you, but we really want you to change up your show. Our players deserve better."

"But they love it," Adams protested. "I'm a performer, I can feel it. You don't understand."

"That may be," Cohen said, as the dealers and assorted staff watched from a distance, "but we really need you to change your act."

"I don't tell you how to run the craps game. You don't tell me how to perform. That's what you hired me for, right?"

"We hired you to do a job," Cohen responded. "And we're telling you you're not doing it the way we want."

"I don't think you understand," Adams continued. "I'm a star. I can sell out clubs anywhere I want. I can…"

"You're right," Cohen reached over, put his hand on top of Adams'. "There is a misunderstanding here." Adams smiled, glad that he had gotten through to this numbskull. "The misunderstanding is, you think you work here. You don't. Don't worry about the show. I want you out of your room, tonight."

"You can't talk to me that way," Adams hissed.

"I just did," Cohen answered, "and you don't work here anymore. You don't work *anywhere* anymore."

Adams left the Sands. Back in Los Angeles, his agent discovered that no club would even take his calls. Not just in Las Vegas— anywhere. Cohen, through his various connections, could make sure that a nightclub didn't get its liquor, a television studio suddenly had union trouble.

Then, finally, the agent got Adams a gig at a small supper club outside Detroit—a far cry from the Copa, but beggars can't be choosers. He opened on Friday night. At 2 a.m. Saturday morning, a blaze ripped through the club.

The message was clear. You didn't fuck with Carl Cohen.

After eight months, Adams sent feelers to the Sands—could he be forgiven?

Cohen was merciful. Adams was allowed back in the Sands family—after Cohen dispatched him to the Cal Neva in Lake Tahoe for a trial run. With a newfound humility—and new material that had Jack Entratter in stitches—Adams again trod the Copa's boards.

Carl Cohen, like many of those who worked in Las Vegas casinos, had grown up in the gambling business. Born in Cleveland, Ohio, in 1913, he was no stranger to the city's gambling underworld—whose leader, Moe Dalitz, would in 1950 open the Desert Inn—though by day he drove a beer truck. Moving to Los Angeles after getting married at 18, he painted ships at the Long Beach Naval Shipyard. Then, in 1941, he and his wife Frances moved to Las Vegas, where Cohen found work at the El Rancho Vegas. This time, he was not driving a truck or slapping paint on metal—he was working the casino tables. Two years later, he bought a share in the resort and became casino manager.

And, for a succession of owners, Cohen thrived in the role, always ensuring that the customers felt taken care of and that the casino made money.

But when Doc Stacher called, you answered, and managing the Sands, already on the rise, was perhaps the best job in Las Vegas. So in early November 1953, it was announced that Cohen had "become associated" with the Sands.

One story that has etched itself faintly into myth has it that Cohen departed the El Rancho Vegas after a public, violent confrontation with majority owner Beldon Katleman. Katleman, the story has it, insisted that Cohen eject a lanky patron wearing jeans and tennis shoes from the casino. When Cohen refused (the shabbily dressed scarecrow was, in fact, Howard Hughes), he and Katleman got into a fist fight. Cohen quit, taking a number of the El Rancho Vegas's dealers and player with him to the Sands, where Jake Freedman was waiting with a job offer mere hours later.

There are several problems with this tale. The first is that it places Cohen leaving in 1955, when Cohen had in fact been managing the

Sands since 1953. The second is that no newspaper or magazine source from the period mentions what would have been a blockbuster story. Third, it is extremely unlikely that Katleman would not have recognized Hughes, one of the nation's most famous celebrities. Fourth no one with any sense would have ever, ever questioned Cohen's judgment in the casino.

Still, there is the possibility that some sort of incident involving Hughes, Katleman, and Cohen served as the pretext for Cohen's move to the Sands. Hughes was definitely in Las Vegas in 1953—he rented three penthouse suites at the Flamingo in May—though he was not in town within months of Cohen's departure from the El Rancho Vegas. More interestingly, Cohen took a two-week vacation to Los Angeles in October, shortly before he announced his affiliation with the Sands. Was he conferring with Doc Stacher, closing a deal that could only be closed in person, and far from Las Vegas? Just after Cohen officially joined the Sands, Jake Freedman returned from his own trip to Houston, where he had secured a $2 million loan that was to be used for a 150-room expansion of the Sands. Freedman had been trying to secure the funds for this project since February, and the timing seems too good to be a coincidence. If that loan could ultimately be traced to Doc Stacher or Meyer Lansky (and, like most money in Las Vegas at the time, that was more than likely), it makes sense that they would want to have the best in the business on hand to protect a sizeable new investment.

Whatever the reasons for his move, by December the Tax Commission had approved Cohen, in return for a $60,000 investment, to become a two percent owner of the Sands. As casino manager and executive vice president, Cohen might have been outranked on paper by Freedman, but everyone who mattered knew the truth: Carl Cohen was now running the Sands.

Cohen didn't just rely on his smarts to keep the casino running smoothly. In May 1954, he had a closed-circuit television system installed in the Sands. Its cameras could focus on each of the ten gaming tables, and showed the action in two sets of monitors—one in the traditional "eye in the sky" catwalk system in the attic above the casino, the other in executive offices. The $40,000 system was, at first, a high-tech supplement to the old surveillance system, which was to station trusted employees on the catwalk, where they could observe, through one-way mirrors, the gambling. Yet it would eventually replace manual observation of the floor.

Rather than hide what some customers might consider an intrusive electronic spying system, Al Freeman issued a press release, and the story was picked up in papers around the country. Jake Freedman, speaking for the casino, assured the press that the system showed only the hands of the dealers and players, along with the chips, cards, and dice, in an attempt to reassure all potential customers that their privacy was protected at the Sands. While casinos are notoriously closed-mouthed about their internal operations, particularly where money is concerned, Freedman admitted that the typical casino lost an average of $100,000 a year to cheating by customers who marked cards and used dishonest dice. Investing $40,000 on an anti-cheating system, then, seemed quite sensible.

Of course, the cameras also let the bosses keep an eye on the dealers and floor staff, without them knowing—Freedman did not tell the press that dealers were confederates in the majority of casino cheating.

Thus, the word went out to the public—and to potential cheaters and the Sands' own dealers—that Carl Cohen had a new weapon on his side, as if they needed any more reason to remain honest at the Sands.

***

The girls were ready to start shoveling the silver dollars.

This was before Las Vegas was a known quantity. When you still had to specify Las Vegas, Nevada, to make certain you weren't talking about the New Mexico town of the same name. Sands publicist Al Freeman and his colleagues at the city's other resorts had a job: let America know what Las Vegas was about, in a way that would make them want to spend their time and money there.

Freeman, born in Philadelphia in 1924, was a Temple University graduate, decorated World War II combat veteran, and reporter for his hometown *Inquirer* who moved into advertising. Working first with Steve Hannigan, who would help set up the Las Vegas promotional machine in the late 1940s, Freeman rose quickly as a partner at George Evans Associates, whose accounts included Frank Sinatra, Dean Martin and Jerry Lewis, and Jack Entratter's Copacabana.

Coming out to work on the Sands opening with George Evans, Freeman chose to remain in Las Vegas, becoming the Sands' publicity chief. He was part of a small but steadfast group of men—they were almost always men—who rose to the challenge of selling Las Vegas.

To do that, you had to subtly broadcast what you could find in the town—gambling, booze, sex—without raising the hackles of those who found such things offensive.

The developing art and science of promoting Las Vegas had begun to coalesce into a formula that would serve the city for generations. The first challenge it met was the gauntlet thrown down by Estes Kefauver and his admirers, whose presence at the federal level into the 1960s constituted an ongoing existential threat. They charged that gambling was un-American, that the men who had built the Strip's growing string of pleasure palaces were on par with communists as public menaces. The publicists knew this wasn't true—after all, these men, their bosses, depended above all on the continuation of the American way of life. Las Vegas must be understood by the general public and the national media alike to be both exciting and safe. This campaign would stretch on for decades, with some variation in technique, but in those early days, the sellers of Las Vegas pitched the battle along five main points.

First, boosters emphasized the abiding wholesomeness of Las Vegas, a town, as boosters liked to point out, with more churches than bars. A small town, where strangers were soon friends. The casinos themselves were staffed by salt-of-the-earth folks who might have been clerks or schoolteachers in any other city.

Second, they promoted Las Vegas as a frontier town out of the Old West, in a land still quite wild. Gambling was part of a Western tradition that put a premium on individuality, independence, and informality. "Come as you are" was a common slogan around then, and it was felt that in the wide-open spaces of the West, one could simply be themselves.

Third was affordability. Thanks to the largesse of big gamblers, who could certainly afford the losses, casinos could offer good food, inexpensive shows (Frank Sinatra himself in the Copa, no cover, no minimum), and small but inexpensive rooms. If they could resist the temptation to gamble, visitors could get a much cheaper vacation than elsewhere. But resisting that temptation would be bad form, when the casino owners were so generous.

Fourth was the power of celebrity. Since Clara Bow attended the opening of the El Rancho Vegas in 1941, Las Vegas casinos had attempted to cash in on the town's proximity to Hollywood. Not only could starstruck tourists see their idols perform on stage; they might share a blackjack table with a film star, have dinner across from a famous television actor, or lounge by the pool with a United States senator. The famous came to Las Vegas to have some fun, and if you wanted, you could do it alongside them. You could commiserate with someone you'd seen in the movies when the shooter rolled snake eyes, bonding in the moment over a misfortune that would become part of a story you'd repeat for years.

Fifth was sex. Las Vegas was hardly unique here, but promoters were particularly ingenious in finding creative ways to photograph attractive women. Those photographs would then be sent to newspapers around the world, and frequently make it into print. Promoters used sex to convince visitors that a trip to Las Vegas was thoroughly American because, after all, there was nothing more American than a pretty girl.

So, it was girls with shovels, looming over silver dollars, at the culmination of an October 1954 promotional sortie to the Midwest.

The trip was a joint production between all the city's casinos, Downtown and Strip, the Desert Sea News Bureau, and TWA airlines. The sole objective: convince the Chicago and Milwaukee populations that Las Vegas was a fun place to visit. TWA was launching a new direct flight to Las Vegas, which would arrive in the desert town about 5 p.m. each day—just enough time to get checked in before heading to a dinner show. Filling those seats meant money for the airline and, of course, the casinos, so as in all cases of mutual benefit, Las Vegas was all in.

On August 30, Freeman and Ben Goffstein, his counterpart at the Flamingo, met with 14 TWA executives at the Palmer House hotel in Chicago. All involved agreed to a rough outline for that fall's profile-raising campaign. A small team of Las Vegas publicists would fly to Chicago, "kick up some noise," and return with a dozen or so print, radio, and television people, who would be treated to a free four-day vacation. At the same time, a massive advertising blitz, orchestrated by the Chicago office of advertising giant BBDO (an inspiration for *Mad Men's* Sterling Cooper), would dominate the newsprint, airwaves, and travel agencies of the Midwest.

Costs for the ad campaign would be split between the Las Vegas hotels and TWA, which was also giving Las Vegas the front page of its travel rate folder. With over a million copies printed, this was a coup for the hotels. Additionally, TWA would send about 11,000 direct mail pieces to high net worth individuals in the Chicago area. Costs for full-color posters, to be placed in every terminal where TWA had a gate, would be split between the hotels and the airline.

Kicking up noise, as Freeman liked to call it, had already become a specialty for Las Vegas publicists. In the past few years, Freeman and Goffstein agreed, they had relied perhaps too much on the power of sex to sell Las Vegas: pictures of pretty girls applying for jobs, relaxing by the pool, playing golf. While providing Chicago papers with cheesecake shots of a Chicago girl enjoying the sights of Las Vegas might have worked in the past, they sensed that this approach was receiving diminishing returns.

"What if," Freeman asked, "we brought out two Las Vegas girls to Chicago, with about $100,000 in silver dollars? We could let people guess exactly how many dollars there were, with the three closest guessers getting a free trip."

Goffstein agreed that this was a fantastic idea. It would not only drum up excitement during the contest itself, but would generate additional stories when the winners took their trip.

"We could put the silver dollars in a department store window. Pinkerton guards standing watch. Have the girls dressed up in Western outfits, handing out guess cards."

The pair further suggested, and the TWA officials agreed, that they should get the newspapers in on the action as well. They could print coupons for readers to send in, with each paper guaranteed one winner. Seven total winners, whose vacations would be spread across the hotels, would deliver far more press than a simple series of cheesecake shots.

A keystone of the campaign was the press junket. For years, casinos had been treating members of the media like visiting crown princes. Provided they had enough reach, newspaper reporters, editors, television anchors, and radio announcers could expect to be flown, housed, entertained, and fed while in Las Vegas, all on the casino's dime.

If a free trip to Las Vegas was involved, most of the "eating press" didn't have to be asked twice. On the contrary; most of them were soon asking if they could bring their wives. It was a bet they couldn't lose: If the answer was yes, their wives would be grateful for the free vacation. If it was no, well, they tried, and there could be no complaining at home since a man's work was his work. To themselves they could rationalize that if by chance they found some temporary companionship in Las Vegas, they could hardly be blamed for taking it. After all, a junket like this was hard, stressful work, and a little relaxation would help them perform better, maybe even get a raise. The wife wouldn't complain about that. If anything, she should be grateful.

More likely than not, it would be the husband asking for his wife, and not vice versa. The media people, as well as their PR handlers, were overwhelmingly male. Three of the 15 personalities invited on the October junket were women: Lee Grossman of radio station WMAQ, Joanne Ruetlinger of Chicago NBC-TV affiliate WNBQ, and Reggie Dombeck, the reigning "Miss Photo Flash," winner of an annual beauty pageant held by the Chicago-area media. And only one of the eight Las Vegas public relations managers assigned as hosts—Geri Nolan of the El Rancho Vegas—was a woman.

So it wasn't surprising that the entire Chicago adventure, while it was supposed to be more elevated than past cheesecake picture campaigns, boiled down to photographing attractive women.

Despite its simple premise, the silver dollar campaign stretched the logistical capability of even the Las Vegas press machine. Although the silver dollars were purportedly flown in from the Silver State, in actuality they were borrowed, interest free, from the First National Bank of Chicago, then trucked to the airport where they were met by a van with three Illinois burros. The "girls" were then photographed coming down the stairs of a parked TWA Constellation, spilling silver dollars from their bags. Additional photos showed them loading the bags onto the burros.

At 10 a.m., the girls, burros, and silver dollars met at Congress and State streets, where they began a procession to the TWA office.

"Just think of it," Goffstein had said, "pretty girls driving the mules loaded down with silver in the middle of a Chicago street—that will make for some great pictures."

Once at the TWA offices, the two Brinks trucks containing the bulk of the money were parked outside, while the currency was transferred to a display in the TWA window. More photos ensued, with girls spilling silver dollars into the window display, followed by guards spilling silver dollars onto the girls, who were now lying on the silver dollars already on display. The girls spent much of the following week handing out guessing cards, passing out promotional balloons, and accompanying the press agents as they toured local television stations. The group even visited the office of Chicago mayor Martin Kennelly, presenting His Honor with a cowboy hat and holster.

Throughout, the Chicago effort remained true to the classic Las Vegas formula, presenting images of sex and wealth in a wholesome,

Western setting. Among the photo shoots was one with "Miss Photo Flash" herself. Goffstein and Freeman's directive to the photographer was instructive. "Place her bust-deep in the pile," they wrote, "as though buried in silver." Another shot would see her placed in the pile, "with head, bust, and legs showing."

On Friday, Gene Murphy and Abe Schiller, who were the Las Vegas publicists on site in Chicago, made sure to have photographers on hand, as the girls assisted in removing the silver dollars from the TWA window. They were to use shovels to pile the silver into bags, and if photographers happened to snap them as they were bending particularly low, well, there wasn't anything dirty at all about that. Good, clean, honest, Western fun.

Then it was time for Las Vegas to host the assorted media personalities, who could deliver positive press just as the TWA/Las Vegas advertising blitz started in earnest. It was perfect timing in particular for Freeman, since Frank Sinatra himself was to begin a week-long engagement in two weeks.

The press flight touched down on the afternoon of Tuesday, October 26. The group started a packed four days with a brief driving tour of Downtown and the Strip, followed by a cocktail party at the El Rancho Vegas in which the Chicago and Milwaukee press met their counterparts in Las Vegas and the publicity people from each hotel. Dinner at the Thunderbird preceded the supper show at the Flamingo, where Ben Blue led a bill that also included Les Brown and his Band of Renown.

That wasn't the end of the night—far from it. From the Flamingo, the group went to the off-Strip Showboat for a special 1 a.m. performance of Minsky's Follies of 1955, backed by the Dorothy Dorben Dancers and Buster Hallet's orchestra, then back to the Silver Slipper for yet another show that began at 2:30 a.m. This was an extravaganza revue featuring burlesque star Sally Rand, former heavyweight boxer Buddy Baer, Swiss yodeler Jean Vallee, and comedian Hank Henry.

As could be expected, Wednesday started late, with a mere dinner at the Sahara and the Peter Lind Hayes and Mary Healy-led supper show at the Sands.

Thursday morning saw a small group head out to Lake Mead and Hoover Dam for boating and fishing, with the full group coming together for a dinner at the Desert Inn and supper show at the Flamingo. Friday had a minimal schedule, with only dinner at the host hotel set in stone, followed by a drive back to the airport for the 9 p.m. flight back to Chicago.

Along the way, of course, the media people were expected to explore all that the city had to offer with their new friends. The press was in town for an average week, as average weeks in Las Vegas go. They might have been introduced to leading cardiac surgeon Sir Russell Brock of Wimbledon, England, who was at the Sands with his wife. Sales managers from 21 airlines were meeting at the Last Frontier; like the Midwestern press contingent, they were feted at all the Strip hotels, with the expectation that they'd be vigorously plugging the wonders of Las Vegas when they went home.

Though all good things must end, they don't always end in style. The press junket did, in a style that perfectly sums up the appeal of Las Vegas in 1954. A small band was playing "Chicago" as the media approached the TWA plane. But they weren't back in the Windy City yet. A pretty TWA stewardess handed each guest several silver dollars so that they could try their luck at a slot machine that had been stationed at the base of the steps under a placard reading "Your Last Chance."

If they didn't hit a jackpot, the male guests got a consolation prize: a Dior bra with a note reading "Just to prove that nobody leaves Las Vegas flat busted!" Press kits had been mailed, and would be waiting when the media people got back to their offices on Monday.

They might have been corny, but such promotions were effective. Within three weeks of the trip, TWA announced that it would be bringing another "Quickie Vacation" press flight to Las Vegas in January. As early as 1954, not even a decade into the serious promotion of Las Vegas, the town's publicists had figured out that a combination of sex, hokey Western kitsch, and freebies sold better than anything else.

***

It was also in 1954 that Jack Entratter made a major change in the Copa. Bandleader Ray Sinatra was leaving. Conducting a Las Vegas house band was a delicate job that balanced skill and self-abnegation on a knife edge. First, you had to be a veteran musician who could command the respect of both your own musicians and the visiting headliner, which necessarily meant a healthy ego. But that ego needed to be confident enough to be sublimated to the headliner's own needs, both musical and emotional, which would themselves be immense.

So Entratter needed to find a bandleader who was good, but not too good; popular, but not popular enough to outshine the featured performers; easy to work with, but no pushover. Luckily, he had already worked with a man who fit the bill: Antonio Morelli. Born in 1904 in Rochester, New York, and spending his early years in Erie, Pennsylvania, Morelli was, from the age of 10, educated in Italy, where he attended the Royal Conservatories of Music in Milan and Parma, focusing on the piano and violin. Returning to the United States at the age of 21, he made a living as a traveling pianist and violinist before transitioning into conducting. Morelli began working the vaudeville and theater circuit around the country, later settling down, with notable stints at New York's Radio City Music Hall and as musical director of the St. Louis Municipal Opera Company.

Morelli first came to Las Vegas in 1953, as conductor for "Oh! Whotta Nite!" a roadshow musical comedy revue featuring one-time vaudevillians Olsen and Johnson. The duo, who had started performing together in 1914, parlayed their manic stage performances into a film career that spanned 15 years, starting in 1930. By the 1950s, they were performing mostly on stage. The show was still evolving when it came to Las Vegas; only about half of its 21 acts had been finalized at that point. The plan was to refine the show as it toured the United States and Canada before hitting Broadway.

The three-week stand at the Last Frontier, in late October/ early November, coincided with a local milestone. To celebrate the completion of Las Vegas High School's new auditorium, the Las Vegas Opera Association presented the city's first-ever night of true opera, as the Los Angeles Conservatory of Arts and Music performed Bizet's *Carmen*. The 1,500-seat auditorium sold out, and Strip showrooms were half-empty, although none of the opera singers had the star power of the Strip's headliners. The resort operators were not panicked, however, and even financially supported the performance, since the Opera Association forecast one or two performances a year.

The *Carmen* sellout was something of an anomaly; Las Vegas audiences were probably drawn to the performance more for its novelty than any abiding love of high musical culture. Yet it made an impact on Morelli. Here was a city, he thought, where a musician could make a living and whose citizens appreciated good music. Nearing 50 with no children, he and his wife Helen were eager to trade the peripatetic lifestyle of a roving conductor with something more stable.

So, in July of the following year, Morelli was all ears when Jack Entratter, for whom he had briefly worked at the Copacabana, asked him to relocate to the desert to serve as musical director for the Copa Room. The city's climate, as well as its cultural openness, was a big attraction. Morelli had long suffered from arthritis and other ailments exacerbated by humidity.

"It's 117 degrees here," he told Helen when he got a chance to place a long-distance call. "But not an ache anywhere. My knees and my back feel great."

With his Continental education, salt-and-pepper hair, and distinctive, waxed-tip mustache, Morelli looked almost like a caricature of the ultra-sophisticated maestro—a definite plus for a Strip showroom. His elegance raised the tenor of Copa performances.

But Morelli, believing that *Carmen* had been no fluke, had ambitions beyond the Strip. Almost as soon as he arrived in Las Vegas, Morelli convinced Entratter to sponsor the Las Vegas Community Chorus, a group that, under his direction, would perform holiday concerts for their fellow Las Vegans. The concerts became a local fixture, giving Las Vegas a touch more culture while helping Morelli feel more at home.

And Helen, who originally remained in New York, began spending more time in Las Vegas. Jaded by Manhattan nightlife, she was nonetheless enthralled when she first flew into Las Vegas at night. From the sky, she saw a tiny row of lights that couldn't hold a candle to New York City. But when she walked in the door of the Sands, the bright lights and the sounds of the slot machines, mingled with the excitement the crowded gamblers, was like nothing she had ever seen before.

After the show, Antonio took her for a walk around the property. Helen was entranced by the groups of olive trees with small lights at their base. This was like nothing in New York, like nothing anywhere.

Yet the next day, in the bleaching sunlight, the Sands, true to its name, looked like a giant pile of sand. Helen had made the mistake of leaving a window open. It was a windy morning, and by the time she'd gotten back from breakfast, the entire room was coated in sand.

Yet there were attractions to keep the Morellis in Las Vegas, beyond the perks that came with Antonio's position atop the Las Vegas entertainment hierarchy. The community concerts, which blossomed into once-a-month affairs, afforded him a position of some importance outside the Copa's stage. "The Toscanini of the desert," Jack Cortez's

Fabulous Las Vegas magazine dubbed him. Morelli felt genuine pride in what he was doing in Las Vegas.

"This is the only city in America," he said after the third Christmas concert in 1956, "where such talent would willingly donate service as a community service."

That same year, he produced "Birth of the Star-Spangled Banner," a musical reenactment of the bombardment of Fort McHenry during the War of 1812. Featuring 125 musicians, 68 singers, and 100 servicemen from Nellis Air Force Base, this was a showcase for all of the city's talent, and another example of the kind of community work Morelli performed.

At first, like many arrivals to Las Vegas at the time, Antonio and Helen hedged their bets. Helen moved permanently in 1957, but they maintained their Long Island home for another two years. After selling their house back East and building a new residence on the Desert Inn Golf Course, the Morellis were hedging no longer—Las Vegas was home.

He then began a series of outdoor concerts known as Shirt-Sleeve Symphonies, in which 125 musicians—who at first volunteered their time but were eventually paid personally by Morelli—performed at Cashman Field from 8:00 to midnight, with cameos by Strip headliners scattered amongst the pops fare.

Always committed to musical education, Morelli worked with schools to provide opportunities for students, and started a fund—the Antonio Morelli Friends of Music Endowment—that gives scholarships to students at the University of Nevada, Las Vegas to this day.

And Morelli continued to excel at the job that had brought him to Las Vegas, conducting the 18-piece Copa orchestra. Morelli would helm the house band until 1972, with billing on the hotel's marquee under the Copa's headliners but above the acts that played the Silver Queen Lounge. Even when headliners brought their own musical directors, Morelli lent a touch of prestige to the proceedings, and with his arrival the golden era of the Copa room truly began. It was a mark of Morelli's influence that, even after he retired from the bandstand, the Sands' house band continued to be billed as "the Antonio Morelli Orchestra," with a series of guest conductors.

The dapper bandleader was one of the finest examples of what the Sands made possible. At the age of 50, despite a long career, he'd had a measure of success but not much standing. At the Sands he was immediately accepted as part of the resort's family, respected, and even deferred to. After decades as a roving maestro, he finally found in Las Vegas the community he had been seeking.

Morelli was able to find such a prominent place so easily partially because he arrived in Las Vegas at exactly the right moment. A decade earlier, and he wouldn't have had the infrastructure to support a community choir and orchestra. A decade later, and someone else would have already founded it. His Las Vegas was a different, smaller city from what it could become—one in which it felt like everyone in the casino business knew everyone else. One in which his Shirt-Sleeve Symphonies were such major civic events that the Strip headliners who walked on for their moment in the limelight were whisked from their stage door to Cashman Field in a patrol car, sirens blaring, lest either the performer or the audience think this was anything less than a big deal. This was a town where everyone was an insider, which meant no one was an outsider.

Maybe he didn't get to wave the baton when the really big stars, like Frank Sinatra, played the Sands—they usually brought in their own musical directors. But the Toscanini of the desert found something more than professional gratification in Las Vegas—he found a home.

Please Be Kind

By 1955, Las Vegas had proven it was resilient, but the young resort was about to face its biggest challenge.

It was success that threatened Las Vegas—specifically, the success of the Desert Inn and the Sands. Both followed the same rough formula: a beloved longtime gambler as the chief owner of record and public well-wisher, with the serious money coming from New York, Miami, Cleveland, and other places. They made making money in Las Vegas look easy—much easier than it actually was.

Players come to Las Vegas because they think they can beat the house—an ambition that, in the long run, can never be realized. Casino developers also think they can beat the odds. Some can, but many can't. Since the birth of the modern casino resort on Highway 91 in the 1940s, through to the multibillion-dollar corporate Strip of today, more casinos than not have danced on the edge of bankruptcy. Plenty have fallen in.

Just as gamblers thrilled to finally be able to shoot craps legally flocked to the Sands, Desert Inn, Sahara, Thunderbird, Flamingo, Last Frontier, and El Rancho Vegas in 1953, would-be casino owners showed up, eying the players packing the tables in the Strip's casinos, then the acres of undeveloped land along Highway 91, with desperate longing. Spending a few million turning a piece of the latter into a swank gambling palace to attract the former was the surest way to make millions.

In August of 1953, as Jack Entratter negotiated for Frank Sinatra to become an owner/featured performer at the Sands, the Tax Commission had before it four applications for casino licenses on the Las Vegas Strip. The Casablanca, to be built on Highway 91 and Race Track Road, was proposed by brothers David and Lou Gensburg, backed by a syndicate of investors including Harpo and Gummo of Marx Brothers fame. The Araby, catty-cornered to the Flamingo, was helmed by the trio of Rhode Island restaurateur Joseph Sullivan, Florida theater-owner Al Gottesman, and Beverly Hills costume jewelry dealer Bob Rice. Los Angeles hotelier Frank Fishman proposed the Sunrise, which would take shape north of the Last Frontier. Across the street, a group of investors led by William O'Connor were seeking to enlarge the Desert Spa motel into a full-fledged casino hotel.

By the following summer, film actor Pat O'Brien had lent his name to the Desert Spa project, which would be known as "Pat O'Brien's Desert Spa." The Casablanca became the Riviera, the Araby the Dunes, and the Sunrise the Royal Nevada. What's more, they wouldn't be the only new casinos to open: Former bootlegger and proficient gambling operator Tony Cornero, whose boats had once coasted the international waters just outside Los Angeles, announced his intentions to open the Stardust, while the Last Frontier's owners began work on the New Frontier, which would replace the hotel's existing casino/theater building and give the property a thorough Space Age makeover. Ed Levinson's Fremont Hotel broke ground in Downtown Las Vegas, even as the Showboat prepared to open on Boulder Highway. At ten stories, the Fremont would be highest building in the state—bigger than the under-construction Riviera. Off the Strip on West Bonanza, in the city's historically black Westside, construction began on the Moulin Rouge, a resort that would be open to both black and white guests—a contrast with the segregation of the Strip and Downtown gambling halls.

Counting the off-Strip properties, the construction boom of 1954 promised (or threatened) to double the number of major casino resorts in Las Vegas over the span of a few months in the following year. That didn't unduly worry Freedman, Entratter, and Cohen at the Sands—after all, they had the players they wanted and they had Sinatra, a casino attraction without peer. To counter Entratter's long list of entertainment contacts, the new casinos looked to differentiate themselves. At the Royal Nevada, entertainment director Eddie Rio hired the Sands' choreographer George Tapps to produce shows that Rio said would rival Broadway. The opening marquee performer was to be opera star Helen Traubel. To add to the sophistication, Rio also brought in the Dancing Waters, a German-designed system that shot 38 tons of water through 4,000 jets in time to musical accompaniment.

The Riviera, by contrast, broke the bank to lure one of the hottest commodities in show business, at least for the demographic Las Vegas casinos were shooting for: Liberace. To get the candelabra-festooned pianist, the Riviera paid him $50,000 per week, more than Jack Entratter had paid to anyone. The New Frontier followed the Riviera's lead, offering Mario Lanza $100,000 for a two-week engagement. As the summer of 1955 inched closer, it looked like the Las Vegas casino industry, barely a decade old, was heading for a major shakeup.

By April 4, when the New Frontier threw open its doors (Mario Lanza, despite his historic payday, refused to perform, though the show went on), the Desert Spa had already fizzled. With insufficient financing, it had opened without a casino in March, and it would soon slide into bankruptcy. The Royal Nevada opened two weeks later, with a dedicated preview night for the "atomic soldiers" of Camp Desert Rock, who were about to be deployed for the much-delayed Apple-2 atomic test. On April 20, Liberace cut the ribbon that opened the nine-story Riviera.

Amid the spate of openings, there were rumblings of trouble. The Tax Commission had refused to license the Royal Nevada unless several of its principles stepped aside. As with Mack Kufferman, these men were found to be "undesirable" because of their associations with operators who were too notorious for even wide-open Nevada. The Riviera, Royal Nevada, and New Frontier struggled financially from the start. The Tax Commission deferred action on the Dunes' license in March.

"Get your house in order," Gottesman, Sullivan, and Rice were advised. The resort's financing was shaky enough that the Commission refused to allow the casino to open unless its owners could prove that it was sufficiently capitalized.

The owners were able to scare up enough cash to satisfy the Commission, opening the new casino's doors on May 23 with a revue show as the main entertainment option—distinctively low-wattage compared to Liberace and Lanza. With only 194 rooms, the Dunes couldn't generate the volume needed to match other resorts. The high-end customers were already locked up by the Sands and Desert Inn—and certainly not about to be wooed by the "Magic Carpet Revue." The Moulin Rouge, which opened on the following day, had better word-of-mouth than the Dunes, but, like the Dunes, struggled financially.

The operators of the Dunes, while they had experience in hotels and restaurants, did not know how to run a Las Vegas casino. They fired, rehired, then fired comedian Wally Cox shortly after his July debut at the casino. Meanwhile, the Clark County licensing board was taking an increasingly hard line, giving the New Frontier's owners 48 hours to "clean up their financial linen." The casino had been issuing conflicting stock certificates, hardly the sign of a well-run operation, and it was only the belief that the New Frontier's closure would cause even more harm to investors and the community (and, no doubt, the elected commissioners) that the board did not immediately revoke the casino's license.

Up and down the Strip, those running the new casinos felt a chill that belied the late-July heat. The success of the Sands had been so quick that it looked as easy as sliding a stack of chips onto the pass line and rolling a string of sevens. But the Royal Nevada, Riviera, Dunes, New Frontier, and Moulin Rouge were close to bankruptcy.

By August 1, the owners of those hotels were seeking new investors or to simply cut their losses and sell out for pennies on the dollar. Making money in Las Vegas was not as easy as it seemed.

***

Unfortunately, the uniformly bad performance of the new casinos did not make investing in Las Vegas—already a bet most mainstream financiers would laugh at—any more appealing. As it turned out, the only people willing to bet money on the success of Las Vegas were those already doing business there. "If you can't beat them, join them," became "If you can't beat them, sell out to them."

The Dunes had already been re-capitalized three times by mid-August. Its owners blamed bad luck in the casino, but the Dunes' losses might have been attributable to something more ominous: skimming. Without a manager like Carl Cohen at the helm, dealers and pit bosses could easily help themselves to a share of the house's winnings. This would have been an annoyance if business was good, but with players already scarce, it was catastrophic.

Compounding the Dunes' problems was the continuing lack of a real draw. The Thunderbird, an unpretentious resort on the Strip in which Meyer Lansky had a secret interest, could get by with a revue featuring "the amazing French piano humorist Rolly Rolls" as its star because it had been cheap to build and had a low overhead. Trying to keep the Dunes afloat with Paris Ala Mode—a "gay and saucy revue" co-starring singer/actress Marion Marlowe (in her Las Vegas debut) and comedian Ben Blue—as the featured entertainment was laughable, when the casino had to pay off not only its $4.5 million construction costs but its operating budget.

Meanwhile, the Sands was featuring a production of the Ziegfeld Follies with a double bill of Metropolitan Opera baritone Robert Merrill and Louis Armstrong as the featured performers. Audiences could enjoy the incongruity of Merrill crooning Fats Waller's "Honeysuckle Rose," followed by Armstrong's interpretations of "Vesti la Giubba" from *Pagliacci*—a vocal treat that no one but Jack Entratter could deliver. Combined with the steady flow of gamblers that Jake Freedman and Carl Cohen produced—and Cohen's eagle-eyed watch over the drop boxes—the Sands was unassailable.

Still, Cohen in Las Vegas and Lansky in Miami Beach—along with Frank Costello in New York, Doc Stacher in Los Angeles, and the unknown others who secretly had a stake in the success of Las Vegas—knew that the specter of struggling hotels up and down the Strip would not enhance their investments. Certainly after *Life* magazine's June cover story ran under the headline of "Las Vegas—Is the Boom Overextended?" it was clear that the entire city's image would suffer for the sins of the newcomers.

By the second week of August, two groups were far along in their negotiations with Sullivan and Gottesman to purchase the Dunes: one consisting of the Sands' chief owners, the other a group headed by former Sands casino manager Ed Levinson. Of course, the two groups were not bidding against each other as such; Levinson had left the Sands under good circumstances, and the Fremont and Sands were to be closely linked for years—no coincidence, since Meyer Lanksy was a major force behind both.

On August 16, the Dunes' Board of Directors officially considered the Sands' bid to buy the property, which would have made Freedman and his compatriots the first group to own and operate more than one hotel on the Strip.

The agreement ultimately hammered out did not see an outright sale of the property; rather, the Sands Hotel Corporation signed a 20-year lease agreement. In return for a monthly rent of $50,000 (with the first year's total, $600,000, paid in advance), the Sands took over the operation of the Dunes, with Jack Entratter now in charge of entertainment for both hotels. Ed Levinson would oversee the casino for the first several weeks, after which he would return his attention to the Fremont, which was scheduled to open the following year.

Al Gottesman put a positive spin on the transaction, angrily denying reports that he and his partners were in over their heads.

"We always planned to build the Dunes as an investment, not something we wanted to operate day to day," he told the paper. "And we cut a very, very good deal with Jake Freedman."

Gottesman issued a further correction: While the *Review-Journal* had reported that he and his partners had spent $4.5 million to build the Dunes, the paper was mistaken. The Dunes, he said, had actually cost $6 million to construct.

Whatever the Dunes' cost, it now had new operators, although final regulatory approvals would not come through until later in the month. The Sands/Dunes deal sparked a wave of speculation: Rumors swirled that the Desert Inn was buying the Royal Nevada and the Flamingo was taking over the Riviera. The last was almost, but not entirely, accurate. Gus Greenbaum, who had retired from operating the Flamingo earlier that year, was content to golf and relax in Phoenix. Chicago mob boss Tony Accardo, convinced that only Greenbaum could reverse the Riviera's fortunes, was initially unsuccessful at persuading Greenbaum to return to Las Vegas. His sister-in-law's murder may have helped to persuade Greenbaum to look after Accardo's interests; in September, the Tax Commission approved his plan to lease the Riviera.

The Desert Inn ultimately balked at taking over the Royal Nevada. Former Sahara executive Bill Miller did, though he was no more successful than the original owners. On New Year's Day, 1956, Clark County sheriff's deputies served a writ for unpaid wages filed by the Culinary Union, sparking a near-riot, as dealers and bartenders, seeing which way the wind was blowing, began pocketing as much cash as they could. The resort closed completely that day. Though it would later reopen under new management, the Royal Nevada never clicked, and was in 1958 incorporated into the Stardust as its southern annex.

The Nevada Tax Commission formally signed off on the Sands/Dunes deal on August 31. The following day, the Sands ran newspaper ads celebrating the marriage between the Sands and Dunes. "The same inspired management that has made the Sands Hotel a living legend takes over operation of the Dunes on September first...your positive guarantee of superlative treatment, service, and entertainment." That was all well and good, but the real news was that none other than Frank Sinatra would be appearing in the Arabian Room, starting September 9.

***

The new operators didn't waste time. Plans for a Lou Walters revue were quickly scrapped, with Jack Entratter announcing that, after Sinatra's opening run, he would be bringing Robert Merrill, Danny Thomas, and other proven Copa hands to the Dunes. In addition, the Arabian Room would feature the same French cuisine that could be found in the Sands' Garden Room. Staff would shift from the Sands to the Dunes, with captains becoming maître d's and promising dealers transitioning to the floor, importing the culture of the Sands.

On the casino floor, Ed Levinson worked double-time to bring the Dunes' games up to snuff. Assisted by Carl Maier, he had to hire dealers, institute cash controls, and bring in players—no easy task.

To reintroduce the world to the Dunes, Freedman and Entratter threw a party, bigger than the shindig that had opened the Sands, bigger than any of the opening bashes thrown that spring. There was more at stake than getting eyes on Freedman and company's latest acquisition. With the sputtering of the Dunes, Riviera, Royal Nevada, and Moulin Rouge, the narrative on Las Vegas was shifting. Rather than being an atomic boomtown, it was increasingly seen as a desert hamlet whose time in the sun had come—and gone. The *Wall Street Journal* ran a piece claiming that there was a recession in Southern Nevada, and while the hometown *Review-Journal* had strenuously "debunked" that assertion, there was concern among the city's most energetic boosters that the future looked bleak.

So Al Freeman cajoled a few dozen members of the press and Hollywood stars to hop a charter flight up to Las Vegas on September 9, a Friday, for a three-day celebration of the new Dunes. When they stepped off the plane, they were greeted by a double-line of showgirls, a typical Las Vegas welcome. This time, however, there was a novelty: a pair of "Nubian eunuchs" waving fans (actually, two Dunes porters from the Westside) and thawb-wearing musicians playing exotic melodies redolent of Cairo or Baghdad (actually disguised members of Antonio Morelli's orchestra, making union scale).

The following night, at a dinner party thrown just for the press, came the climax: a trio of white Arabian horses galloping through a parade of spears, followed by Frank Sinatra gamely striding across the Dunes' front lawn (past an oversized Aladdin's lamp) atop a camel named Irving. The Nubian eunuchs were back at the casino door, and faux Bedouin tribesmen roved the grounds.

Sinatra dazzled, the press scarfed down the champagne and steaks, and gamblers packed the Dunes fuller than it had ever been. Mission accomplished.

But the problems of Las Vegas ran too deeply to be banished by a photo op. As the competition ratcheted up in the summer of 1955, Strip hotels began charging a $2 minimum purchase for entrance into their floor shows—a fantastic bargain, and probably less than most guests would spend, but still, it was a sign that the house was no longer going to spend as freely as it once did. This was a consequence of the doubling of the cost of headline entertainment, though other prices had risen as well: rooms that had once cost $5 to $6 were now $10 to $12, drinks went for 90 cents, and steaks were a staggering $5.

And Jack Entratter had an insoluble problem that not even Al Freeman's most frenetic promotion could paper over: If Frank Sinatra was playing at the Dunes, he was not at the Sands. Entratter could field a deep bench of entertainers, but his pool was not infinitely deep. So, by October the Sands was offering Joey Bishop opening for Peggy Lee, while the Dunes fielded the Kean Sisters and Howard Keel— talented performers, to be sure, but in a different league. In December, Entratter staged a double bill of Dick Haymes and Jerry Lester in the Arabian Room, while Nat "King" Cole charmed audiences in the Copa. Officially, Entratter insisted both rooms were top-notch, down to the Arabian Room chorus line labeled "the world's most exotic harem girls," so as to not upstage or be upstaged by the original Copa dancers, "the most beautiful girls in the West."

So while Entratter could put on great shows at both properties, well, there only could be one Copa Room, and while some visitors might have preferred, say, Maurice Chevalier over Lena Horne, there was little doubt who had more overall appeal. Rather than being grateful at being invited to hear "Livin' in the Sunlight" crooned to them in the Arabian Room, gamblers might wonder why they didn't rate the Copa.

By December it was clear that the experiment was not working out. Jack Entratter denied reports that the casino would be closing as late as

January 14. On the morning of Monday, January 16, however, the casino closed and did not reopen. The Arabian Room went dark as well.

"This isn't worth it," Entratter had told Freedman. "We're working twice as hard on the Dunes as we are on the Sands, and we're getting half the results." On February 1, the Sands surrendered its lease, and the Dunes became, again, somebody else's problem.

The Sands' failure to successfully steer the Dunes into the black, of course, was terrible news for a town that was already buffeted by bad headlines. *Review-Journal* publisher Al Cahlan did his best to put a good spin on a bad situation. Yes, three of the new hotels, the Dunes, Royal Nevada, and Moulin Rouge, were currently closed. But the fault was not Las Vegas, but the new operators themselves. Most of the new casinos, Cahlan argued, "were promotions, pure and simple," with "all sorts of weird deals to get other people's cash." That wasn't uncommon in Las Vegas, but never to this extent; one project, for example, borrowed money at one hundred percent interest.

Cahlan was at pains to point out that the "old" standbys, the Sands, Desert Inn, Flamingo, Sahara, Thunderbird, and El Rancho Vegas, were doing fine. The key, the publisher thought, was perhaps to limit growth (maybe one new major hotel a year), and for the existing hotel owners to pull together and adopt a plan for long-term growth.

And so Las Vegas went into recovery mode. The plan that Cahlan alluded to was the construction of a major convention center that would lift Las Vegas into the next rank of business destinations. Spearheaded by chair of the County Commission George Albright, this effort came to fruition in 1959, after a series of compromises between hotel and motel owners and other business interests.

The success of the Albright Plan went far beyond what even its boldest supporters had hoped. Ultimately, the convention business let Las Vegas fill its hotels reliably during the mid-week, paving the way for the expansions of the 1960s and eventually, thanks to the Sands itself, the mega-resort era of the 1990s.

Things eventually worked out for the Dunes. Under new owners Bill Miller and Major Riddle, the casino opened in June, with a $340,000 bankroll and a low-budget entertainment policy. Initially spurning name entertainment entirely, the resort struggled, but after, in January 1956, debuting Minsky's Follies, the first topless show on the Strip, the Dunes rebounded, remaining, until its 1993 closure, a vibrant part of Las Vegas.

For the Sands' owners, the failed Dunes experiment was naturally a disappointment, but it also confirmed, albeit painfully, what a special place they had created in the Sands.

The Sands was truly one of a kind.

Owner Jake Freedman, wearing his customary cowboy hat, inspects construction on the Sands. Courtesy UNLV Special Collections and Archives.

In its early years, the Sands was an unpretentious collection of low-rise motel wings separate from the main casino/theater building (left). Courtesy UNLV SCA.

Carl Cohen and Jack Entratter guided the Sands to its greatest triumphs from Cohen's 1953 arrival to Howard Hughes' 1967 acquisition of the casino. Courtesy UNLV SCA.

Until the opening of the Regency Room, the Garden Room was the Sands' gourmet dining option. Courtesy UNLV SCA.

Seen here with Kim Novak, Jake Freedman was the Sands' president and public face until his 1958 death. Courtesy UNLV SCA.

Like many other casinos of the era, the Sands offered guests transportation to and from their rooms. Courtesy UNLV SCA.

Cyd Charisse and Dan Dailey, the leads in the 1956 film *Meet Me in Las Vegas,* pose in front of the Sands marquee. The MGM production was an extended commercial for Las Vegas in general and the Sands in particular. Courtesy UNLV SCA.

The two-story Hollywood Park building was typical of the Sands' early rooms. Courtesy UNLV SCA.

Publicist Al Freeman delighted in staging over-the-top photo opportunities, like this scene at the Sands' fourth anniversary celebration in which Jerry Lewis and Jayne Mansfield ended up in the pool. Courtesy UNLV SCA.

Though Freeman's photos often were high on sex appeal, they were just as often wholesome, as this image of a grandmother and young boy poolside demonstrates. Courtesy UNLV SCA.

While slot machines were not in keeping with the glamorous image the Sands projected, they were popular among less serious gambler and were seen as part of the casino's anything-goes fun. Courtesy UNLV SCA.

First known as the Silver Queen, the Sands lounge showcased top performers like trumpeter Jonah Jones. Courtesy UNLV SCA.

The Copa Room was the heart of the Sands. Audiences were within arm's length of major stars like Sammy Davis, Jr., pictured here. Courtesy UNLV SCA.

Ringside seats at the Copa were frequently reserved for celebrity guests. In attendance at a 1964 Frank Sinatra performance, left to right: Sinatra's ex-wife Nancy; Yul Brynner and his wife Doris Kleiner, with Jack Entratter hovering above; Edward G. Robinson. Across, Tommy Sands and his wife Nancy, Sinatra's daughter. Courtesy UNLV SCA.

If You Can Dream

The Sands grew to be more than a mere gambling hall: It was a place people looked to for philanthropic leadership—and photo opportunities.

As the world recovered from the dislocations that followed the Second World War and the continuing struggle against communism, thousands of children were left orphaned. While there were thousands of American parents eager to take into their homes children from Germany, Italy, Greece, Japan, and Korea, there was a shortage of case workers on the ground who could match children with parents.

Actress Jane Russell, who adopted three children herself, hoped to help facilitate adoptions by founding a charity called WAIF (Women's Adoption International Fund). Unable to pay for the program on goodwill alone, Russell turned to the Sands. Publicity director Al Freeman did not fail.

On September 2, 1955 (a week before Frank Sinatra hopped off Irving at the Dunes premiere), the Sands auctioned off a Cadillac Eldorado. Two hundred tickets were sold at a cost of $100 each, netting $20,000 for the fledgling charity. Freeman turned to showgirls to sell the tickets, with Beverly Hills furrier William Baer offering a white stole to the woman who sold the most. Naturally, Russell herself drew the winning ticket, and naturally, it was a press event.

Reports of not just the WAIF raffle but a flood of cheesecake shots, happy vacationers, and surrealist tableaux streamed out of Freeman's office, addressed to every wire service and news office in the land. It might be the now-famous shot of dice-shooters clustered around a craps table in the middle of the Sands pool, a diver caught mid-leap in the background. Or a grandmother enjoying the pool. Or Frank Sinatra and Judy Garland palling around backstage. Or Debbie Reynolds and Jack Benny sitting ringside in the Copa, watching Dean Martin croon.

Las Vegas was fun. The Sands was glamorous. The only way to avoid missing out was to spend the weekend at the Sands.

Staged photos, however, only went so far, which is why publicists up and down the Strip opened their doors to radio, television, and movie producers.

In early 1954, portions of the first episode of the short-lived series *The Lone Wolf* was shot at the Sands, which also provided free rooms for members of the crew. The following year, Edward R. Murrow's newsmagazine show *See It Now* filmed an episode at the Sands. Freedman and Cohen were interviewed in their office, with Entratter captured in the Copa Room. Lena Horne's performance that night was a high point of the show. The crew also filmed action in the casino for over an hour, interviews with a dealer and a pit boss, and reaction shots of the Copa audience.

There was a problem, though. While the publicity that a CBS news crew could deliver for the Sands was appreciated, some did not want to be seen on national television—at least while they were in Las Vegas.

"We've got to be discreet," Cohen reminded Entratter. "We have people out there who don't want anyone to know their full names, much less put their face on the news."

Freeman negotiated a compromise with the CBS crew: A poster advising that cameras were filming for television would be prominently displayed, and before the cameras started rolling, a series of pages would be made over the public address system informing patrons that, if they didn't want to be accidental stars of *See It Now*, they might want to step away from the tables for a while.

Radio, of course, didn't have that problem, and the Sands happily hosted the Dorothy Kilgallen/Richard Kollmar morning radio show several times, despite Frank Sinatra's visceral dislike for the syndicated gossip columnist, as well as other telecasts that brought the sounds and ambiance, if not the sights, of the Sands to households around the nation.

The Sands ended 1955 with a 12-minute segment of an episode of the NBC's documentary series *Wide Wide World* focusing on the varieties of music across the Americas. The David Garroway-hosted show captured Frank Sinatra rehearsing and performing in the Copa Room, along with Freddy Bell and the Bell Boys in the Silver Queen lounge, and Antonio Morelli conducting his orchestra by the pool. Garroway also interviewed Sinatra about a tour he was putting together for Goodwill International, a charity that benefited underprivileged children worldwide.

If Freeman didn't write Garroway's narration, he owed a primo bottle of scotch to whoever did.

"The Sands is never closed," Garroway intoned over shots of people pouring into the casino. "The Sands is the playground of the stars. You may not meet them face to face in Hollywood, but you will at the Sands." Cut to a shot of Bell and his group performing in the Silver Queen. "Every day is Sunday here. So they relax—in the sun, in the lounge—and quite at home like mountain people at a playparty relaxed among their friends."

But that wasn't all.

"There's a music you hear every 16 seconds around the clock. 52 million throws of dice since the Sands opened its door only three years ago. And they wore out 250,000 pairs of dice doing it."

Garroway went on to tell viewers about the 62,000 jackpots that had been hit over the past three years, day and night. "Not that you care if it's day or night," he added. "No clocks, no windows in the casino to distract you from the tempo of living you prefer at the moment." Then a transition to a shot of the Copa Girls, followed by a scrap of Nat "King" Cole performing in the Copa. Here even Freeman probably thought Garroway was going too far.

"Nat 'King' Cole can make you feel like the Sands is a luxury liner, a ship in the desert that floats on warm sand and cold martinis…. Everything is a surprise at the Sands. Continuous music, continuous presence of movie stars, continuous serving of food fit for them, and the girl from Chicago is not a bookkeeper today but the Cinderella of the Sands.

"Continuous gambling, continuous service around and around the pool and milady's chamber, and if the house could possibly arrange it, they would also provide continuous sunshine 24 hours a day." Fade back to Sinatra talking about his tour of Europe on behalf of distressed children. Fade into Sinatra performing again. End program.

The *Wide Wide World* producers had, of course, been guided by Al Freeman in their coverage. In addition to making the shooting locations and Frank Sinatra available, Freeman helped the documentarians with their research. Three weeks before the show aired, Freeman sent writer

Joe Liss a list of 21 facts about the Sands, many of which made it into the show. Even those that didn't provide an excellent snapshot of the Sands in the 1950s. The hotel was the top taxpayer among resort hotels, and had a daily operating expense of $24,000—$14,000 of which was payroll. The Sands had exactly 697 employees, 81 percent of whom were married. Each day, it served these employees 915 free meals. It cost $8,000 a week to keep six musical acts performing around the clock in the lounge. Over 7.7 million people had already visited the Sands, with an average of one person walking through its doors every three seconds. Nearly 1,200 cars were parked at the hotel on an average day. From its four main reservation centers in Los Angeles, New York, Chicago, and Houston, the Sands receive 750 requests a day for rooms, and regularly mailed those who were not fortunate enough to get a room. About 28 percent of the people who gambled at the Sands had never done so before—perhaps eased into the practice by a share of the $12,000 in free drinks the casino poured its gamblers. And, in case a neophyte gambler got lucky, they didn't have to worry about breaking the bank: The Sands kept $485,000 on hand in the casino cage to pay off lucky winners.

With coverage like that, the Sands did not need to buy advertising.

Yet television, while it was increasing its reach, did not have the cache of movies. So Entratter and Freeman, while they were pleased with their work on the small screen, redoubled their efforts to lure a motion picture production to the Sands.

In April 1955, Freeman and Entratter started negotiating with producer Joe Pasternak of MGM Studios. The filmmaker had a script from Isobel Lennart called *Weekend at Las Vegas* and was looking for a casino to serve as host for location shots and the fictional setting. Later that month, Entratter sent the studio a series of color photos of potential filming locations, including the casino, the Garden Room restaurant, the Copa Room, the pool, and the Presidential Suite.

A month later, Freeman received a nine-page script outline. The story begins with rancher Chuck Reynolds driving to Las Vegas in an open convertible, towing a trailer containing his beloved horse Emma. Reynolds loves Las Vegas, even though each of his trips thus far have ended with him selling his car and riding back to his ranch on Emma. But he is happy as he pulls up to the Sands.

"He loves the place—he always has fun—when you gamble, you have to lose, and anyway, *this* time he's going to win!" Chuck is beloved at the Sands. His best friend, a Hungarian blackjack dealer named Bondy as well as casino manager Tom Carr, try to dissuade Chuck from gambling, knowing that he will lose.

By contrast, American-born but French-trained ballerina Maria Clair despises Las Vegas. Performing in a nightclub is below her, she thinks, although her manager, Pierre Duval, is quite happy with the money her Sands engagement will bring in. Clair is described as "a cold girl—remote, distant, aloof, unused to being with people and ill at ease with them." She has never had a boyfriend.

Chuck and Maria meet when Chuck, seeking good luck, reaches out and grabs a random hand while playing roulette. The hand belongs to an outraged Maria. Chuck, however, is thrilled, as he wins a bet for the first time that day. Maria huffs off in disgust, but a few minutes later is bothered by a bellboy, who brings to her a tray full of silver dollars—her share of Chuck's roulette winnings. When she returns the money to Chuck, he wins a slot machine jackpot while holding her hand. Despite her initial coolness, Maria agrees to accompany Chuck on a gambling expedition, to see if she really is a good luck charm. The pair go from club to club, drawing crowds and breaking the bank across town. Along the way, Maria for the first time in her life feels the stirrings of passion, and falls in love with Chuck. Jealous over Chuck's attention being drawn by other women, she leaves him, returning to the Sands in a foul mood.

The next morning, she learns that casino manager Carr, livid at her conduct, wants to cancel her show. Then, he discovers that gamblers, lured by the legend of Maria and Chuck, are flocking to the Sands. Chuck, believing he's hurt Maria, refuses Carr's suggestion that he reunite with her. But after watching Maria rehearse, Chuck is smitten, and persuades Maria to ride out to his ranch, the Lucky Seven, with him. There, she meets Chuck's friends and his mother—described as "a tart little old lady with an Italian-boy haircut." As Chuck and Maria walk around the ranch, chickens start laying eggs, cows begin producing milk, and a partially constructed oil well spurts forth a geyser of crude. A down-home barbeque and square dance conclude the evening, and the happy couple returns to the Sands, very much in love.

But the following day, Chuck's luck vanishes. They have a temporary gloom, but after watching Maria perform on her opening night, Chuck resolves to stay with her, bad luck or not. She agrees to spend six months a year performing and six months on his ranch. Chuck declares that he will never again gamble, as finding Maria used up all the luck he will ever need. End credits.

Not exactly *The Maltese Falcon*, this was a musical comedy intended as light entertainment. By June, plans had solidified enough that the studio sent several employees releases in which the employee indicated they understood that the film, though based in a real casino, was a work of fiction, and that they surrendered all claims that any characters depicted them, and gave MGM full, irrevocable permission to use such a character without fear of a libel action. Reservations manager Nick Kelly, Jack Entratter, Carl Cohen, and others signed. Along with these waivers, Sands management agreed to send three craps tables, four 21 tables, three roulette tables, and 64 slot machines to MGM's Hollywood studios, to create a more authentic portrayal of the casino on film. Shooting the bulk of the casino sequences at the actual Sands was prohibitive, and rather than rely on stock Tinseltown props, which would likely be outdated, Entratter and Cohen agreed that a loan could be arranged, provided they did not run afoul of federal laws prohibiting the interstate shipment of gambling equipment. Transport was arranged, with a police escort.

Of course, not shooting inside the casino would also avoid complications with publicity-shy gamblers. Win-win.

Freeman was MGM's strongest advocate at the Sands. He warned Entratter that Pasternak had delegated negotiations to unit director Sid Bowen, location manager Charles Coleman, and art director Urie McClary.

"Pasternak has ordered them not to argue or linger with any hotel that doesn't seem cooperative," he told Entratter. "I heard that the Flamingo and the El Rancho Vegas haven't done themselves any favors. Right now we are in 65 percent of this film. If we bend over backwards for Pasternak, we can make it 85 percent."

So Entratter and Cohen agreed to be very cooperative, even sending six dealers and a slot mechanic to staff the recreation of the Sands on an MGM soundstage for two weeks, and to accommodate an extended location shoot at the hotel itself. The studio asked the Sands for 15 single rooms to house 100 crew, actors, and executives for the duration, as well as rooms for 75 extras. Some of the technical experts were staying for a whole week, but most of the crewmembers, from Pasternak to the principal actors, were expected to be at the Sands for only four days. The Sands was forced to lease rooms for the crew at the

Royal Palms and Bon Aire motels to accommodate the shoot without closing down the hotel entirely.

By the time principal photography in Los Angeles had wrapped, the film had a new title: *Meet Me in Las Vegas*, though it was occasionally referred to as *Viva Las Vegas*, its title in Spanish-language release.

On September 14, the film's crew began shooting, with a 7:30 a.m. start in the Terrace Room. Pool attendants were instructed to follow the direction of MGM crew in placing the pool furniture that extras would be using. Five gallons of lemonade, with cherries, orange slices, and straws were also required, not for the crew, but to dress the tables. A 2 p.m. shooting moved to the Sands marquee and entrance. Over the next three days, cameras were recording several scenes outside the Sands and in the Dunes' parking lot.

The film itself was a whimsical musical comedy starring dancer Cyd Charisse as Maria Corvier, Dan Dailey as Chuck Rodwell, Agnes Moorehead as Chuck's mother, Lili Darvas as Maria's assistant Sari Hatvany, Jim Backus as Sands manager Tom Culdane, Paul Henreid as Maria's manager, and a host of friends of the Sands who made cameos, often uncredited. Even Jake Freedman was in the film for a second, shaking Chuck's hand when he arrived at the hotel. The Sands itself—particularly the Copa Room—featured prominently, of course, and the plot, such as it was, essentially followed the summary that MGM sent to the Sands for approval in June, with a few characters' names changed. With show business glamor, "authentic" Western living on Chuck's ranch, high stakes gambling, and a bit of culture (the film included Charisse dancing a variety of styles plus musical performances by the Four Aces, Lena Horne, Frankie Laine, an offstage but credited Sammy Davis, Jr., and Japanese child performer Mitsuko Sawamura), *Meet Me in Las Vegas*, like a typical Vegas floorshow, had a bit of everything. When Horne sang "If You Can Dream," dressed in an elegant sleeveless gown and jewels worth more than a high roller's bankroll, it felt that anything was possible in the glamorous world of the Sands.

MGM was even more eager, if such a thing was possible, to turn *Meet Me in Las Vegas* into a marketing bonanza than was the Sands. In December, MGM publicist Howard Herty wrote to Freeman, brainstorming ideas. Maybe Las Vegas and its individual hotels could conduct a national advertising campaign on the film's behalf. Or they could begin mailing Las Vegas postcards to movie editors and reviewers on MGM's list. Perhaps they had some creative ideas for how to decorate MGM's Broadway billboard (Freeman circled this one). Maybe the chamber of commerce could distribute a pamphlet to travel agents nationwide in connection with the picture.

Freeman responded with his own ideas for "Sands exploitation" (his words) of the movie, including advance mailings to the press, a six-month cross promotion with Pillsbury, the Sands funding the distribution of Pasternak's new book, *Easy the Hard Way,* to press, "advertising tie-ups" with favored partners like TWA and the Union Pacific Railroad, and a Sands vacation prize for the theater manager who staged the best promotion. The key, though, was to hold a gala world premiere for the movie in Las Vegas. Insist that all press and spectators arrive in Western dress or spend a few minutes in a makeshift jail in the El Portal lobby. Make it a charity event, with proceeds benefiting the Variety School for Handicapped Children. Further, let the press play (for charity) at an oversized roulette table set up outside the theater; the public could also play, winning a kiss from Cyd Charisse or a dance with Dan Dailey. Naturally, after the movie, the press would return to the Sands for hospitality.

The premiere went off, with typical star power, on Tuesday, February 21. Freeman outdid himself, securing Milton Berle's NBC variety show to broadcast nationwide directly from the Copa—the first color telecast to emanate from Las Vegas. Clips from the film were intercut with action from the Copa, including performances from Jimmy Durante, Eddie Cantor, Peggy Lee, Groucho Marx, the Four Aces, and the Copa Girls. Following the show, a host of stars, including Charisse, Dailey, Ann Miller, Peter Lorre, Fred MacMurray, John Barrymore, Doris Day, Esther Williams, Walter Pidgeon, and Cary Grant, were shuttled down to Fremont Street for the debut screening at the El Portal. The high point of the festivities came when Las Vegas Mayor C. D. Baker presented Pasternak with a commemorative plaque and director Roy Rowland with a 10-gallon hat. Following the movie, the press and stars returned to the Sands, where, in a comically exaggerated chef's hat, Pasternak served "Hungarian" dishes.

Two weeks later, the film's New York premiere at the Astor Theater became a charity event, with proceeds benefiting the United States Olympic Fund, which defrayed the training and travel expenses of American athletes competing in that year's Summer Olympics, held in Melbourne, Australia. This event lacked a direct connection to Las Vegas, outside of the film, so it didn't have the same "hard sell" as the

Berle show. It did, however, keep the movie in the public eye, as did a block-long billboard on Broadway between 45th and 46th streets.

Reviewers generally liked the film. Philip K. Scheuer's *Los Angeles Times* write-up praised Charisse's performance and called out the celebrity cameos. A favorable Hedda Hopper write-up ran under the headline "Cyd's What a Star Should Be." May Tinee of the *Chicago Tribune* praised the sophistication of the film, predicting that it would be a box office smash. Bosley Crowther of the *New York Times* marveled at what a good job the film did at dropping the movie-goer into the fantastic world of Las Vegas. He was less taken with Horne and Laine's contributions than Charisse's dancing, but on the whole endorsed the movie. "An expensive and sparkling production, arranged by Joe Pasternak," he concluded, "endows the whole thing with tourist luxuriance. Oh, boy—what an ad for the Sands!"

***

The good reviews and effusive hometown press for *Meet Me in Las Vegas* might have given the town a morale boost and spurred tourism, but they did not sell many movie tickets; the film ultimately lost money, mirroring a lingering pessimism about Las Vegas itself. Hotel owners and civic boosters put on brave faces, but more objective observers concluded that Las Vegas was in real trouble.

A few weeks after the premiere of *Meet Me in Las Vegas,* Gilbert Millstein penned an article for the *New York Times* that ran under the headline "Cloud on Las Vegas' Silver Lining." After recounting the doom and gloom of the Class of '55, Millstein discussed a *tete-a-tete* with Jake Freedman in "the hushed privacy of a suite of offices upstairs." After demonstrating the Sands' state-of-the-art closed-circuit television system, which Cohen had installed the previous year, Freedman did something that Millstein assured his reader was utterly without precedent.

"Here," said the Sands president, who Millstein described as "a small, seamed man," before producing from his wallet a sworn statement revealing the Sands' recent financial performance: total gross of $8,725,224 in 1953; $9,060,622 in 1954; and $10,347,567 in 1955. Gross gambling win for those years was $5,399,019; $5,256,638; and $6,937,000. If Las Vegas was having problems, the Sands certainly wasn't.

The numbers Freedman showed Millstein, if genuine, show that the Sands was officially pulling in less than $15,000 per day from its casino in 1953 and 1954, and about $19,000 on average in 1955, which shows just how small-scale the gambling trade was. Today, a $15,000 bet on a single hand of blackjack might be business as usual at the higher end Strip resorts. Even assuming that the numbers undercounted gaming win by 15 percent (a probably reasonable estimate for the magnitude of the skim in those days), we get an average daily casino win of under $22,000 in 1955.

One of the common complaints in modern Las Vegas is that the city's casinos have lost their personal touch. In the good old days, they say, everyone was treated like a king. Freedman's numbers give us a good insight into why. If you had a few dozen—maybe 50 or 60 at most—serious gamblers, with only a few on property at a time, each of them would be given special attention. And, when a $400 bet would give pit bosses goosebumps, even players betting $20 a hand were taken seriously. All this made for a friendlier, more intimate reception for gamblers in Las Vegas—particularly at the Sands, where Freedman, Cohen, and other managers and dealers might have relationships with big players going back decades.

With such a narrow player base, the bosses took nothing for granted. The malaise of 1955 had made one thing clear to Las Vegas: For the city to continue to grow, everyone had to pull together, get on the same page.

This was nowhere clearer than in how the county sheriff and casino bosses came to an understanding about law and order.

The casino bosses negotiated, as early as the term of Sheriff Glen Jones, which started in 1943, an unwritten but binding gentlemen's agreement over who was boss. This was an extension of the arrangements between mob money men and desert cowboys that made the Mojave such a hospitable place to run a casino. It was, as Jones explained, quite simple.

"No contract killings. No bullshit in my county," Jones had insisted, as did his successor Glen Leypolt. Ralph Lamb, who served as sheriff from 1961 to 1979, raised the respectful symbiosis between the sheriff's department and the casino bosses to an art form, which might explain why he was the subject of the 2012 CBS television series *Vegas*.

Keeping underworld violence far from tourist-friendly Las Vegas benefited the casino owners as well. But the sheriff exacted another promise from the bosses in exchange for giving them relatively free rein to police themselves: Don't bring in anyone—as a dealer, as a dishwasher, as a shoe shine boy—who would embarrass the sheriff if it became known that he was working in his county.

The bosses were only too happy to oblige, though sometimes mistakes were made. When the sheriff learned of it, the reaction was swift.

Once, for example, the sheriff sent a deputy to the Sands in search of a particular craps dealer. He wore, like most deputies in that time, cowboy boots and a gun. It would have been funny—a real live cowboy, walking around in the ultra-modern Sands—if it wasn't deadly serious.

"You've got a record," he said plainly. "You've got to go."

"Wait a second," the dealer replied. "Let me see what Carl says."

The deputy left. The dealer thought his bluff had worked.

But then he returned with four other deputies. They grabbed the offending dealer and the rest of his crew for good measure, leaving an empty table and an astonished pit boss. The pit boss and the deputies working for Sands security knew enough not to stop them. This was far above their pay grade.

Carl Cohen knew immediately what to do.

He went down to the sheriff's office, hat in hand. Once he made it clear that the offending dealer would be leaving town by sundown, he secured the release of the rest of his crew. Cohen was an almighty force in the casino, not far below the Lord himself, but he knew who ran the county.

Even street-hardened wiseguys were slightly awed by the cowboys.

"You're real tough with a knife or a gun," one of them said to his friend who asked why they gave the cowboys such a wide berth, "but they'll knock you cold fucking bare-handed."

Once, reputed Chicago mob kingpin John Marshall, also known as Marshall Caifano, swung at one of the cowboys who didn't show him the appropriate deference. Connected flush on the jaw. Didn't make a dent. The cowboy smiled, maybe, picked him up by the throat, and carried him out of the Sands.

"How can he do that?" pit boss Ed Walters asked Cohen. "Pick up a guy that heavy, with just one hand?"

"Eddie," Cohen replied, "go out to Lamb's ranch sometime. You'll see these guys throwing around *cows*. After that, a man's nothing."

For their part, the cowboys knew they couldn't bring Frank Sinatra to town, put whole families to work, or make Las Vegas a national headline, and they respected that the casino bosses were, in their own way, tough men who, while they might not be able to rope a steer, were not pushovers. And, without them, there wouldn't be much of a budget for the sheriff's office or anything else in the county.

Secure in the knowledge that each group complemented the other, the cowboys and the casino guys were able to work together for the mutual benefit of everyone—tolerance and prosperity. Cowboys, mobsters, show business guys, all living in perfect harmony. Las Vegas was, when you came down to it, the most all-American town in the nation. It would solve its own problems.

***

As Las Vegas recovered from its crisis of confidence, the Sands continued to take the spotlight, hosting, for example, the world premiere of Paramount's *The Joker Is Wild.* The 1957 film, a biography of comedian Joe E. Lewis, starred Frank Sinatra, so the Sands threw open the doors to over dozen reporters, many with their spouses, who could be counted upon to favorably mention the hotel in their reporting on the hard-hitting news of the movie opening. Freeman also reserved 16 rooms for Frank Sinatra and his closest friends, including lyricist Sammy Cahn, whose "All the Way" as sung by Sinatra would garner that year's Academy Award for Best Original Song, and Dean Martin and Peter Lawford, who would soon become notorious playmates of Old Blue Eyes.

The premiere itself was more than a red carpet followed by champagne—Freeman turned it into a 24-hour bash, which he hailed as a worldwide first. Starting with a 6 p.m. cocktail party in the Sands' Emerald Room, a second-floor conference center with a plush, deep-green carpet, guests were treated to dinner and a show in the Copa headlined by popular soprano Marguerite Piazza. The media were then ferried down to the El Portal. In front of the theater, the Strip's hotels staged a mini parade of stars, many of whom came up on stage as the Variety Club presented awards to Lewis and Sinatra.

The actual movie began at 10:30. Following the film, guests were invited to a private party thrown for Sinatra and Lewis at the El Rancho Vegas, where Lewis had been a fixture for years. Upon staging back to the Sands early that morning, the press was free to enjoy as much food and drink as they could consume, on the house, with a car back to their chartered flight leaving at exactly 5 p.m.

Freeman and Entratter could afford to give rival Beldon Katleman's El Rancho Vegas some of the spotlight because there the El Rancho Vegas was not really competition for them. Lewis was a beloved character, but he was no Frank Sinatra, and the Opera House was no Copa.

The Sands' profile reached something close to the zenith of *Meet Me in Las Vegas* in late 1957, when CBS favorite *I Love Lucy* (technically, *The Lucille Ball-Desi Arnaz Show*, as the hour-long version was formally known) shot an episode set (although not filmed), in part, in the hotel. Called "Lucy Hunts Uranium," the episode centered on Lucy's attempts to claim a $10,000 bounty by discovering a uranium strike in the Mojave. The Ricardos found themselves in Las Vegas because Ricky was performing in the Copa Room. The episode lacked the immersive presentation of the Sands that distinguished *Meet Me in Las Vegas*—outside of two exterior shots of the building, focused on the famous marquee advertising Ricky's performance, there was no footage of the actual Sands, although the hotel loaned the production some of its monogrammed bedsheets to dress a hotel room set.

But there are some interesting things in the episode, which garnered impressive ratings on its first airing on January 3, 1958. One is an establishing shot of a sign reading "Welcome to Las Vegas," over a year before Betty Willis' famous sign was installed at the south end of the burgeoning Strip. The second is the presentation of Las Vegas, which mixed Hollywood glamor (guest star Fred MacMurray and his wife, June Haver, just happen to be staying at the Sands) with the raw-boned Western surroundings: grizzled prospectors riding burros feature prominently in the story. The revelation that Fred MacMurray had lost $100 playing nickel slots got a big laugh from the studio audience. The plot features the usual elements of a misunderstanding leading the characters into progressively more madcap antics. Still, there is one fascinating tidbit—Ricky says that he is able to join the uranium hunt because "Jack Entratter canceled the show." This suggests that the audience would be familiar enough with Entratter to catch the reference. "Lucy Hunts Uranium" might not have driven as many people to call Sands reservation centers as *Meet Me in Las Vegas*, but it is evidence that Entratter—and the Sands itself—had a secure place in the American consciousness.

***

In early 1958, it looked like Las Vegas had rebounded from the disasters of 1955 and the Sands had distanced itself from the Dunes fiasco. But good fortune only went so far. In late 1957, Jake Freedman began complaining of chest pain. "The Colonel," as he was respectfully known, was no stranger to poor health: He had suffered from arthritis for years, and several decades of the late-night lifestyle of a gambling operator were hardly conducive to wellness.

Each December, the Sands threw its customary gala anniversary party. Hosted by inaugural headliner Danny Thomas, the evening consisted of a performance by Sammy Davis, Jr., dancing by the Copa Girls, and the cutting and consumption of a giant cake. The casino's president was conspicuous by his absence.

Freedman managed to drag himself to the Sands' New Year's Eve celebration, where, as was his habit, he gave away $50,000 in silver dollars to casino-goers. But his health didn't improve with the new year. A week later, he checked into Mt. Sinai Hospital in Los Angeles. On January 19, while undergoing surgery for a ruptured artery in his chest, Freedman passed away. He was 64 years old, and left behind a widow, Sadie, a son, Nathan, and three grandchildren.

Three days later, more than two hundred friends paid their respects to Freedman, packing into the tiny chapel of the Groman Mortuary in downtown Los Angeles. Rabbi Max Nussbaum of Los Angeles delivered a eulogy emphasizing Freedman's charitable work. Bernard Cohen, rabbi of the Las Vegas Jewish Community Center, also spoke. Fellow Las Vegas casino owners and managers, including Moe Dalitz, Wilbur Clark, Al Parvin, Abe Schiller, Beldon Katleman, and Louis Lederer, attended, with a large delegation from the Sands headed by Entratter and Cohen. A host of Hollywood admirers, including Frank Sinatra, Danny Thomas, Tony Martin, Loulla Parsons, and Joe Pasternak, paid their respects.

Freedman's *Review-Journal* obituary recounted his twin successes in horse racing and oil, his generosity, and his triumph at the Sands. Though born in Russia, he was thoroughly a Westerner.

"Ironically, Freedman will be buried in a tuxedo," the obituary claimed, "even though his lavish wardrobe included 67 Western outfits and 75 cowboy hats—a Freedman trademark."

Freedman was laid to rest in his family mausoleum in Houston's Beth-Israel cemetery. It was in Las Vegas, though, where his legacy lived on. That July, Sadie accepted an award from the counsel general of Israel in recognition of her late husband's tireless work for the United Jewish Appeal. And, for years, he was fondly remembered throughout the town for his generosity and incredible gambling appetite.

The biggest tribute to Freedman, however, came at the Sands. On the afternoon of his funeral, from 2 to 3 p.m., all gambling ceased in the casino—the ultimate sign of respect. Then, the dice started rolling and the silver dollars started clattering again. Freedman would have approved.

Something's Gotta Give

Jake Freedman's passing did not much change life at the Sands. Though president of the casino, he did not make many substantive decisions. Like Wilbur Clark of the Desert Inn, he could charitably be called a spokesman for the group that owned the casino, less charitably, a figurehead, and even less charitably, a mascot. Any important decisions relating to the hotel and entertainment had been made, from day one, by Jack Entratter. He was assisted by Archie Loveland, a hotel veteran who had worked at one point with Cohen at the El Rancho Vegas. Loveland came aboard in May of 1957, taking a role that was subordinate to Entratter, though he had the kind of gravitas that made his word carry far. Carl Cohen, of course, held sway in the casino and represented the Sands in several community matters. He was frequently the one tasked with passing out checks to charity groups, of which there was a seemingly endless stream, from the Helldorado Parade to the many community concerts Antonio Morelli staged to an ecumenical array of religious benefits.

In 1952, the conventional wisdom was that the Sands, with most of its capital and managerial expertise coming from the East, needed a Westerner at the helm to pacify the locals, even though the role was mostly ceremonial.

But by 1958, the Sands, and its investors, were in a much different place than they had been a mere six years earlier. The casino was now, arguably, the most successful in Las Vegas. In 1952 Estes Kefauver was still a vital force in American politics, and it seemed possible that the federal government could turn against Nevada's experiment in commercial gaming. Over the ensuing six years, Kefauver's anti-gambling campaign, while successful in clearing out illegal gambling in other parts of the country, had proven no match for the Silver State. When campaigning for the vice presidency in 1956, Kefauver flat-out repudiated his earlier opposition to Nevada gaming, opining that he had always really believed gambling was best left to the wisdom of the states. Internally, Las Vegas casinos had faced down the challenges of the 1955 crash and emerged stronger. No one could imagine the town without the casinos of the Strip, particularly the Sands.

So it was decided—as these things were always decided, far from the public eye—that a Westerner was no longer needed at the helm of the Sands. Jack Entratter had earned his spurs over the previous half-decade by bringing entertainment legends to Las Vegas. Carl Cohen, a Las Vegas resident since 1941, was practically a native. So Entratter became president, with Cohen promoted to vice president. The Monday following Freedman's funeral, the Sands Board of Directors confirmed the decision.

One subtle sign of the shift from West to East was the renaming of the Silver Queen to the Copa Lounge. At the hotel's opening, the name was an homage to Nevada's reputation as the Silver State. But, after five years in business, Entratter renamed it after the main showroom. From a marketing point of view, that made sense. After all, the Copa was famous from coast to coast, and the Silver Queen sounded more like a steamboat than a hip cocktail lounge. There were other changes. The Garden Room, under the supervision of Chef Sui, expanded its Chinese food service from "dinner" through 6 a.m. Previously, Chinese food was only available after midnight. Within a few years, Al Freeman was boasting that the Sands served more Chinese food daily than the three top Chinese restaurants in San Francisco, combined.

All told, there was more continuity than change for the Sands in 1958. In keeping with the general shift toward convention bookings in Las Vegas, the hotel lined up several groups, including the National Licensed Beverage Association, which held a special officers' dinner in the Sands' Emerald Room in conjunction with its 1,000-delegate, four-day convention; the Kern County Chamber of Commerce, which held a three-day "selling safari" in which it tried to sell the California county to the rest of the world (apparently Las Vegas was a better place to do this than Wasco or Bakersfield); the Cincinnati Automobile Club, which had a brief meeting in the aftermath of the AAA convention held in Arizona that year; the Japanese Steel Association, which spent three days meeting with American steel executives and catching Danny

Thomas in the Copa Room; and, in what was surely a triumph for all involved, the Pacific Coast Meat Jobbers, who broke away from their multi-day conference to enjoy a cocktail party in the lounge. It might not have been the most glamorous group, but it did bring 700 guests to the Sands during an otherwise-slow week.

In these years, the Sands' management began placing much more emphasis on the hotel part of the operation. One casino-related change was the 1959 arrival of baccarat, which Frank Sinatra had played in the south of France and, which, he assured Cohen, would be a great draw for sophisticated international players. Cohen investigated for himself, comparing *chemin de fer*, in which players bet against each other, to a version known as *punto banco* in which players bet against the house. As *chemin de fer* had underwhelmed gamblers at the Stardust the previous year, he installed a doubled-lobed baccarat table in an alcove renamed the Deauville Room. Players bet against the house, streamlining the play. The game was unfamiliar enough to Las Vegas that the casino ran newspaper ads stressing how easy to learn and exciting to play it was, and the casino even offered to teach players the rudiments of the game as late as the 1980s. Still, it was hoped that European tourists would flock to the game.

Complementing his focus on filling rooms, Entratter continued to push the Sands' entertainment. Having brought in rising star Johnny Mathis in 1957, just off the success of "Chances Are," the impresario pulled off another coup when he wooed Judy Garland to the Copa for the first time. Al Freeman worked overtime promoting her arrival at the Sands. Her two-week stand, consisting of two hour-long performances a night, was hailed as a milestone for the Sands and Las Vegas.

For the opening night of "Miss Show Business," Entratter and Frank Sinatra chartered a special train, which ferried a large group of Garland's closest Hollywood friends for a two-day junket centered around the October 1 VIP-only debut performance. This was, Freeman assured reporters, the largest group of movie stars and celebrities ever gathered in Las Vegas. The 600 guests who packed the Copa past capacity enjoyed not just Garland's scheduled performance, but also an unscripted, impromptu 20-minute singing and ribbing session with her dear friends Frank Sinatra and Dean Martin.

The Sands seemed to be on the verge of a genuine star turn. After the hotel's appearance in *I Love Lucy*, it seemed like the Sands might even get a show of its own. In late 1958, Entratter talked with Lucille

Ball and Desi Arnaz about the possibility, but it never went further than that. While the Sands was fine as an occasional location to give an episode a star rub, from a practical standpoint a series set at the Sands— even if filmed on a Hollywood soundstage—would be a hard sell on both sides. The networks, though they had no problem with giving Las Vegas occasional coverage, might balk at investing in a show set there. For his part, Entratter would likely have insisted on strict creative control. He and Freeman as a matter of policy struck any references that could be potentially construed as reflecting negatively on the Sands or Las Vegas as a condition of featuring the hotel in any production. Writers and producers working under the pressure of a weekly series likely would have objected to this level of editorial interference.

In any event, the Sands show did not take off, although it is intriguing to imagine what might have been had a program set at the hotel replaced *Guestward Ho!* at Desilu. That sitcom, about a New York family who replaces the New York City rat race with life on a New Mexico dude ranch, enjoyed a single 38-episode season in 1960-1, airing on ABC. Still, even without a network show to call its own, the Sands had near-universal brand recognition. The Sands was everywhere, and nothing but good times were on the horizon.

***

In the summer of 1960, the Sands enjoyed what might have been its finest hour, hosting "The Summit" meeting that in the public consciousness became known as the Rat Pack and appearing prominently in *Ocean's 11*. But amid the good times, there was tragedy. On August 27, Jack Entratter was driving a group—Al Freeman, the hotel's chief engineer Bernard North, and David Ormont, president of the Terminal-Hudson Electronics Corporation—from the Sands out to Lake Mead for an afternoon of waterskiing. Skis were strapped to Entratter's station wagon, and Ormont, a longtime friend of Entratter's who was staying at the Sands with his wife, Evelyn, was already wearing his bathing suit.

According to witness Jimmy Humphrey, the station wagon passed him headed east on Desert Inn Road and did not even attempt to stop for the sign at the intersection with Sandhill Road.

At the same time, Doris Jean Jones was driving north on Sandhill. Jones t-boned the station wagon, which rolled, crushing Ormont's skull, killing him instantly. Freeman and North were thrown from the vehicle and injured seriously enough to require hospitalization. Entratter walked away from the crash unscathed, while Jones suffered a head injury, fractured pelvis, and broken leg.

Sheriff's deputies at the scene declined to issue a summons.

Three days later, however, Clark County District Attorney Jack Cherry filed involuntary manslaughter charges against Entratter. The sheriff's report claimed that Entratter had disregarded the stop sign while speeding down Desert Inn at 50 miles per hour. Entratter, who was briefly jailed during the two-day investigation, retained Harry Claiborne as his defense attorney. Claiborne was one of Las Vegas's premier defense attorneys, claiming among his clients casino owners, those suspected of mob ties, and even celebrities, and had been Jake Freedman's advocate in hearings before county and state officials while the Sands was still under construction.

Entratter, in addition to being instrumental in the death of his friend and the hospitalization of two Sands employees and an innocent bystander, was now facing serious charges. But, as always, the show went on. Two weeks after the accident, he presided over a pair of weddings at the Sands—that of Los Angeles physician Max Shapiro and Jewel Hood, and of Frank Sinatra's daughter Nancy and singer Tommy Sands. Freeman, still in the hospital recuperating from a serious head injury, was not able to work his usual magic with the press; instead, Las Vegas News Bureau chief Jack Pepper, assisted by Entratter and Eleanor Roth and Ruth Steinberg, did the public relations honors.

Ten days after the Sinatra/Sands nuptials, a preliminary hearing before Justice of the Peace Oscar Bryan began. Claiborne fielded 13 witnesses in defense of his client—no mean feat for an accident that involved five people, one of whom was dead. While Humphrey, the lone witness, maintained that Entratter had been speeding and did not brake at all, Al Freeman, who had recovered sufficiently to offer testimony, disagreed.

"I felt a definite braking action," he testified, insisting that Entratter lost control of the car due to "washboard" conditions on the unpaved road. Washboard roads develop ridges of gravel and dirt that impede driving, as decreased contact with the road surface can lead to drivers losing control of their vehicle.

On Monday, October 3, Justice of the Peace Bryan rendered his decision on whether Entratter would face trial for the accident.

"There is no way legally that this man could legally be bound over on the evidence that was presented here," he told a courtroom packed with friends of Entratter. "There is no evidence here, nothing.

"I'm dismissing this case. If anyone isn't happy about that, they can bring it to the grand jury, the district court, or for that matter the Supreme Court."

The courtroom erupted with applause.

After the decision, which the *Review-Journal* claimed "erased for all time the stigma of highway homicide" from Entratter, the Sands president was far from conciliatory.

"There was never enough evidence proving negligence on my part," he said. "I do not feel that I should have been formally charged.

"I feel it was because of my position as an executive that these charges were lodged against me. If a man with many traffic violations gets off for $20, it just doesn't seem fair that I should have to put up with the torture I went through since the time of the accident."

Here, Entratter was referencing a recent case where a driver with a history of bad behavior was only fined $20 for his role in a fatal accident.

"I'm driving a car which kills a man I've known for 25 years and injures three others. I felt terrible about the accident, and then I'm faced with this charge of manslaughter. I feel the negligence was on the part of the County. The road where the accident happened was dangerous. I wasn't driving fast and I was not drinking. The accident was one of those unfortunate things. These past weeks in court have been torture."

Though he knew in his heart he had done nothing criminal, Entratter had still been anxious.

"You never know what might happen in a court of law. Circumstances can be twisted and before you know it you are really in hot water."

Entratter did not believe that he had faced the charges by accident, though.

"I feel that the accident took place during a time when a political position was at stake, and I was tossed into the act as a political football. Had the accident happened at a different time and it was someone else driving, I'm sure things would not have been handled the same way."

This may have been a reference to upcoming local elections, or even to the Nixon/Kennedy presidential contest, in which Entratter and the Sands had taken a strong interest.

In any event, Entratter was cleared of criminal wrongdoing, but the threat of a civil suit hung over him. Entratter suffered a larger tragedy when, on May 13, 1961, his wife Dorothy died from a coronary occlusion. He commemorated her by establishing a children's home in Jerusalem, Israel in her name, which was dedicated by Frank Sinatra (who had written a sizeable check to fund the center) the following year.

In July 1961, Jones and her husband Vernon sued Entratter for $70,000. The suit never went to trial. But in November, Ormont's estate, with presumably greater resources for a legal battle, brought suit for wrongful death against Entratter, Jones, Clark County, the Board of County Commissioners, and Press Lamb, the county road superintendent. The claim requested $250,000 in damages plus $4,751 in funeral expenses.

There was no quick resolution of this case. In early 1963, District Judge John Mowbray dismissed the case on grounds of government immunity. Ormont's estate appealed, and the Nevada Supreme Court reversed the decision, allowing the litigation to proceed. By the time it was ready for trial in June 1966, the case was amended to increase the potential damages. Just after a jury was empaneled, however, the plaintiff and defendants agreed to an out-of-court settlement.

After nearly six years, Entratter could put the accident behind him. But fighting first a criminal then an extended civil action likely took its toll on the showman. No matter how competent his attorneys, he still had the cloud of an impending trial looming over him for years. Ironically, this was center of what is called the "Rat Pack era" of Las Vegas, when the Sands was at its most prominent. A few months after the Ormont suit was settled, Caesars Palace would open, threatening the Sands' place as the elite Las Vegas resort. By the end of the year, Howard Hughes would take up residence in town, auguring massive changes in how Las Vegas casinos were owned and operated.

Entratter's guilt in the accident had been exonerated by a justice of the peace, but he certainly paid a heavy price for his actions on that summer day.

***

From the 1941 opening of the El Rancho Vegas, Las Vegas resort hotels advertised themselves as places where anyone was welcome—provided they had spending money, of course. A big part of the appeal of Las Vegas in general, and the Sands in particular, was that paying guests could rub shoulders with anyone—interesting vacationers from around the world and Hollywood stars alike.

The Strip wasn't universally welcoming, though. If you were black, you would find that no casino hotel on the Strip or gambling club Downtown would accept you as a guest, and your avenues for advancement as an employee were limited. Men could be hired as porters and women as housekeepers. New arrivals found they could not rent or buy a home anywhere but on the Westside. While the prospects for earning a living were better than they were in the sections of Arkansas and Mississippi that many African Americans left for Las Vegas, for them the Mojave was not the carefree paradise that press releases made it out to be. Las Vegas may have been freer, perhaps, than the Deep South, but it had a reputation as "the Mississippi of the West" for a reason.

For their part, those who enforced the color bar in Southern Nevada claimed to do so not out of deep-seated racist convictions, but because the presence of black patrons would drive away less enlightened Southerners, who made up a big proportion of gamblers, particularly at the Sands. This didn't, of course, explain the systemic residential, social, and economic segregation that defined Las Vegas at the time, but it might have made the waiters and doormen on whom it fell to politely (or not) remind African Americans of their place feel a little bit better about themselves.

Las Vegas had not always been segregated; in the 1930s, black-owned businesses could be found in the Downtown area. When the City Commission approved the first commercial gaming licenses in 1931, it requested applications from black gambling operators who would run an establishment catering exclusively to their own race. Such a business was duly licensed on Stewart Street. But as the city's population grew during the Second World War, racial segregation became the rule, and black-owned businesses moved to the Westside. This included bars and gambling clubs. By the mid-1950s, as the rest of the country was slowly moving away from segregation in the aftermath of *Brown vs. Board of Education*, Las Vegas was becoming more segregated.

Even at its Las Vegas height, segregation could be softened by the powers of wealth and celebrity—to an extent. Every Las Vegas casino hired black singers and musicians to perform, but as a rule they were not permitted to mix among patrons after the show, as white entertainers were encouraged to do, and they were usually forbidden from staying on property, instead relegated to taking rooms at an over-priced, under-appointed boarding house on the Westside.

Louis Armstrong—by the 1950s an elder statesman of American jazz and popular entertainment—learned this firsthand. He and opera star Robert Merrill became friends during their joint performances in the Copa, as Armstrong regaled Merrill with stories of the opera houses he had visited during his European tours.

So it was natural that they would want to unwind after the performances together, as show people do. In Europe this wouldn't have been a problem. In Las Vegas it was.

Trying to enter the Flamingo for a late supper, Merrill was welcomed warmly—after all, he was a marquee-topping star.

Armstrong was not.

"I'm sorry, Louis, but we can't let you in," the maître d' said apologetically. "You know how it is." Still, he beckoned for Merrill to take a seat.

"It's okay, Bob," Armstrong said. But it wasn't.

"I won't be eating here," Merrill responded, and left with Armstrong. They ended up in Armstrong's rooming house on the Westside, enjoying Southern dishes that Armstrong's wife Lucille had whipped up.

Lena Horne was recognized as a talented singer and actress when she headlined the Sands. She even had a featured number in *Meet Me in Las Vegas*, along with Frankie Laine. And she was allowed to stay in a room while performing in the mid-to-late 1950s—in recognition of her celebrity, perhaps, but also of her white husband. She was not, however, allowed to swim in the Sands' pool, and her sheets were laundered separately from those of other Sands' guests.

Similarly, Sammy Davis, Jr. had insisted his family members be allowed to watch him perform at the New Frontier in 1955 (they were hailed as the first black audience members in the young history of the Strip), but he himself did not have run of the casino. Even at the Sands, this was initially the case. During his first appearances there, he entertained his friends post-show in the second-floor Emerald Room. On one level, it was a chance for him and other show people to unwind in public, but out of the public eye. On the other, it was a way of satisfying Davis while keeping a black man out of the casino.

The Emerald Room played a minor role in one of Davis's most painful encounters with racial bigotry. In 1957, Davis became involved with Kim Novak, then a rising young actress under contract with

Columbia Pictures. Studio boss Harry Cohn, fearful that audiences would reject a white actress who dated a black man, allegedly, through underworld associates, let it be known that if the dalliance wasn't ended, Davis would be beaten severely. To show that he and Novak had no future, Davis must get married immediately—to a black woman, of course.

Chicago mob boss Sam Giancana reportedly relayed word that while Davis was safe in Chicago and Las Vegas, he and his friends' protection did not extend everywhere. Davis chose to marry Loray White, a dancer who was then performing at the Silver Slipper. On January 28, 1958, the pair were married in a civil service in the Emerald Room. Jack Entratter hosted the reception, with a three-tier cake provided by the hotel.

In mid-1958, Davis was more popular than ever with Copa audiences; they demanded encore after encore. Bowing to popular demand, Jack Entratter permitted Davis to stay onstage longer, impersonating Frank Sinatra and Jerry Lewis, or just doing a little hoofing. But this meant the guests weren't at the crap tables.

"Nice concert you did in there, boy," Carl Cohen remarked to Davis in the casino that night. To anyone watching, Cohen and Davis were the epitome of brotherly love; Cohen had a smile on his face and a meaty arm around Davis, who was smiling just as broadly. But the message was clear: Make sure the audience was "out here" when they were supposed to be. Davis might be the one the crowds were screaming for, but he wasn't so big that Cohen couldn't call him "boy."

There were plenty of people who Davis didn't have to take that kind of abuse from. Cohen wasn't one of them. The show ended on time from then on.

Still, that this exchange even took place the way it did was a mark of the special status that Davis enjoyed. Most black performers were encouraged to return to their dressing room and their accommodations on the Westside after the show. That Davis was even allowed to walk through the casino, much less hold a conversation with Cohen there, was out of the norm for Las Vegas, much less other parts of the country.

Further, that the story of Davis being granted the privilege of performing overtime and speaking with Cohen on the casino floor was published in Les Devor's "Vegas Vagaries" column, whose Sands items were more or less dictated by Freeman, indicates that not only did

Cohen and Entratter feel comfortable hosting Davis in the casino, but that they wanted to publicize it, only a few months after his wedding to White. The message was clear: Davis was welcome at the Sands.

But they also publicized that Cohen called Davis "boy."

Because of this, and countless other indignities, voices in the black community began to insist on the desegregation of Las Vegas, for better opportunities in housing and employment. The Sands had a role in this struggle.

In 1952, before the hotel opened, Entratter hired James Gay III—known to his many friends as Jimmy—as a personnel consultant. Gay had established himself as a central figure in the Westside community within a few years of his moving to Las Vegas from Fordyce, Arkansas. High school classmates with Alabama football legend Bear Bryant, Gay earned a degree from the Arkansas Agricultural, Mining, and Normal College at Pine Bluffs before attending mortuary school in Chicago. He returned to Fordyce and operated a mortuary, but soon set off for Las Vegas with his wife, Hazel, who had owned a barbershop, beauty parlor, restaurant, and record shop in Fordyce.

A college-educated businessman in Fordyce, Gay found working in Las Vegas mortuaries closed to him, so he took a job as a cook at Sill's Drive-In. He also began serving as director of the Jefferson Recreation Center at Jefferson and D Streets on the Westside. He briefly worked as an assistant physicist at the Nevada Test Site before coming to work at the Sands.

At the Sands, Gay received a full-time salary to assist in the hiring of personnel. Initially hired for a three-month stint, Gay ultimately stayed with the Sands for 18 years. When he left the company he was director of communications for all Hughes Nevada properties. Gay's unofficial job was to liaison with the black community of Las Vegas, smoothing over any difficulties that might arise. Gay was respected by the Sands' management; he was a member of the Sands' delegation that attended Jake Freedman's Los Angeles funeral service. He boasted among his friends celebrities and politicians black and white. Governor Grant Sawyer in 1958 appointed him to the Nevada Athletic Commission, the body that oversaw boxing in the state.

Few black Las Vegans, though, were afforded the same opportunities as Gay. Even Gay found himself denied credentials by the State Board of Embalmers because of his race. The local NAACP became increasingly confident as, across the United States, barriers fell. In the late 1950s, the group held a series of boycotts targeting Westside businesses that did not hire black employees; these were successful. But the hotels and casinos of the Strip and Downtown still remained out of reach.

Nationally, NAACP chapters used boycotts and sit-ins to pressure businesses into integrating. But neither tactic would work on Strip hotels. As blacks were already not customers, a boycott was impossible. And even the most radical crusader for social justice knew that even the thought of occupying space at a casino's tables without playing was something close to sacrilege in Las Vegas.

So instead, the president of the Las Vegas NAACP, Dr. James McMillan, decided to stage a protest.

While not as bad as keeping paying customers away from the blackjack tables, the thought of a march down the Strip horrified the powers that be in Las Vegas. To shine any light on the negative aspects of their city seemed a terrible betrayal. This was the town that had come together in the face of a Congressional investigation into gambling, circled the wagons, and emerged stronger, had been boosting and spreading the word for over a decade now, securing magazine spreads and prime time coverage. Now, to have the press report on Las Vegas in the same breath as Montgomery or Little Rock—to encourage that kind of scrutiny was perverse.

Yet McMillan and other NAACP leaders, including David and Mabel Hoggard, Woodrow Wilson, Donald Clark, and Bob Bailey, held firm. If the city's casinos did not take meaningful steps to integrate in the next 30 days, they would flood the Strip with hundreds of picketers.

Mayor Oran Gragson begged McMillan to cancel the protest. Even though he grew increasingly skeptical of the support he could expect from the Westside's churches, McMillan refused. He understood that, in the absence of economic power, he had one weapon to wield against the power structure: publicity. In the hands of Al Freeman and his counterparts, it had essentially made Las Vegas. The casino owners knew that it could also destroy.

For his part, Jimmy Gay had a simple message for Jack Entratter: I'm not crossing any picket line. Neither, was the implication, would the Sands' black employees, and possibly even entertainers.

Gamblers to the core, the men who ran the casinos of Las Vegas were used to figuring the odds. Segregation had on its side the force of habit and the possibility that white Southern gamblers might not want to visit an integrated resort. But it would also mean protests and division, plus the possibility that black entertainers would refuse bookings, and that image-conscious business groups would cancel their conventions. On the positive side, eliminating segregation would remove awkward moments when a Nat "King" Cole or Dorothy Dandridge performed. And, it bore saying, black guests' money was just as green as that of whites.

So the gamblers, led by the Desert Inn's Moe Dalitz, decided to integrate. Like every other decision in Las Vegas, it had more to do with business than social or even personal concerns. On March 26, 1960, members of the NAACP and the Las Vegas business community, along with a host of politicians from the governor to the sheriff, announced that the city's hotels, casinos, and gambling clubs would henceforth be integrated.

The Sands was on the leading edge of the drive toward integration. The hotel began hosting an annual fashion show staged by the Alpha Rho Chapter of the Gamma Phi Delta Sorority. A national charity effort that raised $250,000 in 1959, the local effort was headed by Sarann Knight Preddy, who herself played a major role in the integration of Las Vegas. Knight Preddy had been a Westside resident since she moved to Las Vegas in 1942 at the age of 22. She opened a gambling club in remote Hawthorne, becoming the first black woman to receive a Nevada gaming license before returning to Las Vegas, where she again made history, breaking the color barrier by becoming a dealer at North Las Vegas' Jerry's Nugget. The event, at which Jimmy Gay represented the hotel, became a yearly fixture at the Sands.

A measure of the casinos' new concern for civil rights—or at least their concern that they be perceived as evincing a concern—came in April 1968, after the assassination of Dr. Martin Luther King, Jr. Five Las Vegans—including Woodrow Wilson, the state's first black legislator, Reverend Donald Clark, and Jimmy Gay—represented the city at Dr. King's funeral in Atlanta. But an even greater tribute took place in Las Vegas, as, for two hours, all casinos in the city and on the Strip were closed. This was only the second time the gambling had stopped across Las Vegas in the wake of a tragedy—the first was after the assassination of President John F. Kennedy. At the Sands, the dice had been stilled and the roulette wheels stopped in honor of Jake Freedman a decade earlier, putting Dr. King into respected company.

That's not to say that Las Vegas became a racial paradise overnight. It took a federal consent decree to force casinos to make more than token efforts at hiring black employees in more than menial positions. But the Sands' commitment to integration was sometimes personal. In 1967, one of Jimmy Gay's daughters was getting married. Over the years, the Sands had hosted events—birthdays, weddings—for executives and friends of the hotel, as a mark of respect and appreciation. In recognition of his long service to the Sands, Entratter offered to throw Gay the most lavish wedding the casino had seen yet.

Jack delivered. A sit-down meal for over 800 guests, with dignitaries like Nevada Governor Paul Laxalt, Senator Howard Cannon, and Las Vegas Mayor Oran Gragson, the reception was hosted by Danny Thomas, the Sands' perennial spokesman. The hotel picked up the entire $30,000 tab. After all, this was family.

"I've never seen a more beautiful wedding," Gay said to friends. "The only difference between this and President Johnson's daughter's is that hers was on national television."

It was a small moment in the grand scheme of things—certainly not enough to offset years of systemic injustice—but for Gay, the wedding meant something deeper. Once denied a license to practice his trade because of his skin color, he was now shown an honor as high as any.

If the Sands had not been especially brutal in its application of Jim Crow, it wasn't exceptionally eager to see it gone, either. Once it was gone, however, the hotel's managers were quick to leave the past behind, adapting quickly to the new reality. As a business, as an institution, it might have been a microcosm of America.

$\mathcal{M}$e and My Shadow

Since its opening, Danny Thomas had been, on paper, the premier celebrity spokesman for the Sands. He was the casino's debut act, emceed the casino's annual anniversary party, and was generally given first mention in any coverage of Sands events at which he was present. After the opening, Jack Entratter moved quickly, signing 14 of the top 18 nightclub draws to three- to five-year contracts. Entratter did not invent the nightclub residency, but in Las Vegas he perfected it. Stars worked three- or four-week stints in the Copa, with 8 p.m. and midnight shows in the relatively intimate Copa Room. They were well-paid—though Entratter tended to be tighter with the purse strings than other entertainment directors. In lieu of higher pay, he could offer the stability and prestige that came with a Sands contract.

Entratter wasn't content to rest on his laurels; he was constantly seeking out new talent and adopting the Copa's lineup to meet shifting tastes. Granted, he didn't put Elvis or Carl Perkins onstage—gamblers, after all, weren't known for their love of rock and roll—but he did phase out opera in favor of popular singers. He was the first in Las Vegas to book rising stars like Paul Anka, Nancy Ames, Buddy Greco, Corbett Monica, Frankie Randall, Lana Cantrell, and Diahann Carroll. Being invited into the Sands family was a sign that a performer had arrived.

Entratter also welcomed non-performing celebrities. This included, at various times, film stars like Humphrey Bogart and Lauren Bacall, Marlene Dietrich, Kirk Douglas, David Niven, José Ferrer, Marilyn Monroe, and Jack Lemmon; baseball players from Joe DiMaggio on down; and gossip columnists such as Louella Parsons.

It wasn't just well-known personalities who got the star treatment at the Sands. The hotel was equally eager to accommodate government and military panjandrums. In the summer of 1958, Dr. Dhia Ja'afar, the head of Reclamation and Public Improvement in Iraq, maintained headquarters at the Sands while he visited Hoover Dam. The following year, the hotel nearly hosted Marshall Konstantin Verhshinin, the commander of the Soviet Air Force. Though things had gotten enough along that Al Freeman had blocked out rooms (the marshal would have had the Governor's Suite in the Santa Anita building, not Sinatra's favored Presidential Suite), the visit was ultimately scrubbed.

The real star of the Sands as the 1950s turned over into the 1960s, though, was Frank Sinatra.

Officially, all celebrities affiliated with the Sands were friends, and it wasn't uncommon for them to attend each other's performances or even jump on stage when the occasion warranted. But, in late 1959, a group coalesced around Sinatra that, at least to the public, shared more than even the usual goodwill Sands stablemates had for each other.

Like Frank Sinatra, Dean Martin was long a performer at the Copacabana in New York. Indeed, Jack Entratter billed him and Jerry Lewis after they first performed together at Skinny D'Amato's legendary 500 Club in Atlantic City. The duo began performing at the Sands in January 1955. By October of that year, they had earned sufficient trust of the Sands management that they were permitted to engage in an outrageous stunt.

Killing time at the Sands while waiting for their plane to be ready (the duo wasn't even performing, just stopping in for a brief vacation), Martin, native of Steubenville, Ohio, and a onetime dealer at its illegal casinos, started dealing cards playfully at an empty blackjack table. When a few gamblers sat down, Lewis flipped cards to them, with Martin peeking at Lewis's hole card and suggesting how players finish their hand. When they still lost, he slid them silver dollars and $5 and $25 chips anyway. Martin paid players who did legitimately beat the house two to four times more than their bet. He also politely encouraged players who'd been "lucky" to give up their seats to new arrivals, who thronged the table as word got out.

After 35 minutes, Martin and Lewis had emptied the table's chip tray. On paper, the Sands was down $74,895. But Entratter was beaming.

"That $75,000," he told a *Review-Journal* reporter, "is nothing compared to the $2 million in goodwill the boys just made for the Sands. Of course, we're glad their plane finally got here. Six hours of that would almost be financially embarrassing."

After Martin and Lewis split in 1956, the former Dino Crocetti continued to play the Sands. Though superficially Martin and Sinatra were both Italian-American crooners of roughly the same age, they had drastically different personalities. This much was apparent to even casual fans, but Sands employees, who knew them offstage, saw it up close. Martin was generally relaxed, content with showing up when he had to, getting paid, and leaving others alone. When Dean was coming to town, everyone smiled. Business would be good, and things would go more or less according to plan. Sinatra, on the other hand, was unpredictable. He might tip the maître d' $500 for having a piano brought into the Garden Room, or something might trigger his infamous temper.

One night, Sinatra and ten of his friends were ordering Chinese food at the Garden Room. As was his custom, Sinatra ordered chow mein with no mushrooms. Maître d' George Levine cautioned the captain taking the order to tell the chef the noodles were for Sinatra— he would know, above all else, to not let one mushroom touch the bowl. Between the table and the kitchen, the captain forgot, or he couldn't be bothered. Chef Su-Pong made a heaping bowl of chow mein with mushrooms. With a flourish, the captain removed the silver dome from the bowl and presented the chef's finest to Frank.

When he saw the mushrooms, Sinatra screamed and threw the bowl over his head—it clanged off the wall, scattering noodles everywhere. Levine, despite himself, laughed. Sinatra then chased the maître d' into the kitchen.

"You want to fight?" he demanded.

"Frank, I'm a lover, not a fighter."

With that Sinatra laughed, hugged Levine, and returned to the table, leaving a generous tip. An apology, of course, was too much to ask for. If it wasn't mushrooms in his noodles, it might be a hamburger that was too well-done, or a writer (Harlan Ellison, specifically) not dressed well enough.

Sinatra, though he tried to incorporate jokes into his act, didn't have Martin's natural comic timing or easy delivery. His idea of a good joke was to throw a cherry bomb into a friend's toilet. He gave his friends "affectionate" nicknames: Martin was "Dago," Joey Bishop was "Hebe," and George Jacobs, his long-serving black valet, was "Spook." One of his favorite gags was to duet "Me and My Shadow" with Davis walking behind him.

Martin was usually the butt of his own jokes, which endeared him in ways that Sinatra did not.

Once, for example, Martin was walking by the dealers' break room while a baseball game was on. The dealers were watching the action on an antiquated set with rabbit ears that couldn't quite get decent reception—the picture was snowy and intermittent. Some of the dealers who had money on the game were upset that the Dodgers' pitcher couldn't find the plate, throwing ball after ball.

"Whaddya expect?" Martin asked. "He can't see the plate through all those wiggles."

Martin went down to the porte cochere, turned to a bellhop, and said, "Let's get a TV." They got in a Sands station wagon and drove to a local store.

"I want a TV, one that gets baseball," he announced when he walked in.

"They all do," the owner replied. He wheeled out from the back the largest and most expensive set he had in stock, with an oversized antenna.

"You sure that one gets baseball?" Martin asked.

"Yeah, of course it does," the owner replied. Martin paid. As the bellhop wrangled the set into the station wagon, the owner looked more closely.

"You're Dean Martin, aren't you?"

"No, no, I'm not," Martin said as he got into the station wagon.

The next day, around 4:00 p.m., Martin walked into the dealers' room. The dealers, now watching the game on their new set, broke into applause as Martin looked confused—hey, what did I do?

Just then, the pitcher split the plate with a fastball. Those with money on the game cheered.

"Of course he's throwing strikes now," Martin cracked. "He can finally see the plate."

Laughs all around. Without missing a beat, he turned to pit boss Ed Walters.

"Eddie, what are you doing up here? Get back in the casino before someone robs the place."

Maybe because they were so different, contrary to their public image as frequent drinking buddies, Martin and Sinatra did not socialize much offstage.

That wasn't so for Sammy Davis, Jr., who began performing at the Sands in March 1957. Though into the 1960s his act was officially billed "The Will Mastin Trio," his "uncle" Mastin and father usually performed only one dance number with Davis at the start of the show, with the junior member spending the next 50 minutes singing, doing impressions, and dancing. Clearly, he was the star, though his own sense of obligation to his father and Mastin kept them in the act longer than they probably should have been.

Davis felt indebted to Sinatra in ways that Martin did not. He credited Sinatra's featuring the Will Mastin Trio at a 1947 New York concert with supercharging his career. Having confronted prejudice in both show business and the U.S. Army, Davis was grateful that Sinatra fought for him to share not just the stage, but also restaurant tables and hotel suites, with him. Despite his penchant for racially insensitive (by today's standards) humor, Sinatra earned a reputation as one of the most racially progressive white entertainers of the 1940s and 1950s. Billy Eckstine became the first black singer to perform at New York's Copacabana in 1950 at Sinatra's urging. He insisted that his arranger Sy Oliver stay with him at whites-only hotels. He integrated his orchestras, and in 1956 drew kudos from the black press for his support of Nat "King" Cole after a racially motivated attack on the singer in Birmingham, Alabama. Though he joked onstage that audiences might not be able to see Davis because of his skin color, his commitment to racial justice was by all accounts sincere. The two became even closer following Sinatra's support of Davis after the November 1954 car accident that cost him his left eye and might have ended his career.

Decades later, the union of Sinatra, Martin, and Davis, along with Joey Bishop, Peter Lawford, and a host of associates, would be known as the Rat Pack. The original Rat Pack, of which Sinatra was a member, had coalesced around Humphrey Bogart and Lauren Bacall—Bacall in 1955 said the group looked like a pack of rats after returning from a debauch at the Sands. The Sinatra-led group was branded the Rat Pack by gossip columnist Dorothy Kilgallen, who wrote a typically negative item about Sinatra and his mates staying up drinking "like a pack of rats." Sinatra responded by calling Kilgallen out during his act. "Lucky you only have to read her column, that you don't have to look at her face," he told a Sands audience. "You'd throw up."

Sinatra himself never used the term "Rat Pack," nor did anyone at the Sands. He preferred calling his chums "the Clan," but Davis disliked that name due to its associations with the Ku Klux Klan. The group's earliest performances were branded "the Summit," in reference to the

September 1959 meeting between U.S. President Dwight Eisenhower and Soviet Premier Nikita Khrushchev at Camp David and a planned May 1960 meeting between the pair that was canceled after the Soviets shot down Francis Gary Powers' U-2 plane during an overflight of Soviet airspace.

With Sinatra, Davis, and Martin all under contract at the Sands, it only stood to reason that the trio would end up on stage together. That kind of star power, on one stage, in a room with fewer than 600 seats— this would be the hottest ticket in history.

What would become the stuff of legend, "the Rat Pack in Las Vegas," started as a way for Sinatra to cross-promote his appearances at the Sands and a movie he'd taken on.

In 1958, Lawford and his wife, Pat Kennedy, bought a story about a heist orchestrated by a band of former GIs from director Gilbert Kay. It just so happened that Frank Sinatra's Dorchester Productions owed Warner Brothers a movie, and he didn't need much convincing. The script endured several re-writes, though much of the final film—*Ocean's 11*, of course—ended up being improvised on-set.

A four-week location stint in Las Vegas started on January 18, 1960 with a three-day shoot at the Riviera. The film's production, it was announced, was headquartered at the Sands, where Frank, Dean, Sammy, Peter, and Joey performed onstage from January 20 through February 16.

Al Freeman, who is credited with the idea of uniting the group onstage, whipped up a frenzy around the group's appearances, promoting them as the greatest event in the history of show business.

"Star lite—star bright—which star will shine tonight?" asked a Sands advertisement.

"Every show is different—but you can count on at least two—usually five of these great stars onstage at the same time," Freeman enthused.

"One night, we had Sinatra, Dean Martin, and Sammy Davis all singing into one microphone at the same time—and across the stage came Peter Lawford chased by Joey Bishop waving a big butcher knife—little 'schticht' like that—some even more hilarious—you'll see any show you pick to go to the Sands these nights."

As can be imagined, putting on two shows a night with that level of energy, when combined with Sinatra's minimum required after-hours carousing, did not leave much in the tank for filming. For that reason, director Lewis Milestone presided over a relaxed shooting schedule, at least where the principals were concerned—generally, the starring five were on set between 3:00 and 6:00 p.m., with morning calls a rarity, outside of one 5 a.m. shoot featuring Sinatra, who worked only six days after the initial Riviera shoot, usually for less than two hours a day. That was fine for Sinatra and the others, who were more interested in having a good time than producing grand cinema. Their after- and before-hours antics earned coverage in entertainment columns across the country, raising anticipation for the film before shooting had wrapped.

But it wasn't all wine and roses. Richard Benedict, who played robber "Curly" Steffens, was robbed of $25, taken from his hotel room while he was filming. Other stars found ways to get themselves into trouble.

One day Richard Conte, who played Anthony Bergdorf in the film, asked pit boss Ed Walters for $200 of the casino's money to play with. Walters gave him the chips—after all, the guy was a movie star who had to be good for it. Conte was feeling important. In some of the press coverage of the movie's production, he had sixth billing. After all, if Sinatra and Martin could take chips at will, why couldn't he?

"You can't give Conte $200," Burky Gorelnik, another casino boss, told Walters. "He'll never pay it back."

Walters returned to the table.

"Excuse me, sir," he said, "but I'm going to need that $200 back."

"Do you see $200 here?" Conte asked, looking quizzically at the table, as many of his chips were mysteriously no longer visible.

Realizing that he'd screwed up, Walters called Carl Cohen and explained the situation.

"Eddie, stay by the table and I'll be right there," Cohen said.

As Cohen approached the pit, everyone wanted a word. Graciously, he made his way past the well-wishers and to Conte's table.

With a smile on his face, Cohen walked up to Conte, embraced him, and pulled Walters close.

"Richard," Cohen said in a voice just above a whisper, "pay the $200, asshole."

Still smiling, Cohen took a few steps away before turning around. "Still on for golf tomorrow?"

"Of course," Conte replied, as nonchalantly as he could.

"Great, we'll get Cesar Romero and Buddy Lester out there, too."

Conte returned the $200, a tight-lipped smile the whole time. Any bystander would have seen nothing amiss. That was Cohen's art: to get results without causing anyone to lose face.

Ocean's 11, even more than *Meet Me in Las Vegas,* was a feature-length advertisement for Las Vegas. Where the Cyd Charisse film had an extended sequence at a ranch, almost every frame of *Ocean's 11* is either set in a casino or features characters talking about what they're going to do once they get to Las Vegas. The plot revolves around racketeer Spyros Acebos' plan to simultaneously rob the Sands, Sahara, Flamingo, Riviera, and Desert Inn at the stroke of midnight on New Year's Eve. Danny Ocean, played by Sinatra, is a former 82nd Airborne sergeant who recruits ten of his former brothers in arms (the titular 11) to put the plan into practice.

With members of the group stationed at each casino, the transmission tower supplying electricity to Las Vegas is detonated at midnight, just as revelers are singing "Auld Lange Syne." Since the casinos' backup generators were wired to the cashiers' cage doors rather than the lights, the former soldiers walk in and grab bags full of cash, which they stow in dumpsters. Garbage truck driver Josh Howard (played by Sammy Davis, Jr.) picks up the cash. All looks good, but, alas, former gangster Duke Santos pieces the plan together and the Eleven, when their ingenious plan to smuggle the money out of Las Vegas and away from Santos goes up in smoke, are left with nothing for their troubles except for the thrill of having tried.

"Show me a man without a dream and I'll show you a man that's dead…real dead," Davis sings as he and the rest of the cast walk past the Sands. The final shot, Davis smoking resignedly in front of the Sands marquee bearing his name along with that of Sinatra, Martin, Lawford, and Bishop, drove the point home: To live, to really live, you had to take chances. Preferably at the Sands. Try your best, but don't expect to leave with the house's money—or your own.

Released on August 4, 1960, *Ocean's 11* was an ode to the Las Vegas that Sinatra had, in good measure, built at the Sands. Unusual for films of its time, it had a cross-country debut, with 200 theaters opening the film simultaneously, which may have been a record.

The film's world premiere, held of course in Las Vegas, had come the previous night. Luckily, Martin was in the middle of a stint at the Sands, and the rest of the cast flew in for the gala. At this point, Al Freeman had gotten the art of the movie launch down to a science: a cocktail party in the Emerald Room for 60 of his closest friends in the eating press; a complimentary dinner show at the Copa, with Martin assisted by his famous friends; followed by a convertible parade to Fremont Street, where Sinatra's quintet performed for a crowd estimated at 10,000 in front of the El Portal theater. The film itself was almost secondary. Freeman even succeeded in wrapping the "Welcome to Fabulous Las Vegas" sign with a banner promoting the movie.

Despite the fireworks and the novel distribution strategy, the film earned tepid reviews. William Leonard of the *Chicago Tribune* called it "a delirious picture in full color and slightly larger than life size, with 'name' stars playing bit roles, the neon lights of Las Vegas flashing in the background, and cops and robbers in half-hearted flight and pursuit. Nobody wins—and nobody deserves to win." He concluded that the show was "a comedy rather than a thriller, with an ironic finish."

Bosley Crowther found the movie amusing but morally offensive. He was dismayed at the "surprisingly nonchalant and flippant attitude towards crime" maintained throughout *Ocean's 11* and shocked that the movie suggested there was nothing inherently wrong with taking what was not yours. The critic also felt that the script vastly underestimated the difficulty of robbing Las Vegas casinos, so it was clear that, if the movie was making a joke, he didn't get it. Yet another Gotham critic declared that "if this picture can be parlayed and advertised and publicized into a great success of names and décor, then they've gotten away with real murder. If not, and the public ignores one of the truly emptiest displays on record maybe some of these many talents will be forced to go to work."

Despite the dubious reviews the film pulled in $5.5 million in domestic box office, earning a spot as the eighth highest-grossing film of the year. Ironically, this was just about the same total that the eleven robbed from Las Vegas casinos in the movie. *Ocean's 11* success led to a series of Sinatra-led ensemble films, including *Sergeants 3*, *Robin and the 7 Hoods*, and *4 for Texas,* none of which was hailed as a cinematic masterwork, each of which earned money.

As a vehicle for the Sands, *Ocean's 11* was perfect. Years later, long after Sinatra had graced its stage, when the Sands was gone, the film was a time capsule, capturing that moment when the world, it seemed, was ringside at the Copa.

***

It was through Frank Sinatra that the Sands, heretofore religiously apolitical (there were gamblers and vacationers in both parties, so why take a stand?), went all in for John F. Kennedy in 1960.

Kennedy was no stranger to Las Vegas. He first visited the town in early 1956, as a guest of Wilbur Clark of the Desert Inn. He returned that September to speak on behalf of Democratic presidential candidate Adlai Stevenson, staying with Clark, as he did again for a weekend in November 1957.

Sinatra had publicly stumped for Democratic candidates since FDR. In 1955 he met Kennedy at a campaign rally, and the two became friends. When he was in Washington, Sinatra had an open invitation to stop by Kennedy's suite at the Mayflower Hotel. Starting in the summer of 1958, Sinatra reciprocated, hosting Kennedy at his Palm Springs home. While there, he did not much discuss matters of state, instead talking about sex, having sex (chiefly with prostitutes), and doing lines of cocaine with his brother-in-law Peter Lawford, with whom Sinatra had become close friends, mostly due to the Englishman's Kennedy connection.

When Kennedy came to Las Vegas on February 7, 1960 to speak at the Convention Center and meet potential convention delegates, Sinatra, in the midst of filming *Ocean's 11*, invited him to see his show at the Copa.

"Ladies and gentlemen," Sinatra introduced his friend from the stage, "Senator John F. Kennedy, from the great state of Massachusetts, the next President of the United States!" Kennedy received a standing ovation. Sinatra even made him part of the act. As he often did, Sinatra picked up Davis and made an announcement.

"I'd like to thank the NAACP for this wonderful trophy." This usually got laughs (and was sadly typical of Sinatra's onstage repartee with Davis). This time, though, Sinatra deposited Davis on Kennedy's lap.

"It's perfectly all right with me," Davis quipped, "as long as I'm not going to George Wallace or James Eastland."

Sinatra introduced Kennedy to Judith Campbell, a call girl who had previously been a guest at his Palm Springs home. He had arranged for her to sit alongside Kennedy that night, at a table with Peter Lawford and Pat Kennedy. The two evidently sparked. According to Campbell, the next day they had a three-hour lunch on the patio suites 509 A and B in the Churchill Downs building, which were usually reserved for Sinatra, but for this occasion had been provided for Kennedy. The pair enjoyed Sinatra's show that night, sitting together at Jack Entratter's table.

Then, it was on to business. In the wee hours of February 9, Kennedy was the guest of honor at a small party in Sinatra's suite. According to Davis, Sinatra delivered $1 million in cash to Kennedy before the presidential hopeful boarded his private plane en route to Oregon, money raised by the Sands' owners and their friends to support Jack's primary campaign.

The owners' support was due to more than Jack's youthful appeal. Reportedly, Joseph Kennedy had enjoyed good relations with the criminal underworld since Prohibition. Sinatra provided a direct connection to Sam Giancana, a conduit through which the Kennedys made an offer: Help get Jack in the White House, and he would see to it that the pressure remained off, and Cuba's Fidel Castro deposed, reopening the nation to American business interests, including those of "the boys," whose Havana casinos had been quite lucrative.

With this understanding, organized crime—and those tied to it— threw their support behind Kennedy whole-heartedly, delivering cash, hustling primary delegates, and applying pressure at just the right places. In lockstep with his friends from Chicago, Sinatra became Kennedy's biggest celebrity campaigner, even recording a new rendition of his hit "High Hopes," with lyrics by Sammy Cahn proclaiming, "Jack is on the right track."

Sinatra was able to forge an even closer link between Kennedy and the mob. Shortly after their time together at the Sands, Kennedy and Campbell began a physical relationship at New York's Plaza hotel, one that would last for two years. Shortly after she began her tryst with Kennedy, Sinatra introduced her to Sam Giancana at Miami's Fontainebleau hotel; she promptly began seeing him as well. She later claimed to have ferried messages between the pair. Although the veracity of that claim has been disputed, no one has questioned that Campbell was seeing both men simultaneously or that Sinatra introduced her to both.

Back at the Sands, Sinatra pulled everyone he could onto the Kennedy bandwagon, whether they liked it or not. Martin dutifully made noises in support of the candidate, though he privately thought Kennedy, at best, the lesser of two evils. Sometimes this came out in public.

"What did you say his name was again?" Martin blurted into a microphone at the Copa one night, after one of Sinatra's lengthy tributes to Kennedy. But, with the big bosses and Sinatra equally gung-ho for JFK, work was work.

After the election, the underworld was far from pleased with Kennedy's appointment of his brother Bobby, who had pledged to rid America of organized crime, as attorney general. Sinatra bent over backwards to placate the campaign, pressuring Sammy Davis, Jr. to delay his marriage to Swedish actress May Britt until after the election. Davis obliged, and Sinatra served as best man at the November nuptials.

As a thank-you for his public and private campaign help, Kennedy asked Sinatra to produce his inaugural gala. It seemed like the former teen idol from Hoboken was about to become a frequent guest at the Oval Office.

He didn't. The problems started when Sinatra put together an all-star lineup of American entertainers to fete the new president the night before his inaugural, which naturally included his friend Sammy. After all, who better to serenade Washington on behalf of America than a black Jew with a Puerto Rican mother?

Joseph Kennedy disagreed, barring Davis from the event. JFK's secretary Evelyn Lincoln called Davis with the news just three days before the scheduled performance. Sinatra himself was not assigned a seat at the actual inauguration despite his having raised $1.5 million to pay off the campaign's debts the night before. He was incensed but could do nothing.

The final break between Sinatra and Kennedy came in March 1962, when Kennedy spurned Sinatra's invitation to spend a weekend at his Palm Springs home, instead enjoying the hospitality of Republican Bing Crosby. Sinatra had spent thousands of dollars renovating his digs to accommodate a presidential visit and had dreams of his home becoming a "Western White House" for Kennedy. But Bobby, Jackie, and others around Jack insisted that Sinatra's ties to mobsters made him an unacceptable host, although those mobsters believed they had put Kennedy in the White House.

Sinatra's exile from Kennedy's inner circle was a taste of things to come for both him and the Sands. Far from enjoying the support of a friendly administration, both would become targets of the federal government.

***

While Entratter, Cohen, and everyone at the Sands were thrilled with the attention Frank Sinatra brought to the hotel, it wasn't a relationship without strain. Sinatra got into the habit of treating the Sands like his personal boarding house, promising friends and potential friends comped rooms without asking anyone at the hotel. He did not, for the most part, endear himself to the hotel's staff, and both Entratter and Cohen came to view Sinatra as someone to be tolerated and placated. It was not just his celebrity that held them in check; he was also, probably, fronting for organized crime interests whose continued support was necessary for the Sands to remain successful.

In October 1959, frustrations hit a new level when Sinatra's publicity agency, Rogers & Cowan of Beverly Hills, volunteered a pair of Sands rooms for a promotion around Sinatra's upcoming single, "Talk to Me." Freeman learned fairly late that he would be responsible for providing rooms for the winner of an essay contest and their hometown DJ. Freeman was understandably chagrined that he would be losing two rooms during what was sure to be a big weekend.

"Al, most of the brunt of the promotion is falling on Capitol Records," Guy McElwaine of Rogers & Cowan assured Freeman. "They're the ones supplying two hi-fi sets and paying for posters in 75 key radio markets. All we're asking for is two rooms for two nights when Frank opens."

"Not just rooms," Freeman responded. "Food and beverage, too."

"But Frank's picking up the transportation himself," McElwaine countered. "And you've gotta believe we're going to be working overtime to promote the Sands Hotel on this campaign."

It went without saying that Frank Sinatra at the Sands in 1959 needed no extra promotion, and after all that Freeman had done to spread the word over the previous seven years, he might be forgiven for getting upset at the intimation.

"Frank and Hank Sanicola have already approved this," McElwaine continued, referencing Sinatra and his longtime manager. "I hope you find your way clear to approve it too."

McElwaine then sent Freeman a follow-up memo, extending his best wishes to Jack Entratter and Freeman's assistant, Eleanor Roth. He made sure to copy Frank. The intimation was clear: Frank wanted this, make it happen. Put that way, it was hard to say no.

Sinatra became more of a liability in the summer of 1963.

Nevada gaming regulators in the early 1960s faced pressure from two sides. First, by this point casinos—particularly those on the Las Vegas Strip—had become essential to the economic well-being of the state. From that perspective, no one wanted to look too closely at where the money to build casinos came from, or where the profits went, since, more likely than not, organized crime was involved at some point.

On the other hand, allowing mobsters to openly set up camp would invite federal scrutiny, which would be a disaster. So in June 1960, the Gaming Control Board issued the "Black Book," an 11-name list of people who were not allowed to even set foot in Nevada casinos.

"The notoriety resulting from known hoodlums visiting Nevada gaming establishments," the document explained, "tends to discredit not only the gaming industry but the entire state as well. In order to avoid the possibility of license revocation, your immediate cooperation is requested in preventing the presence in any licensed establishment of … 'persons of notorious or unsavory reputation' including the above individuals."

Sinatra's friend Sam Giancana was among those named in the Black Book. There was one problem: How do you exclude an owner from his own casino?

In 1960, Frank Sinatra had bought a 49.5 percent interest in Lake Tahoe's Cal-Neva lodge. Perhaps not coincidentally, Joseph Kennedy also owned a share in the North Shore casino through a front. Sinatra himself was almost certainly fronting for Sam Giancana. Redubbed Frank Sinatra's Cal-Neva, the club reputedly yielded suitcases full of skimmed cash that made their way to Giancana. Certainly, Sinatra was committed to making the Cal-Neva a success. The following year, he added a new showroom, with better acoustics than the old one, which he named the Celebrity Room. He himself was a frequent performer and brought in other top stars.

Giancana was a frequent guest at the resort, including a stay that overlapped with Marilyn Monroe's shortly before her death in the summer of 1962. In that year, events drew the attention of the Washoe County sheriff's office, the Gaming Control Board, and even the FBI. The husband of an employee died in an automobile mishap that authorities suspected, but could not prove, was no accident. A man was shot in the casino's entrance; the shooter fled but was eventually located in the Carson-Tahoe hospital, badly battered. He claimed to have fallen from a horse, though his doctor noted that it must have been a very, very tall horse. The casino's direct involvement couldn't be proven, but the delay between the time of the shooting and the first call to law enforcement, as well as the fact that the shooter was a casino employee, suggested otherwise. Further, the feds were investigating reports that women had been flown from San Francisco to Lake Tahoe to participate in prostitution at the Cal-Neva.

Meanwhile, under Robert F. Kennedy, the Justice Department was taking an active interest in Las Vegas. In the summer of 1961, Kennedy planned to assemble a federal strike force that would raid and close all of the major casinos in Las Vegas. Needless to say, this would obliterate the state's economy, Democratic Governor Grant Sawyer's career, and any chance the Democrats had in the state for generations. Governor Sawyer flew to Las Vegas to personally remonstrate with the attorney general, who remained aloof, although the previous summer he had begged Sawyer for his help in securing his brother's nomination. Sawyer then went to see the president himself, who was noncommittal but apparently convinced; the raid never happened. Still, it was clear that Bobby hadn't forgotten about Las Vegas, and would need only the smallest pretext to bring the full weight of the Justice Department down on it.

So, in the spring of 1963, Nevada regulators were concerned about Sinatra as a casino owner. As they began to consider the relicensing of the Cal-Neva, they shared their concerns with Sinatra attorney Mickey Rudin, requesting that Sinatra "take more care" in selecting the top executives of the resort. Rudin relayed that Sinatra was amenable. Indeed, he appeared to comply, by appointing an experienced hotel operator to the casino's top spot.

As the Board later learned, the supposed manager was actually a figurehead, and the resort continued to be run by Skinny D'Amato, who, despite his many successes at his Atlantic City nightclub and reputation as a pillar of that community, raised the hackles of Nevada regulators due to the interest both the FBI and the IRS had expressed in his businesses. Having barely escaped catastrophe at the hands of Bobby Kennedy, no one in Nevada was about to stick their neck out to protect anyone the feds came after.

It just so happened that Sam Giancana was near the top of the feds' list. The federal government had subpoenaed him to testify before a Chicago grand jury. He took the Fifth. The U.S. Attorney took the extraordinary step of offering him complete immunity from prosecution for anything he discussed; perhaps more fearful of upsetting his partners than a prison sentence, he again took the Fifth. The government began contempt proceedings against Giancana, with the FBI keeping him under 24-hour surveillance.

Giancana took the Bureau to court, arguing that their constant surveillance was an invasion of his privacy and, even worse, had thrown off his golf game. The alleged mobster won a court order stipulating that the G-men must remain at least one foursome behind Giancana as he golfed. In protest against these restrictions, the FBI turned over its surveillance of Giancana to the Cook County sheriff's office, who lost Giancana within a few hours. It was July 1963, and no one in the federal government had any idea where the reputedly most dangerous mobster in the nation was.

Giancana, who set up shop at the Cal-Neva, did not try to keep a low profile. One night, while relaxing with Phyllis McGuire and her manager in their cabin, Giancana became enraged at a comment the manager made. He began beating the man, while McGuire slammed her high heel shoe into his head. Sinatra and his valet, George Jacobs, staying next door, heard the commotion and entered the room. Sinatra prevented Jacobs from attempting to break up the fracas, instead calling for security guards. When the dust settled, he had Jacobs drive Giancana to the Chairman's Palm Springs home.

The manager, who had nearly lost his eye to Giancana's diamond ring, told the authorities that both Giancana and Sinatra had issued "Mafia death threats" to him. Naturally, this only added to the files the Gaming Control Board was assembling on Giancana's links to Sinatra.

When the Board's agents became aware that Giancana had been at the Cal-Neva on July 30, the mobster was gone. Two days after notifying the FBI that Giancana had apparently been in Nevada, the *Chicago Sun-Times* ran a front-page story detailing the allegations. Despite the publicity, the investigation ground on, with Gaming Control Board chief Edward Olsen attempting to interview Sinatra in Las Vegas while his compatriots quizzed several employees at the Cal-Neva.

The Cal-Neva interview yielded nothing—D'Amato declined to talk, and no one else could shed light on Giancana's whereabouts, past or present. Sinatra, staying at the Sands, did not take Olsen's call, although Jack Entratter suggested Sinatra would prefer to speak at the Sands.

"That may be more convenient for him," Olsen replied, "but it's in the best interest of the state for him to come to my office."

Sinatra did stop by Olsen's office a few hours later, placidly admitted that he'd seen Giancana in passing at McGuire's cabin. No, he hadn't had a real conversation with him, much less seen him deliver a beating. No, he hadn't asked him to leave.

"I see Sam a few times a year," Sinatra said. "We play golf sometimes, and he stays with me in Palm Springs. I don't see what's wrong with that."

"He's on our list of excluded persons—don't you see that associating with him can discredit Nevada?"

"Fine. I won't talk to him in Nevada. But I'll talk to whoever I want to anywhere else. I know people on all walks of life."

"But can't you see that..."

"This is a way of life, and a man has to lead his own life."

"It's not just Giancana seeing his girlfriend; your club has done many favors for him. Don't you recognize this could jeopardize your license?"

"That's a possibility, but you'd have to take whatever steps you want to."

Sinatra denied that he'd witnessed a fight at McGuire's cabin, but declined to do so under oath, at least until he'd talked with his attorney. When he left Olsen's office, neither of them was happy.

By the end of the month, the allegations that Giancana had been at the Cal-Neva—and that the state was investigating him—became front-page news in Las Vegas. Sinatra's accountant Newell Hancock called Olsen.

"Frank is irritated" he started, before relaying an offer for Olsen to have dinner with Sinatra at the Cal-Neva, then stay for the Sinatra/ Martin double bill. Olsen declined.

A half-hour later, a woman called Olsen and asked for him to hold the line for Mr. Sinatra. Frank then personally invited Olsen to dinner.

"I just told Mr. Hancock no," was the response.

"Why?" Sinatra asked.

Olsen replied that such a meeting would not be in the best interests of Nevada gaming.

"You're acting like a fucking cop. I just want to talk to you off the record."

"Why can't you just come to my office?"

"I don't want to deal with reporters."

"There'll be no reporters here unless you call them."

"Listen, Ed, I haven't had to take this kind of shit from anybody in the country and I'm not going to take it from you people. I want you to come up here and have dinner with me. Bring your shitheel friend, La France." This was investigator Charles La France, who had been conducting interviews in Tahoe. Olsen then motioned for La France and Guy Farmer, a Gaming Commission employee, to pick up extensions and listen.

"It's you and your goddamn subpoenas which have caused all this trouble. It's all in the papers."

"Only the Board and the people subpoenaed knew about them. We did not put them in the papers."

"You're a goddamn liar. I'll bet you $50,000 they were in the papers."

"Mr. Sinatra, I don't have $50,000 to bet."

"You're not in the same class with me."

"I certainly hope not."

"No, just don't fuck with me. You can tell that to your fucking Board and that fucking Commission, too."

"Why don't you call me back when you're not so emotionally overwrought?" Olsen suggested.

"You asshole! You know, I have plenty of other businesses. I barely make anything from the Cal-Neva. But it means something to a lot of the little people who work there."

"Maybe everyone would be better off if you concentrated on those enterprises and let Nevada gaming to other people."

"I might just do that, and when I do, I'm going to tell the world what a bunch of fucking idiots run things in this state. C'mon, come up and have dinner with me. Just think about it."

With that, Sinatra hung up the phone.

Three days later, two Gaming Control Board agents performing a routine investigation of the Cal-Neva's count reported that D'Amato had attempted to bribe them with $100 each, placed in the crook of one of the agent's arm. The agent threw the bills on the table.

"Aww, you can take that," D'Amato explained, apologizing for their inconvenience earlier that week. After a great deal of back-and-forth, the agents succeeded in returning the bills to D'Amato, then fled the property, promptly reporting the matter to Olsen.

Olsen had a staff attorney draft an order calling for Sinatra's license to be revoked. He brought it, along with supporting memoranda (including one that detailed Sinatra's colorful phone call), to Governor Grant Sawyer's office.

"I'm going to file a complaint against Frank Sinatra, asking for his license to be revoked," Olsen said.

"Why?"

Olsen showed him the information, walking him through the sequence of events.

"When?"

"As soon as we work out the legal details."

"Well, you'd better be right."

On September 11, Olsen filed a complaint, alleging that Park Lake Enterprises, Inc., the company through which Sinatra owned the Cal-Neva, had violated several gaming regulations. It detailed Giancana's numerous visits to the property earlier that summer, specifying how the reputed mobster was served food and drinks by casino employees, given a Cal-Neva car to drive, and generally given run of the property. Worse yet, Sinatra had refused to end his association with Giancana. Compounding that, he had in the phone conversation with Olsen "maligned and vilified the State Gaming Control Board, the Nevada Gaming Commission, and members of both Board and Commission by the use of foul and repulsive language which was venomous in the extreme." Other counts dealt with alleged malfeasance by other Cal-Neva managers.

Nevada regulators weren't the only ones who demanded that Sinatra cut ties with Giancana. As the drama in the Silver State unfolded, Sinatra was in the midst of negotiations with Jack Warner that would see Warner Brothers buy his label, Reprise Records. A typical studio boss of the era, Warner was used to getting his way. He would absolutely not tolerate part of the Warner family having public ties to someone like Giancana. So, he made an ultimatum: ditch your "Chicago" friends, or you're not moving onto my lot.

Initially, Sinatra fought the complaint, hiring Harry Claiborne to defend him against the Board's allegations. Claiborne promptly began filing motions and taking depositions.

Meanwhile, the president himself, perhaps thinking fondly of his February 1960 weekend at the Sands and the friends he'd made there, made at least a half-hearted attempt to help Sinatra. As the governor rode with him to his planned speech at the Convention Center on September 28, 1963, Kennedy had a question for Sawyer.

"What are you guys doing to my friend Frank Sinatra?"

"Well, Mr. President," replied Sawyer, "I'll try to take care of things here in Nevada, and I wish you luck on the national level."

That ended the conversation.

Whether it was because Claiborne told him he had a hopeless case, because JFK's cavalry had failed to arrive, or because of Jack Warner's threat to nix the Reprise deal, Sinatra gave up the fight. On October 7, Claiborne's office issued a statement in the singer's name.

In it, Sinatra claimed that he had six months earlier made the decision to prune his business interests, liquidating his non-entertainment holdings. Though he was "surprised, hurt, and angered" by the Board's request to revoke his license, he acknowledged that under the letter of the law, the license was a "revocable privilege." As he was leaving the state anyway, he instructed his attorneys to announce that he was withdrawing from the gaming industry entirely.

He ended by expressing his hopes that the industry, which he had worked so hard to build up, would continue to grow and prosper.

As a result of giving up his license, Sinatra was also forced to sell his shares in the Sands. Whether he really owned those shares or was fronting for others, he was proud of his stake in the casino, of being able to call himself "an owner" of the most successful casino in Las Vegas. On his end, Giancana was livid that Sinatra had thrown everything away because he couldn't control his temper.

"That bastard and his big mouth," Giancana said. "All he had to do was keep quiet, apologize, let the lawyers handle everything. But no, he had to make that phone call, run that big mouth. Now we're out of the whole place." Giancana estimated that Sinatra's intransigence had cost him nearly a half-million dollars.

Within days, the Gaming Commission approved of Sinatra selling his 9 percent interest in the Sands for $391,500. Sands Hotel, Inc., bought the stock, which was placed in escrow pending the transaction's closing at the end of the year. Frank Sinatra was no longer an owner of the Sands. His controlling stake in the Cal-Neva wouldn't be quite as easy to dispose of, as he spent the next several years trying to sell his interest in the resort, which the Gaming Commission had insisted he place in trust. He had the worst of both worlds: lingering legal and fiscal responsibilities with none of the perks of casino ownership.

"Anyone want to buy a casino on the Lake?" he would ask during his Copa performances well into 1966, garnering a chuckle from the audience.

But the story did have an amusing post-script. In early 1964, Ed Olsen accompanied friends of his from California to Sammy Davis, Jr.'s late show at the Sands. As he was leaving the showroom, his friends spied Davis, and rushed up to him, declaring how much they loved his performance.

Davis turned to the couple and said, "Give me a minute alone with your friend. We have something to talk about." Olsen prepared for a fight.

"That little son of a bitch, he's needed this for years," Davis told a shocked Olsen. "I've been working with him for 16 years, and nobody's ever had the guts to stand up to him." The pair parted friends, with Davis inviting Olsen to join him and May Britt for dinner the next time he performed at Harrah's Lake Tahoe—an invitation that Olsen appreciated but never consummated.

At the Sands, as always, life went on. But the federal government's interest in the casino went far beyond Sinatra. Even as the Gaming Control Board labored to maintain a firewall between the Sands, a major employer in Clark County, and Sinatra's interests in the Cal-Neva, the FBI was conducting a clandestine investigation of its own in Las Vegas.

That investigation would become public in a way that would make *Ocean's 11* look like a tightly plotted thriller.

*G*onna Build a Mountain

In the early 1960s, Las Vegas was in the middle of a major building boom. No new resorts opened, but many of the Strip's hotels added rooms, and throughout the town apartments, shopping centers, and houses were springing up almost overnight. This was a city moving ahead, and those who stopped risked being left behind.

With 465 rooms in 1962, the Sands was one of the smaller resorts on the Strip, with about 50 rooms in a cluster of non-descript two-story buildings. The Stardust, which had opened in 1957, had by this point more than a thousand rooms. The Tropicana had added 150 rooms to its original 300 and was considering expanding again. The Sahara had added the first of its high-rise towers and was building a second, even taller, one. The Dunes had already expanded once and was in the process of adding its own tower, the Diamond of the Dunes.

Late in 1962, the Sands' owners, licensed and unlicensed, agreed that their hotel needed to grow. They hired Julius Gabriel, a Las Vegas architect, to design a room expansion that would keep the Sands current. The new addition, named the Aqueduct, was to be larger, housing 83 rooms and suites. It looked different from the other hotel wings, with a concave curve centering on a swimming pool echoing, perhaps, Miami's Fontainebleau, with its own putting green as well. Three stories high, it was clad in pink and white tile and concrete.

Rather than compete on volume, the Sands opted to go upscale, offering the kinds of accommodations that no other resort could. The expansion's ten biggest suites averaged 1,600 square feet each, huge for the time. The top ones had private swimming pools. These were rented to the public for the sky-high sum of $115 a night. By comparison, a decent room could be had elsewhere on the Strip for $10 per night.

Twelve "Petite Suites" had a king-size bedroom and queen-size living room separated not by a wall, but by a step up and drapes. Depending on their theme, the suites had fixtures like Italian marble tabletops, Spanish chandeliers, and Moorish décor. The bathrooms, which had sunken Roman tubs and separate showers, even had bidets—perhaps the first rooms in Las Vegas to boast this European custom.

At $1.1 million to build and another $500,000 to furnish, Aqueduct was, Jack Entratter announced, "perhaps the costliest public accommodation in America."

The Aqueduct suites were about more than gold tiles and Moorish carvings. Maids were available 24 hours a day, ready to do more than just clean rooms—they were expected to pack and unpack for guests as well. To keep room service trays out of sight and to preserve the wing's posh image, special closets were built into the hallways to allow them to be stowed.

Guests didn't have to worry about walking the considerable distance from the casino to their room; a brand-new Buick Riviera stood ready to transport them around the clock.

Opening in April 1963, the Aqueduct suites and rooms were the first phase of an even more ambitious expansion plan. This was no time to stand still: Across the street, the Sans Souci was being reborn as the Castaways, a Polynesian-themed, 488-room resort hotel and casino. The Clark County Board of Commissioners approved an even bigger potential rival: a $10 million, 1,000-room hotel casino, which Sacramento builder Jack W. Greene planned next to the Castaways. While Greene's dream never materialized (he and his partners would be suing each other within the year as the project collapsed), at the time it appeared that the Sands was in danger of being overshadowed.

The second phase of the Sands' growth promised to reinvent the resort for the new Las Vegas. Other hotels were going vertical, with the Desert Inn, Stardust, Sahara, and Riviera planning new high-rise expansions. All told, casino owners were spending $50 million to add capacity. It was time for the Sands to go upward: Its new rooms wouldn't be put in a two- or even three-story building, but in a tower on top of its casino building.

Going further, the resort's footprint ground floor space tripled. The casino would be doubled in size, while the Copa added an upper tier of tables and booths, giving it 120 more seats. At the same time, the backstage facilities and dressing rooms were expanded. The Copa Lounge would be replaced by the Celebrity Theater, a 350-seat terraced venue with a stage capable of revolving and moving up and down.

In dining, a new gourmet restaurant, the Regency Room, replaced the Garden Room, which was reborn as the Garden Court adjacent to a new Terrace Room. A barber shop, beauty salon, jewelry store, and his-and-her clothing boutiques would add to the resort's amenities. The convention facilities, too, were to be dramatically expanded, with a convention hall capable of hosting as many as 2,000 people at once. It could be configured as a movie theater, performance venue, or as many as nine individual meeting or dining rooms. After the new hall opened in September 1965, it hosted a typically diverse array of groups, from the Ford Motor Company to the National Bituminous Concrete Association to ABC-TV's Board of Governors.

All told, the Sands was investing $9 million to reinvent itself—twice what it had cost to build the resort in 1952. And it wasn't going to be ahead of the curve when it finished, either. The Dunes would have a 24-story tower, 1,000 total rooms, and a 15-story neon sign that cost $100 a day to keep lit. Just to keep up meant the Sands had to grow—quickly.

The 17-story Sands tower, Entratter told the press, would bring the hotel to 777 rooms. The tower itself was to be a cylinder rising into the sky; its rooms would be wedge-shaped, with a window-wall looking out. The top-floor executive suites would boast 20-foot ceilings.

Architect Martin Stern, Jr. designed the ambitious expansion. He was one of the chief figures behind the Strip's increasingly vertical skyline. Stern, who had worked as a commercial architect in Los Angeles, first came to Las Vegas in 1953 to create an expansion for the Sahara. He designed a second expansion there three years later and, in 1959, the Sahara's first tower. He then planned the Sahara Tahoe, his first ground-up casino commission, before being asked to expand the Sands. After the Sands, Stern would go on to design the International and MGM Grand, two Kirk Kerkorian-owned casinos that defined resort design for a generation among a series of expansions and new properties, mostly in Las Vegas, Reno, Tahoe, and Atlantic City.

The project called for extending the Sands' main building farther south to accommodate new casino and retail space and to serve as the base for the new tower, and adding convention space to the north. To accommodate the convention space and back of the house facilities, the Sands bought the Kit Carson motel. Spreading the Sands' footprint to the south presented one logistical challenge: Two of the existing low-rise hotel buildings, Belmont and Arlington, stood in the way. Instead of demolishing them and simply building a larger tower to make up for the 100 or so rooms that would be lost, the Sands' bosses decided to move them about 50 feet to the south, taking the place of a parking lot that formerly stood between them and Churchill Downs.

Work started in September 1964, with the demolition of most of the Kit Carson motel and the Terrace Room, the jacking up and sliding south of the Belmont and Arlington buildings, the demolition and infill of the Terrace Pool, and the construction of a climate-controlled promenade that re-used heating and cooling units salvaged from the Kit Carson. Then came the construction of the convention space and Copa addition. By November, work on the tower had begun. In January, work on the casino itself started, with care taken to ensure that customers could still gamble without interruption. By May, work on the restaurants commenced.

To handle the greater traffic the new rooms and space would bring, Stern dramatically expanded the casino entrance, giving it a round colonnade with a 35-foot ceiling. The hotel got its own lobby and lounge, with an expanded new porte cochere able to accommodate eight cars simultaneously unloading passengers and luggage.

Stern didn't do much to update the décor: Earth tones still dominated, giving the new Sands a visual link with the old, but his new layout pointed the way to the future of casinos. Originally, the main casino building was separate from the rooms; guests, as a matter of course, would walk outside or be ferried in a golf cart or even a Buick to get to their bed. In Stern's new design, though, 400 of the hotel's rooms were connected to the casino and convention facilities by an air-conditioned promenade. Casino resorts were growing up.

"All the warm decor and features of the Sands have been retained," Jack Entratter said. "Although there is a new and fashionable look to the Sands Hotel rising skyward, there is still an integrated design with all the charm of the existing facilities."

In January 1966, the Sands celebrated the dedication of its new tower and expanded space with a series of performances by Frank Sinatra, backed by the Count Basie Orchestra, in the Copa Room, with a special dedication dinner party for VIPs on January 7. We have an idea of what the night would have sounded like thanks to *Sinatra at the Sands with Count Basie and the Orchestra*, featuring arrangements by Quincy Jones, recorded at the end of the group's four-week stint and released on Sinatra's Reprise label.

That weekend, while it celebrated a new beginning for the Sands, marks the last triumph for the original casino. The Sands was on the cusp of a new era.

***

While they were planning their expansions, the Sands' managers were checking up and down the Strip: What were the Desert Inn, the Dunes, the Sahara, the Flamingo, the Tropicana doing? Those were their competitors. But their real enemy was Bobby Kennedy.

Starting in 1961, Kennedy authorized the use of hidden microphones—"bugs"—to procure intelligence that informants had been unable or unwilling to provide. He and his organized crime squad suspected that the mob was skimming thousands from Las Vegas casinos each month but were unable to uncover any actual evidence of the practice. While they were picking up a fair amount of gossip about petty rivalries among the casino managers and reputed mobsters behind the skim, they had been unable to penetrate the count rooms and procure actual proof that this was happening.

The usual method of flipping low-level criminals to build cases against their higher-ups proved virtually useless in Las Vegas. Those involved, through either loyalty or fear, owed more to each other than the federal government. Developing an undercover agent into a figure with enough trust to be allowed into the inner circle could take years, if not decades. The only way, Justice was convinced, to learn the truth about the mob and skimming was microphone surveillance, abbreviated in FBI-speak as "micsur."

For more than a decade, federal investigators had been probing organized crime and were hot on the trail of several mob bosses, including Sam Giancana of Chicago. The Bureau identified another axis of organized crime that ran through New York, New Jersey, and Los Angeles. The key figure here was Doc Stacher, who resided in Los Angeles but who had come up in New Jersey. In early April 1961, the Bureau bugged his room at New York's Hotel Pierre for a week. The G-Men then switched their focus to his rooms at the Beverly Wilshire

Hotel where they installed microphones that remained in service indefinitely.

Stacher, living up to his nickname of "the Brain," was well aware that he was being watched. One summer day, seeing two suited agents sweltering while watching him from a balcony while he lounged poolside, he waved them over.

"Put on some shorts and get in the pool with me," he suggested. "You're never going to learn anything about me from all the way up there."

Carl Cohen, investigators believed, was Stacher's chief contact at the Sands. To get to Stacher, they launched an intelligence-gathering campaign directed at Cohen. On August 9, 1962, the Los Angeles Field Office installed a bug in Cohen's apartment on North Doheny Drive in Beverly Hills. Despite having already cultivated two informants in the field, agents were no closer to proving that Cohen was funneling money to Stacher, though they were optimistic that bugging Cohen's apartment, which a "reliable source" had assured them was the site of many high-profile meetings, would finally provide proof.

That optimism was misplaced. Cohen did not talk business in his apartment, any more than Stacher did at the Beverly Wilshire—at least when he knew that cops might be listening in. Knowing that he was "hot," Cohen then sold the apartment's furniture and abandoned it.

The investigation then switched its focus to Las Vegas, where the FBI field office had, in the previous year, begun its own aggressive electronic eavesdropping operation. Agents there created a business front called the Henderson Novelty Company, which ostensibly provided a "musical rental service." Instead, Dean Elson, the head of the office, leased 25 phone lines from the Central Telephone Company that were billed to the Henderson Novelty Company and paid for in cash. They used those phone lines to install listening devices on telephones and via hidden microphones in offices at the Fremont, Desert Inn, Stardust, and Dunes. Trying to penetrate the Sands, though, agents chose a homier target.

Cohen, like Jack Entratter, lived at the Sands. He and his wife, Frances, occupied an apartment in the Rockingham building. Given his hours, such a short commute was sensible; Cohen was generally in the casino from late afternoon until past midnight, and was usually present for the count that concluded all three shifts. So, on February 19, 1963, agents surreptitiously entered his apartment—"trespassed" was the strictly technical term—and installed two listening devices: one in the living room, one in an adjacent room that served as a gym.

The Bureau's timing was awful. The Cohens chose to have their apartment remodeled at just that moment, so that for the next month all the agents heard were hammers and saws. Then, shortly after they moved into the renovated apartment, Cohen departed for Mt. Sinai Hospital in Los Angeles, where he sought treatment for his chronic heart condition.

Finally, on May 3, agents began to get the goods on the Cohens' domestic life. Cohen told an unknown caller that he was getting ready to take a swim and catch some sun. As work continued on the apartment, Frances ordered lunch from room service. The same thing that she had for breakfast: toasted bagels, lox, cream cheese, toasted English muffins (well done), and coffee. Possibly incensed at the idea of second breakfast, the FBI agent listening in typed "This is lunch?" on the transcript. Frances then showed her guests the gym, demonstrating each piece of equipment, and called out to ask Carl, in another room, if he had a towel. He did, and soon left for the pool. Twenty-five minutes after Frances called room service, her lunch arrived, and she spent the next three hours gossiping with her guests and talking about dinner plans.

The following morning, agents listened as Mr. and Mrs. Cohen discussed their adventures in modern dentistry, a conversation that culminated in them comparing how many teeth they had remaining. Mrs. Cohen, apparently, won that round when she revealed to her husband that she only had nine of her own teeth in her bottom gum. Perhaps inspired by the sad fate of her departed seven lower teeth, she then began working out in the gym. At 2:37 p.m., Frances had friends visit, and the agents found it impossible to understand anything as they all talked over one another. At 3:55 p.m., an unknown male, presumably a hotel employee, came to the apartment, and agents clearly made out Frances relaying orders about the hotel's critical infrastructure.

"This chair is hardly stuffed," she complained. "It feels like I'm sitting on iron. It's a lovely chair, but I wish it had more stuffing."

There were no more pertinent conversations recorded that day, or on the following days, unless you were to count the Cohens discussing their dog, Frances working out, Frances talking with her friends, Carl saying that he was going to the pool, or Frances watching television. On May 12, though, agents learned of major dissension in the ranks at the Sands.

"We ordered these steaks well done, and they're still walking around," Frances protested to room service. Unable to get a satisfactory answer, she handed the phone to her husband, who had just started watching television.

"Get two well done steaks up here," is all he said before hanging up.

Two days later, a memorandum from Dean Elson, Special Agent in Charge of the Las Vegas office to FBI Director J. Edgar Hoover, admitted that "no significant information" had been developed from the eavesdropping. Still, he requested a 60-day extension for the bug because in Las Vegas, you never know.

The assistant director recommended in a May 27 message that, despite the continuing lack of pertinent information, the surveillance be extended.

"Even though we have been endeavoring to penetrate the Sands Hotel Operation for a number of years, this is the first highly confidential source we have been able to establish," he wrote. Even though the source may not produce as anticipated, it was worth continuing.

"A source in contact with Sands personnel is especially desirable since informants have reported that Sands Hotel officials have a contact in the Justice Department, and we know that certain information has apparently been leaked to Nevada gamblers. Cohen himself made a trip to warn [redacted, but probably Stacher] that he was 'hot.'"

Those with a naïve faith in the powers of their government would have been dismayed had they read Cohen's FBI file. The greatest police agency in the free world, with over 16,000 staff at its command, had for years been unable to learn the secrets of a gambling house on the Las Vegas Strip. Worse yet, it wasn't entirely sure that the agency itself hadn't been breached by its targets.

That was possible, though it was equally likely that "the Professor" Stacher had deduced that the two suited men wilting in the sun each day as they watched him at the Beverly Wilshire pool were law enforcement agents and had communicated this to his friends, suggesting that they be discreet in everything they said—they already knew, from decades of habit, to write nothing. By this point, he was vigilant about the threat of bugging, even telling his nephew that a workman who repaired the nephew's heating unit had placed a bug in it. Only an idiot would talk openly about skimming—or anything more substantive than their dinner plans—knowing that the FBI was listening. Joseph Stacher and Carl Cohen were not idiots.

So while FBI agents insisted that microphone surveillance was the most powerful weapon they could bring to bear against the evils of organized crime, they had to admit that it wasn't exactly paying off. At the Sands in the summer of 1963, as the pressure from the attorney general mounted, their last, best hope was a pair of microphones that, to date, had produced only chatter about fitness equipment, steaks, and dental misfortunes.

Elson put off the lack of information gleaned from the bug in Cohen's apartment to its interminable renovation, but it was another renovation project that brought the FBI's eavesdropping program to light. In October 1962, via a Central Telephone employee, the FBI bugged the phone on Ed Levinson's desk in his Fremont Hotel office. A few months later, Levinson decided that he wanted to move his phone. Installer Al Kee came in on his day off to do the work. While relocating the telephone, he discovered the bug and immediately notified Levinson. They were able to trace the line back to the switchboard and learned that it had been leased to the Henderson Novelty Company.

Levinson discovered the wiretap on April 28. Whether that had anything to do with Cohen's reticence to talk business in his own home is unknown, but on June 25, FBI agents finally heard something worth recording: an unknown voice saying "1-2-3-4" while testing telephone equipment, apparently looking for bugs. The agents immediately deactivated both listening devices. The office debated whether to break into Cohen's home again to retrieve their bugs, but fearing that they might walk into a trap, declined. All was quiet for two weeks, when a local citizen that agents had been grooming as a potential informant asked a single question.

"What are you doing to Carl Cohen?"

The agents denied all knowledge of anything to do with the Sands boss.

"He found three bugs in his apartment, and a tap on his phone. Were you behind it?"

Over the summer, other bugs were discovered at the Stardust and Dunes, and at the home of the Stardust's Johnny Drew.

As the wiretaps became front-page news, the FBI refused to comment. Sheriff Ralph Lamb denied that his office was behind the bugs. Some suggested that they were the work of rival gaming operators.

On September 4, Cohen's attorney Harry Claiborne (who had surely built a wing of his house on fees accrued from the Sands by this point) filed suit against the Central Telephone Company, charging that the company had "purposefully, willfully, and maliciously" furnished telephone lines connected to the bugs in Cohen's suite, knowing full well that the lines would be used to eavesdrop and record conversations without Cohen's knowledge. Claiborne cited a Nevada law that clearly declared that such unauthorized intrusions of privacy to be prohibited. He was asking for $750,000 in damages.

Newspaper reports of the lawsuit combined it with the recent discovery of bugs in Major Riddle's Dunes office.

On a related note, a confidential informant told his FBI handler that he was present at a September meeting with Sands personnel. Among other things, they discussed Sinatra's ongoing struggles with the Gaming Control Board.

"I don't care what happens to him," someone said. No one disagreed.

"He's been nothing but a problem for years," someone else volunteered.

So it was decided, Frank was out.

Also at this meeting, it came out that Cohen, by paying "a large sum of money" to a phone company employee, had been able to learn everything about the FBI's electronic surveillance.

The informant was, however, unable or unwilling to reveal who the employee was, how much he had been paid, or any real details.

SAC Elson was not entirely convinced that the meeting had taken place, much less that their informant had been present. While he had long considered the possibility that the "hoodlum element," with their vast wealth, might compromise the wiretapping program, he didn't believe that any of the three phone company employees his office had worked with would be so venal.

"I do not feel," he wrote to Hoover himself, "that any of these three individuals could be bought off with any sum of money."

Perhaps another employee had come across the FBI's lines by chance, then. Or perhaps it was misinformation from Cohen. In any event, he would remain alert and inform his superiors immediately if he learned more.

Meanwhile, officials at the Central Telephone Company were concerned, though they initially promised to "hold firm" against Cohen, perhaps even filing a counterclaim for defamation against him. They weren't entirely resolute, particularly should other hotel owners file suit, or the company continued to take a beating in the press. As can be imagined, the revelation that the phone company helped plant spying devices in the home of a paying customer—one who, thanks to his charitable work, was a leading citizen, no less—did Central Telephone no favors.

The FBI's floundering surveillance program (by the time Cohen filed his lawsuit, all microphone surveillance had been discontinued) was becoming a political liability as well. The night before President Kennedy's visit to Las Vegas, Republican Lieutenant Governor Paul Laxalt charged that Nevada was "teeming with federal agents," the result of Attorney General Kennedy's "premeditated plan" to make himself "a tin hero" at the expense of the Silver State. The Republican Party would, he guaranteed, not stand for that.

"Our state just wants to conduct its business without Bobby Kennedy's phone tapping," he said, protesting federal intervention in the state's biggest industry. Nevada had gotten its house in order with its own anti-mob efforts, like the Black Book, though Laxalt admitted the list of excluded persons might be incomplete.

"We might suggest some Washington-level names to be added," he quipped.

Claiborne, for his part, did not directly accuse the attorney general or the FBI of planting the bugs that had been discovered in his client's home, instead placing the blame solely on the phone company. FBI Assistant Director Courtney Evans speculated that Cohen didn't want potentially embarrassing recordings the FBI might have to introduce at trial, though he imagined that Cohen, who knew the FBI had heard nothing of value, had already factored this in before filing suit.

Central Telephone, in its October 2 response to Cohen's civil complaint, denied everything. SAC Elson of Las Vegas advised his FBI superiors two days later, though, that his contacts there were convinced that, should the matter go to trial, the FBI would likely be involved. The company's legal counsel speculated that Claiborne would subpoena telephone employees and records that would reveal the true nature of the Henderson Novelty Company. Moreover, the telephone company's insurance agency, which would presumably be on the hook for a $750,000 judgment should Cohen prevail, would undoubtedly insist on transferring as much of the blame as possible to a third party. The Bureau had to start making contingencies, he argued.

With public opinion building behind him, Cohen seemed to have both the telephone company and their secret client over a barrel. But scarcely a week after the company filed its brief denial in court, Cohen had Claiborne withdraw his suit, with prejudice, without any explanation.

Cohen's withdrawal mystified Dean Elson and everyone in the FBI's leadership who scrambled to learn why Cohen had abandoned a solid legal action, pressing agents to canvass any and all informants. At first, no one could answer, though by the end of the month one agent was told that Cohen felt he'd achieved enough simply by filing the suit.

"I embarrassed the phone company and the FBI," he reportedly said. "That's all I wanted to do."

Given the costs of hiring Claiborne, that was an expensive moral victory for Cohen.

But the bugs continued to plague the FBI. After Cohen withdrew his claim, Jack Shaw, chairman of Nevada's Republican Party, accused the Democrat-run federal government of spying on "a large number of our state's prominent and most respected citizens in the gaming industry."

Shaw, picking up Laxalt's earlier criticisms, did what Cohen and Claiborne had not.

"The reports that we Republicans got were that it was the FBI," he told the *Las Vegas Sun*.

"I don't think he knew what the FBI was up to, but Governor Sawyer should be very concerned about this," he continued. "We need to keep gambling in Nevada controlled by the state instead of the federal government."

In November, Democratic Senator Howard Cannon got into the act, referring to Cohen's wiretapping during John R. Reilly's nomination hearing. Reilly, seeking a post on the Federal Trade Commission, was currently the head of the Executive Office for United States Attorneys in the Justice Department. This line of questioning did not produce any information embarrassing to the Bureau, but it did show that the matter was not going to be forgotten.

Other casino owners were not as magnanimous as Cohen. In February 1966, Edward Levinson and the Fremont Hotel filed for the second time a $6 million lawsuit against Central Telephone and four FBI employees, including Dean Elson, charging them with invading his privacy. Levinson had withdrawn a previously filed suit, believing that the Justice Department could pressure the IRS into ending its investigation into his taxes. When the IRS refused to call off its investigation, he refiled.

With Levinson represented by well-connected D.C. trial attorney Edward Bennett Williams, the case received national publicity, thanks to syndicate columnist Drew Pearson's coverage. Cohen joined the suit, requesting $2 million for the FBI's eavesdropping in his home, while Stardust executive John Drew's wife filed for $1 million in damages. That September, the Central Telephone Company admitted that it had leased the wiretap lines to the FBI.

Seeking re-election that fall, Grant Sawyer publicly lambasted the FBI for placing a bug "in the bedroom" of Carl Cohen—apparently, it had a better ring than "gym/den." Pearson's coverage of the case earlier that year had reported that the Bureau had placed a bug in Carl and Frances's actual bed, something that the FBI could not publicly deny without admitting that it had bugged his living room and gym.

In early 1968 the civil cases fizzled, and maybe coincidentally the federal government dismissed tax evasion indictments against Levinson and others at the Fremont and Riviera. Still, the cases were heralded as a "major embarrassment" for the FBI, and the first indication of just how widespread federal eavesdropping had become. And a major part of the story started with Carl and Frances Cohen's apartment at the Sands.

The continuing strain of the federal investigation, as well as Cohen's long-standing heart trouble, may have contributed to his diminishing role at the Sands. He had already ceded the role of casino manager to Sandy Waterman, who had come to the Sands via Sinatra's Cal-Neva, but still monitored the daily counts. In the summer of 1964, he began to defer to Waterman and others on matters of procedure.

In that year, he spent increasingly long periods away from the Sands, living at health spas in Miami and North Jersey for extended periods, ostensibly to lose weight. Some of his travels, though, were on behalf of the casino; he attended a Palms Springs golf tournament, likely recruiting gamblers, and traveled with Entratter to New York in the fall to seek additional funding for the in-progress tower expansion. He made several trips to Los Angeles, probably to speak with Doc Stacher, who had been indicted on tax evasion charges the year before and would, the following year, be deported to Israel, effectively ending his influence at the Sands.

Stacher's tax suit ensnared the Sands. In September 1963, just as Cohen was about to file his lawsuit against Central Telephone, United States District Judge Thurmond Clarke ruled that, as they had sufficient grounds to fear possible self-incrimination, six Las Vegas casino figures were within their rights to assert the Fifth Amendment before a Los Angeles grand jury investigating Stacher. Among the four were Cohen, Sands treasurer Aaron Weisburg, and Charles Kandel and Leo Durr, also casino employees.

A great deal had changed since December 1962 when, on the Sands' tenth anniversary, Entratter was re-appointed as president and chairman of the board, Cohen was promoted to executive vice president, and Frank Sinatra was made a vice president.

While Cohen and the others managed to avoid being ensnared in the Stacher trial, they certainly felt the government's pressure. They had made the Sands into the most successful casino in Las Vegas. But Las Vegas was changing, and neither Entratter nor Cohen were getting any younger. Even with a modern expansion, the Sands was a step behind the competition. Turmoil in the behind-the-scenes ownership sparked by Stacher's departure only exacerbated problems. It seemed likely, as 1966 began, that Cohen, Entratter, or both might leave.

No one, though, could have predicted what was about to happen to the Sands or Las Vegas.

Ain't That a Kick in the Head

It all started because the reporters in Boston were too nosy.

Howard Hughes, by 1966, was a man who liked his privacy. He inherited a fortune as a teenager thanks to his father's drill bit patents, and he used that wealth as a springboard to fame. He established himself as a Hollywood producer, aviation pioneer, and canny businessman whose holdings would include tens of thousands of acres of land and a variety of operations.

Yet Hughes was not well. While he had once enjoyed the Hollywood nightlife and had spent many late nights gambling in Las Vegas (he was a frequent guest at the Flamingo for several years), in the late 1950s he became increasingly reclusive, preferring a darkened bungalow at the Beverly Hills Hotel to the bright lights of the Sunset (or Las Vegas) Strip.

Hughes' withdrawal from public life could have been due to a variety of factors: an addiction to painkillers following air crash-related injuries; a desire to avoid being served with lawsuits; mental health issues; or, probably, a combination of all three. In any event, one of the wealthiest men in the world now preferred living in hotels on a semi-permanent basis. Although he owned more land than he could measure, he chose to live in hotels rather than a private residence.

The Beverly Hills Hotel had been perfect at first—ideally situated to keep tabs on his film and aerospace investments—but in early 1966 he moved to Boston, where he took up residence in the Ritz-Carlton.

But Boston was too humid, too germy. And *Boston Globe* reporters were asking too many questions about what Hughes was doing in the city. So he began to look for another place to get away from it all.

Las Vegas Sun publisher Hank Greenspun convinced Hughes—and his right-hand man Robert Maheu—that Las Vegas was the best place in the nation for a billionaire with a penchant for privacy. After all, it was the ultimate company town. No state taxes on personal or corporate income. Privacy? The sitting governor was buying campaign ads attacking the federal government for having the nerve to snoop on the men skimming casino money for the mob. Hughes already owned well over 20,000 acres of land in the area. It was close enough to Los Angeles to keep tabs, far enough to have some distance. Yes, Las Vegas would be perfect for Howard Hughes.

At first, it looked like Hughes would be staying at the Dunes, but in the end it was the Desert Inn, still owned by Moe Dalitz and associates, that hosted the billionaire. On November 27, following a continent-spanning train journey, Hughes arrived at the Desert Inn shortly before dawn, toted through the casino and into an elevator on a stretcher. He settled into a suite on the top floor of the St. Andrews tower, which would be his home for the next four years.

Once in Las Vegas, Hughes set out to dominate. He succeeded, bending everyone from the Desert Inn's chefs to the state's governor to his will. Greenspun even argued, in a *Sun* editorial, that the people of Las Vegas should give the genius billionaire the "private space" he craved, and called the rival *Review-Journal* to task for reporting that Hughes had secretly arrived in Las Vegas, presumably the exact sort of story that any newspaper would seek out.

As New Year's Eve approached, Dalitz wanted Hughes' party out so he could fill his hotel with high rollers. Hughes wanted to stay. Maheu called Jimmy Hoffa, who called Dalitz, and explained that it would be in his best interest to allow Hughes to stay through the New Year. Still, it was clear that Hughes was not welcome at the Desert Inn. Incredible wealth has its privileges: Maheu suggested that Hughes simply buy the Desert Inn.

Hughes had the benefit of a bottomless (by Nevada standards) bank account. He was also under pressure to shelter from taxes a half-billion dollars in cash he was sitting on after settling a lawsuit over his ownership of TWA. It made sense that he would then binge-buy as much Nevada real estate, including casinos, as he could. Even though it was difficult to separate Hughes from his eccentricities by this point, the general idea to maximize his footprint in Las Vegas made perfect sense.

Maheu tabbed two men with helping him negotiate with the Desert Inn's owners. One was Edward Morgan, an attorney and former FBI agent. The other was Johnny Rosselli, a Los Angeles mobster with a reputation as a fixer. Maheu had met Rosselli when, at the behest of the CIA, he coordinated efforts to assassinate Cuban dictator Fidel Castro. When the sale closed, Morgan received a massive legal fee, part of which he shared with Rosselli.

Having bought the Desert Inn, Hughes decided to buy as many casinos as he could. Many of the city's casino owners, never sentimentalists, were happy to talk with Maheu about selling. For the right price, anything was for sale, but some owners were more motivated than others. Perhaps the most motivated were at the Sands. In fact, even before Hughes had closed the Desert Inn deal, rumors swirled that the Sands was about to be bought by a Houston-based group and that Jack Entratter would leave to run the Frontier, whose new owners had run into licensing difficulties.

Doc Stacher's deportation had left a void. He had been the main link between the money that had built the Sands and Carl Cohen. Certainly, Cohen hadn't been flying down to Los Angeles every few weeks to make social calls. With Stacher gone, the possibility of more funding for additional expansions—something that all Las Vegas casinos were considering in the late 1960s—disappeared. What's more, it created uncertainty about the future. And, if there's one thing Cohen and the other bosses detested, it was uncertainty. Watching your customers lose thousands each night will do that.

So when Maheu called, Entratter and the rest of the Sands leadership was receptive. Most of them were old-time gamblers who had been in the business since Prohibition. The Sands had given them legitimacy. Las Vegas had given them a community. But, on a daily basis, running the Sands was a grind. In Al Freeman's press releases it looked so glamorous—Jack shaking Hollywood hands, Carl handing out checks to B'nai Brith, Pop Warner football, St. Rose DeLima Hospital. The executives who had their conventions and vacations at the Sands probably fantasized about trading places with Entratter and Cohen, but on a daily basis they probably had more freedom and clearer exercise of authority than anyone at the Sands.

While the public believed the jobs of the Sands brass to be glamorous and privileged, the reality was that Entratter, Cohen, and the others worked long, odd hours, lived at the hotel, and were consumed around the clock by both the challenges of operating a casino in a competitive market and maneuvering in the mob-linked underworld. There was a reason that Cohen was spending more time away from the Sands than at it these days.

Of course, in the negotiations, it was an entirely different story. The casino was the most profitable anywhere, ever, and was poised to dominate both in entertainment and in gambling for years to come.

Unlike the haggling over the Desert Inn, which threatened to break down at several points and took the better part of three months, serious negotiations between Hughes—as with the Desert Inn, conducted via Morgan and Rosselli—were relatively quick and painless. On July 23, a Sands spokesman announced that Hughes had paid about $15 million to buy the Sands.

The Sands did not slow the velocity of Hughes' buying spree. He soon bought the Castaways (which Maheu snapped up with cash left over from the Sands acquisition), the Frontier, the Silver Slipper, the unopened Landmark, Krupp Ranch, Spring Mountain Ranch, Warm Springs Ranch, Alamo Airways, the North Las Vegas Air Terminal, and local CBS affiliate KLAS. This was on top of the forty square miles of land he already owned west of Las Vegas.

In the new management structure, Jack Entratter and Carl Cohen served as senior vice presidents, responsible for entertainment and the casino, respectively, while retired Air Force Major General Edward Nigro stepped in as senior vice president and, effectively, general manager of the resort. Nigro, a classmate of Maheu at Holy Cross College, had just stepped down as commander of Sheppard Technical Center at Sheppard Air Force Base in Texas. A World War II and Korea combat veteran, Nigro had risen through the Air Force ranks before leaving to work for Howard Hughes.

Maheu brought around him executives who formed the core of what became known as Hughes Nevada Operations, hiring those with experience outside of the hotel business. Former Las Vegas FBI Special Agent in Charge Dean Elson, for example, joined the team, now supporting the same casino managers he'd illegally wiretapped a few years before. Walter Fitzpatrick and Henry Schwind came from the IRS, another federal organization that was not beloved in Las Vegas. Former LAPD officer Jack Hooper headed up security for Hughes Nevada.

On the surface, the new leadership simply grafted itself onto the Sands. About a half-dozen other now-former shareholders with various executive positions, including Charles Turner, Sandy Waterman, General Charles Baron, Charlie Kandel, and Bucky Harris, continued to live on property in their suites, just as Cohen and Entratter did, although over the ensuing decade most of them would leave for greener pastures. Nigro began to assume some of the civic functions that Cohen had once performed, assuring the local NAACP that the Sands was committed to nondiscriminatory hiring one week, awarding Hughes Nevada scholarships to aspiring college students the next. Indeed, under Maheu, the Hughes team outstripped the old owners' community efforts. In late 1968, a Las Vegas High School student was seriously injured in a Reno game. When Maheu learned that his parents couldn't pay for the costs of transporting him back to Las Vegas, he authorized one of Hughes' private planes to bring him home.

Las Vegas was still a small town, and such interventions went a long way in establishing goodwill with the locals. Almost overnight, Hughes had become the state's biggest employer, with an estimated $175 million spent on buying businesses and property by the end of his second year in town. He owned a piece of Clark County larger than the incorporated City of Las Vegas. There was no mistaking it: Las Vegas had a new boss.

***

The new regime quickly "improved" the Sands' procedures. The biggest changes were around casino credit, traditionally an area in which Cohen and the other managers relied more on their estimations of a gambler's honor then the metrics a bank officer would use to assess a potential loan. Credit was an intensely personal matter, and, again, one of honor. At this time, money loaned for gambling purposes was not legally collectible in Nevada. Theoretically, you could sign a marker for $100,000, lose it all, and pay nothing. Granting credit was an act of faith. The serious gambler's credit reflected not only his net worth but also the management's opinion of his trustworthiness. To be granted credit at a Las Vegas casino was the ultimate sign that a gambler was respected. Asking for $10,000 and being told that you were good could bring a happy tear to a rough customer's face. Being denied credit, well, that told you just where you stood.

In the Sands, as in most other Las Vegas casinos, known gamblers did not typically sign for the money they were lent. If, on occasion, a gambler didn't pay his marker, Cohen made it clear that they would not be having a second conversation. That usually worked wonders. If a gambler tried to quibble with Cohen or credit manager Bucky Harris about how much he'd asked for ("I know you say I borrowed $40,000, but I clearly remember asking for $30,000"), he earned himself a one-on-one with Carl Cohen.

"The first one we'll give to you," he would tell the gambler. "The second one, we'll talk about. There will be no third one."

So when a gambler asked for credit, his pride, his entire identity, was on the line. To be shaken off, that was a humiliation like no other. But to watch the dealer turn to the pit boss and hear, "Mr. J. is good," was as fine a feeling as any imaginable.

Serious players, and those wealthy enough to lose serious money, would never be addressed by name. They came to the Sands for discretion. The head of the New York Stock Exchange or the vice president of Manufacturers' Bank didn't want his name shouted across a crowded casino, didn't want his room in his name, didn't even want to be addressed respectfully by his full name at the table. The most anyone would say was an initial.

The Sands didn't have many formal structures, but it ran exceedingly well. Credit disputes were rare. Serious cheating was surprisingly rare as well. No regular player would dare take a shot against the casino. They knew that, as much of a degenerate gambler that they were, as many angles as they knew, the men dealing to them and especially the men watching the action were deeper degenerates who had seen more angles.

If someone who walked through the door tried a move, they were dealt with harshly and never seen on property again. What happened? No one really wanted to find out.

The Hughes regime made it clear they would not be nearly so sentimental about money, or so lax in formal procedures. At midnight, when the sale officially closed, the new owners walked into the casino, accompanied by their own security and accountants. They locked down the casino and cage, and began accounting for every dollar.

Within two days, the new managers had posted a new set of procedures for granting credit. All customers, even Mr. Hughes himself should he choose to patronize the casino, had to show a picture identification to receive credit. They also had to sign before they received their chips.

Within a month, all the big players had gone.

"I'm not going to give my *name*," one player told the pit boss, who shook his head sympathetically. It was as if he'd been asked to pose for pictures with one of the young women who'd accompany him back to his room.

The new management also insisted on bringing in their own accountants to count the casino's money. This was not how it had been done. In the old regime, the casino people had counted the money—accountants were the people they gave their numbers to.

"What a world!" one of the old-timers remarked to his friend as they watched the accountants file into soft count.

The new regime came in to put the Sands in order, regularize procedures, and make sure that all the money was legitimately accounted for—no more suitcases going to Doc Stacher in Beverly Hills or Meyer Lansky in Miami. They did just that, but at a higher cost than they could have guessed.

At the end of Hughes' first year, the management proudly told the gaming staff that, as a result of their new systems, the casino had shown a profit of just over a million dollars for the year. Sure, the old hands had grumbled, but they couldn't argue with those kinds of numbers.

When the new faces left, one of the old-timers asked a question.

"How do we tell them we used to make that every month?"

***

No one was less happy with the Sands' new ownership than Frank Sinatra.

The singer was in the doldrums of a long, long losing streak. Once a heartthrob to bobby-soxers, he had crossed 50 as rock and roll swept the world, making him something worse than irrelevant: antiquated. He'd had to give up his casino interests and his associations with guys like Sam Giancana but wasn't any closer to becoming a Hollywood power player. Jack Warner even issued a statement to the effect that, while the Reprise purchase had left Sinatra with a sizeable interest in the studio's music division and an office on the lot, he had never considered appointing him as his successor as head of Warner Brothers.

It felt like a lifetime since he'd produced an inaugural ball for the president.

Worse, he no longer reigned as a god king at the Sands. He was still the star attraction on the Copa stage—his sets with the Count Basie Orchestra showed him at the peak of his powers—but he was now merely an honored guest and no longer an owner, no longer a friend of the friends of the Sands. The days when he could commandeer a block of rooms were over. Worse yet, he knew it.

Throughout his career, Sinatra struggled with dealing with adversity. His long history of threatening to punch reporters (threats which, more than once, he delivered on) speaks to his anger issues. His friends and lovers knew that their relationship with him was entirely conditional: be seen talking to the wrong man or the wrong woman, fail to show him his due respect, disappoint him in any way, and you were out. Forever.

While the Sands had been Sinatra's Las Vegas home since 1953, while his performances there benefited him and the hotel, nothing was guaranteed. He had left Columbia Records, which had made him a star in the 1940s, and Capitol Records, whose albums made him a legend in the 1950s. Once Sinatra wasn't an owner, there was no guarantee he'd stick around.

Still, it looked like Entratter could keep Sinatra in the fold. He hosted Frank's July 19, 1966 wedding to Mia Farrow in the Presidential Suite, picking up the couple at McCarran Airport himself in a Sands limousine. And Sinatra continued to pack the Copa.

But there was an uneasy undercurrent after Howard Hughes bought the Sands. The two had been rivals for Ava Gardner in the 1940s and never got on after that. Sinatra liked to style himself as a businessman, a mogul—he embraced Dean Martin's nickname "Chairman of the Board" unironically—but Hughes was the real article, a force even more powerful than a chairman, so mighty he didn't even need a title. He was just The Man, HRH when it needed to be official.

Howard Hughes' casinos were making steps toward greater cost and cash controls. Gone were the days when Martin and Lewis could give away $75,000 worth of chips in a half-hour. Not a cent moved without someone signing for it. This was not to Sinatra's liking. It was bad enough not having run of the place. But to be reduced to serving as an employee, having to answer to clerks, that was humiliating. That his old enemy Howard Hughes was his ultimate master was galling. Hughes made his displeasure with Sinatra clear when he refused to buy out Sinatra's remaining stake in the Cal-Neva (which the singer continued to own as a passive landlord), even as he was buying, it seemed, every room with a roulette wheel in Nevada.

Further, the Sands—sad to say—was losing its luster. Caesars Palace, which opened on August 5, 1966, had already begun siphoning high rollers away from the Strip's former top spot. Some of the behind-the-scenes owners at the Sands who'd left when Hughes assumed control had interests in the new resort. With its over-the-top Roman theme, Caesars Palace made the Sands, despite its recent additions, feel like an artifact. You could get great food in the Regency Room, but you couldn't have a goddess pour you wine and massage your temples, as you could at Caesars' Bacchanal. Sensitive to being thought old hat, the last thing Sinatra wanted was to be tied to yesterday's news.

Not usually one to suffer in silence, Sinatra did just that to make a point. On September 4, 1967—Labor Day—Sinatra disappointed a packed Copa Room when he failed to step onstage for the 8:15 dinner show.

"I can't do the show," he told Entratter. "Sore throat."

Entratter reached out to Sammy Davis, Jr., who hopped on a plane in Los Angeles. He was onstage before 10. Al Freeman announced that Davis was ready to fill in for the rest of Sinatra's engagement, although he assured reporters that Frank would be ready to sing again on Wednesday. Meanwhile, some speculated that Sinatra was about to sign a contract at Caesars Palace.

Tensions reached the boiling point that weekend.

Sinatra, as Freeman had promised, returned to the stage. But he wasn't the biggest star at the Sands.

Given the Sands' long ties with Houston, it was perhaps inevitable that the stars of the space program, which was headquartered in Houston, would be welcomed at the resort. The previous summer, a half-dozen astronauts (including the ill-fated Apollo 1 crew of Gus Grissom, Roger Chafee, and Ed White) had caught Red Skelton's act at the Copa. They met with him backstage to compliment him on his astronaut pantomime routine and pose for pictures. As national heroes, members of the Apollo programs were considered among the most important of the VIPs who visited the Sands, and each visit was given the full Al Freeman publicity treatment, with photos and captions sent to the usual media suspects.

On September 6, another delegation of astronauts arrived: Wally Schirra, Don Eisele, Walt Cunningham, Gene Cernan, Tom Stafford, and Jack Swigert. These were the primary and back-up crews for Apollo 7, the first manned Apollo mission, which launched a year later (John Young in the interim replaced Swigert in the backup crew).

Naturally, the astronauts caught Sinatra's show. Photos were taken of a grinning Jack Entratter standing by their table in the Copa Room. Sinatra serenaded the future moon-men with "Fly Me to the Moon." This was, the audience could feel, a special night, a once-in-a-lifetime thrill.

But the night turned awful shortly after the final curtain.

Under the previous administration, Sinatra had a virtually unlimited credit line—after all, he would probably blow most of the money anyway, and you couldn't put a price on the boost he gave the casino when he was playing. Plus, he was an owner.

Not anymore. Word had come down, supposedly from The Man himself, that Sinatra's tab was closed.

Earlier, Sinatra's wife Mia had lost $20,000 at the tables; Sinatra had asked for $50,000 to try to win it back. He lost it all and may have said words to the effect that he didn't intend to pay it back. So when Sinatra approached the pit and asked for another $50,000 to share with his new astronaut friends, he heard a word he hadn't before at the Sands: no.

To his credit, Sinatra took the refusal in stride, not wanting to lose his temper in front of America's space heroes, who suddenly had an early morning and weren't all that interested in shooting dice anyway. No problem. Sinatra left the casino with Mia, and everyone in the pit breathed a bit easier.

But this stung, and the more he thought about it, the angrier he got. *He* was the one who had made the Sands a success. *He* was the one everyone came to see. *He* was the reason there was anything more than a pile of sand in this godforsaken place. To be publicly humiliated like that—it was just too much.

Sinatra returned that morning, enraged.

"I'm going to break both your legs," he screamed at a hapless pit boss. "If you weren't so old, I'd bury you!" he shouted at grave shift boss Dave Silverman. He'd threatened reporters, co-stars, waiters before. But now he cursed the entire resort.

"I built this place from a sandpile, and before I'm through that's what it will be again!"

Outside, he climbed aboard a golf cart with Mia, possibly intending to drive back to their suite and finally get some sleep. He wore a shoebox on his head to shield his eyes from the harsh morning sun. He threw the cart into gear, peeled off in a huff, then swerved, driving it smack dab into the lobby's plate glass window, which shattered.

Sinatra's valet George Jacobs, who had a front-row seat to his employer's blow-up, later insisted that his boss hadn't meant to drive through the glass—after all, he and Mia could have been seriously hurt. Perhaps even angrier that he'd lost control (literally and figuratively), Sinatra then whipped out his gold cigarette lighter and tried to set the lobby's couches and drapes on fire, to no avail.

He then flew back to Palm Springs with Mia. After sleeping, then consulting with Dr. Jack Daniel's, he called Bob Maheu.

"I'm done with you," he said. "I'm not singing at the Sands anymore."

Luckily, Entratter had Davis on standby, and the versatile performer was ready. The Copa would not be dark that night.

Perhaps even more steamed that the show was apparently going on without him, Sinatra flew back to Las Vegas the following night, Sunday. Initially, he put on a show of contrition, apologizing to the pit crew for Saturday morning. Still, he wanted some answers about his credit, he realized as it got later and he got drunker. He picked up a phone, asked to be connected to Jack Entratter. Mr. Entratter was unavailable, which was not unreasonable given the late (now, early) hour. PBX Supervisor Frank Scher put a call through to Carl Cohen, who did not answer. Sinatra then threatened to pull out every wire in the second-floor switchboard room if he did not immediately speak to Entratter or Cohen, who he was convinced were dodging him.

Sinatra then flagged down a Sands deputy, insisting he be given access to the switchboard room, presumably so he could call Entratter directly.

"No," the deputy said. When Sinatra insisted, he simply said, "I don't work for you."

"You're pretty tough with that gun," Sinatra responded. "I'll shove it up your ass."

Somehow, Sinatra found the switchboard room on his own. He pounded on the door, screaming to be let in. The door remained closed. Now accompanied by his longtime friend Jilly Rizzo and another acquaintance, Sinatra returned to the lobby. Finally, he learned, Cohen agreed to meet with him. It was sometime after 5 a.m.

Sinatra was already sitting at a table in the Garden Room when Cohen walked in. Still clearing the cobwebs after being awoken abruptly, he had pulled his suit pants on over his pajama pants, which were sticking out just above his shoes.

"Frank, Frank," Cohen started, trying to calm Sinatra, who would have none of it.

"Fuck this place," Sinatra yelled. "What the hell? I built this joint, and this asshole tells me I can't have a marker? What am I, a bum?"

"Frank, it's not our joint anymore. You've got to sign for the money. We've got accountants looking at everything, Haskin and Sells. The guys in the pit are just following instructions."

"You son of a bitch!" Sinatra screamed. "You cocksucker. You motherfucker."

Cohen sat, impassive.

"What are you nervous about?" Sinatra asked him.

"Jesus, Frank, you just got me out of bed."

"Really, what are you so nervous about?" Sinatra asked again, thinking he had Cohen on the ropes.

"I'm through with this bullshit. We'll talk when you're sober," Cohen said, pushing his chair back to get his considerable bulk up.

"I'll get someone to bury you, you kike motherfucker," Sinatra screamed, as he flipped the table, splashing Cohen with the coffee that had been set out for them.

Purely on instinct, Cohen threw a jab that nonetheless had his full weight behind it. You never forget how to throw a punch, especially when you've just been scalded and insulted.

Cohen's fist, like Sinatra's golf cart, found its target precisely, regardless of the intention. Sinatra went down, his lip split, what felt like pieces of teeth loose in his mouth.

"Get him, Jilly, get him," Sinatra begged. Cohen gave Rizzo a quick look that said, "There's so many places in the desert, they'll never find you."

"Not him, Frank, not him," was all Rizzo said.

Sinatra was so angry that he got up, picked up a chair, and tried to attack Cohen. He only succeeded in smacking an intervening Sands deputy in the head, sending him to the hospital for stiches.

His work done, Sinatra left. Hours later, he signed a contract with Caesars Palace, who would pay him $3 million total—at an industry-leading $100,000 per week—to headline the Circus Maximus theater. Caesars' owners also reportedly agreed to buy Sinatra's stake in the Cal-Neva, at which he would also perform.

Sinatra's departure from the Sands was front-page news in Las Vegas and reported on from coast to coast. "Frank Sinatra Loses Teeth During Strip Hotel Brawl," read an above-the-fold headline in the *Review-Journal*. Columnist Don Digilio, one of the many journalists who had felt Sinatra's sting over the years, did not hold back.

"Singer Tony Bennett left his heart in San Francisco," Digilio began, "and Frank Sinatra left his teeth—at least two of them—in Las Vegas."

Sands employees who declined to be identified told the tale of Sinatra's rampages, universally backing Cohen.

"As far as I'm concerned," a bellman said, "Carl Cohen is a national hero."

A Sinatra representative put out a statement denying that Sinatra had even been punched, claiming that Sinatra had spent Tuesday night out on the town, an impossibility if he'd really had his teeth knocked out. Sinatra's dentist A. B. Weinstein, however, admitted that he'd repaired two caps that had been knocked loose from his patient's front teeth. Sinatra's agent finally admitted that, with so many witnesses, they could not deny the fight had taken place.

Clark County's sheriff's deputies investigated the mayhem, interviewing about a dozen witnesses but not Sinatra himself, who had left town. Ultimately, District Attorney George Franklin neglected to file charges against the singer, although he maintained that, per the investigators' report, three misdemeanor charges could be laid against him. But, as no police officers witnessed the fracas and no one was willing to file a complaint, he would not be hauling Sinatra into court. Still, he put the former Sands owner on notice.

"I don't feel Sinatra should have the right to tear a hotel apart or run wild. If he gets out of control he should be handled like anyone else," Franklin said.

"The next time Sinatra is in town," the district attorney concluded, "regardless of whether he is performing, we are going to check his actions."

Though Cohen was cheered nearly unanimously (Earl Wilson and Hank Greenspun were the only journalists to offer Sinatra any support in the press), Sinatra leaving was disaster for the Sands. While he didn't succeed in quickly luring Dean Martin and Sammy Davis, Jr. to Caesars Palace, he left a void at the Sands. One FBI informant even told his handler that the entire weekend's antics had been carefully staged to allow Sinatra to break his Sands contract and sign at Caesars Palace, where the alleged mobsters the Bureau was surveilling reportedly had large interests. Many of the Sands' former players departed for Caesars Palace, and the Sands never recovered. It took nearly 30 years, but Sinatra's prophecy of doom eventually came true.

If the ruckus was planned, it's not likely Sinatra getting slammed in the kisser was part of the bargain, but, as von Moltke said, no plan survives contact with the enemy. Still, Sinatra leaving marked the definite end of an era at the Sands. Though Martin and Davis would hang on for a few years (Martin would ultimately leave for the Riviera, where he acquired a share), the Sands was no longer Frank's house.

While Sinatra leaving was a catastrophe, him staying might have been worse. Under Hughes, even Entratter and Cohen were on borrowed time, though Hughes was indifferent at worst to them: They were mere hired hands, for the most part beneath his attention. He actively loathed Sinatra, though, and relished the chance to twist the knife. Even if Cohen had extended him credit indefinitely, something would have made Sinatra leave.

When the dust settled, it at first looked like business as usual at the Sands, with Sammy filling in at the Copa. The casino, if anything, enjoyed an even better reputation locally. Far from being shunned by the community, Cohen was embraced. For years he'd been involved in several local charities, so it was natural that, a few weeks after he decked Sinatra, he be named general chairman of the St. Jude's Ranch for Children's annual "Nite of Stars" dinner show. If anyone could sell tickets to the gala, he could.

Ominously, though, the benefit show wouldn't be held at the Sands, the usual place of pride for such events. No, this year the St. Jude's trustees decided to hold their bash at Caesars Palace.

The old Sands was gone. What would come in its place, no one knew yet.

12

Luck Be a Lady

The writer was blowing through an awful lot of money, the boys in the pit saw. It wasn't unusual for customers to lose big, but the writer was losing so outrageously that it became a topic of conversation in the dealer's lounge.

"Writing must pay a lot better than dealing," was the consensus.

But it didn't. At least not for this writer, not yet.

Mario Puzo had loved gambling since he was a kid. Growing up poor, to an immigrant Italian family in Hell's Kitchen, New York, he was introduced to the allure by Christmastime card games. He later recalled cheating his brothers "with childish simple-mindedness," dealing himself the ace of spades from the bottom of the deck to win their Christmas envelopes. He didn't do it for gain (Mario would buy them presents with the money), but because he had to win.

For Puzo, gambling was a mystical experience.

"What non-gamblers do not know is the feeling of virtue when the dice roll as one commands, he later wrote. "And that omniscient goodness when the card you need rises to the top of the deck to greet your delighted yet confident eyes. It is as close as I have ever come to a religious feeling. Or to being a wonder-struck child."

Puzo graduated to double-dealing poker to the rough crowd that congregated in his neighborhood streets. His first exposure to Nevada gambling came in 1939 when, as a teenager doing a stint in a Lovelock, Nevada Civilian Conservation Corps camp, he lost his $23 bankroll in Reno. After catching sleep on a backroom table reserved for bust-outs like himself, he caught a ride back to Lovelock on a freight car.

"No money in my pockets, no worries in my head," he later reminisced.

Following his World War II military service, Puzo took a job as a file clerk in the New York Veterans Administration, where fellow clerk Salvatore "Sally Rags" Ragusin introduced the aspiring writer to the sports and horse-betting demimonde. After a few gambling adventures together, the two went their separate ways, as Sally Rags pursued a career as a professional sports bettor and Puzo graduated from writing for pulp magazines to publishing two critically acclaimed but slow-selling novels.

Frustrated by the commercial failure of 1965's *The Fortunate Pilgrim*, a highly personal tale of an Italian immigrant family in pre-war Hell's Kitchen, Puzo agreed to write a novel about organized crime, one that would sell a lot of copies, even if it wasn't great literature.

"I was forty-five years old and tired of being an artist," he later wrote of his decision. "Besides, I owed $20,000 to relatives, finance companies, banks, and assorted bookmakers and shylocks."

Hearing that his onetime friend was now a writer, Rags reconnected with Puzo, convincing him to take a Las Vegas gambling trip over New Year's Eve 1967/68 to get color for his in-progress novel, which touched on Las Vegas. Rags, who was booked at a sold-out Caesars Palace, used his connections to get Puzo a room at the Sands. The writer was impressed, but Rags was apologetic.

"I'm sorry that's the best I can do, but it's a busy weekend," he confessed. "The place has really gone downhill in the past year—me and my friends never stay there anymore. But it was the only place with rooms available."

That "Gambler's Halloween" (as Puzo termed New Year's in Las Vegas), Rags and his friends were at Caesars Palace.

"A few years ago, this would have been at the Sands," he told Puzo. "We used to joke that if the Sands burned down on New Year's Eve, J. Edgar Hoover would have to lay off half the FBI."

Puzo got his color for *The Godfather*, and a profile of Rags for the February 25, 1968 *New York Times Sunday Magazine* to boot, but that was not his only trip to Las Vegas. He spent a great deal of time at the Sands, losing badly at roulette and vacuuming up all manner of mob stories for his novel (which he wrote entirely from "research" rather than personal experience with the Mafia).

An earlier stay overlapped with that of David Janssen, then at the height of his fame, playing Richard Kimble in *The Fugitive*. The television star was drunk, playing blackjack poorly, and causing trouble.

Pit boss Ed Walters put a call into Carl Cohen, as everyone did when a situation demanded delicacy.

"Eddie," Cohen told Walters when he arrived, "when I get through with him, he'll think he won an award."

Cohen went over to Janssen, conversed with him *sotto voce.* Janssen and his gofer got up from the table.

"Eddie, we're going to get something to eat," he called to Walters.

"Carl, that's unbelievable," Walters said to his boss. "He was screaming at everyone who tried to calm him down."

"Well, sometimes you gotta be nice, sometimes you gotta be...not so nice."

"But what did you say to him?"

Cohen smiled at the small knot of casino personnel that had gathered.

"I made him an offer he couldn't refuse."

Cohen's finesse of Janssen was, naturally, the dealer's gossip for the next few days. One roulette dealer excitedly told the tale to Puzo, still losing happily. He was already soaking up plenty of details for the book—he'd learned about "Superman," a well-endowed Havana performer, from a dealer who'd worked for Lansky there, and plenty of other anecdotes, legends, and just-barely-believable stories that brought life to his story of a mob dynasty.

Puzo, of course, put Cohen's words in the mouth of his Don Vito Corleone, the mob godfather modeled at least partially on Carlo Gambino, who was himself familiar with the Sands. He'd come out to check on his investment but was spooked by the phones. When someone in his suite picked up their extension, a light went on the phone in his room. Was someone listening in? He and his bodyguards were moved to the 6th Street home of a pit boss, who got to stay in the Sands suite for his troubles.

All of those great stories didn't change the fact that Puzo was $17,000 in the hole, and Carl Cohen was not going to let him return to New York without making good on his losses. Playing roulette for six to eight hours a stretch, Puzo quickly blew through his bankroll. Hearing that he was under contract to write a surefire best-seller, Jack Entratter himself authorized extending him credit. But, as Puzo kept losing and word got to the Sands that he wasn't exactly careful with his money (he'd run through the first $100,000 of his $410,000 advance in three months), Cohen decided that enough was enough.

Producer Bob Evans, a Sands gambler and friend, came to the rescue, paying off Puzo's marker so that the writer could finally leave Las Vegas. The price was that Paramount got the rights to make a *Godfather* movie for much less than Puzo could have held out for.

"I needed the cash," Puzo later wrote. "Let me say now that the fault was mine. But I never held it against Paramount that they got *The Godfather* so cheap."

After he had made his first million from *The Godfather*, Puzo returned to Las Vegas. In November 1969, when Puzo's book had already climbed the best seller list, gossip columnist Earl Wilson included an item about him. Puzo, he said, "a dedicated gambler who loses $ by the buckets, is writing his next novel about Las Vegas. It's a subject he knows very well."

Puzo had already written about Las Vegas—before *The Godfather's* release, he wrote a gambling guide for the Christmas issue of *Holiday* magazine—but the Las Vegas novel never happened. He did, in 1976, publish a non-fiction book, *Inside Las Vegas*, that delved into the history and current set-up of the gambling town. It was Puzo's love letter to the city.

By the time *Inside Las Vegas* came out, Puzo said he had stopped gambling. But he admitted that he was as hooked as anyone else, albeit on a smaller scale. He wasn't the kind of guy to win $100,000 and then lose it all. Those men, he said, were almost affectionately known as degenerate gamblers.

"But in my very worst days I was only a mildly degenerate gambler which gives me an understanding, I think, of the syndrome," he wrote. "It's not that you want to lose what you have won. It's just that you cannot believe it's possible to lose. When winning you are convinced God loves you."

Puzo stopped gambling, he confessed, because he'd been cut off by every casino in town.

"I hereby affirm and swear," he wrote, "that I owe a fortune in markers to the casinos, every penny of which they won fair and square.... But the day they cut off my credit and made me pay cash for chips was the day I broke my gambling habit."

The conclusion of his article about Sally Rags was, perhaps, Puzo's elegy to the fleeting success that is all the best any gambler can hope for.

"Sally Rags, expert gambler though he be, sweet guy and all, was never going to find his long-sought-for 'middle,'" he wrote. "Like everyone else, he would have to settle for a small and temporary edge."

What was true for gamblers was true for casinos. By the early 1970s, it was clear that the Sands, which ten years earlier had seemed destined to rule Las Vegas forever, had only enjoyed a small and temporary edge.

***

Howard Hughes had come to Las Vegas to get far from the madding crowd, but he also wanted to be an emperor. He could twist governors, senators, perhaps even presidents to his will. And at first he seemed to get his way: Frank Sinatra left the Sands almost immediately, though he remained an irksome presence down the street at Caesars Palace. He was able to buy a major chunk of Nevada's gaming industry without having to make an appearance in front of the Gaming Commission— the presence of his proxies and a personal phone call with Governor Paul Laxalt were enough to waive that requirement. Just before Sinatra's teeth met Carl Cohen's fist, Hughes announced plans to build a massive, space-age airport to the west of town that would accommodate the coming age of supersonic jumbo jets. Las Vegas would become the new gateway to the entire American Southwest. For a man of Hughes' wealth, few things were impossible.

I will remake you in my image, Hughes whispered to Las Vegas, and all I ask is your devotion.

But Hughes wasn't the only one with big plans in Las Vegas. Kirk Kerkorian, who had worked his way up from very little to amass a fortune in aviation, was taking a third look at the casino business. He'd invested a bit in the New Frontier and lost it all in 1955. A few years after that, Jay Sarno approached him with plans to build Caesars Palace on a piece of land Kerkorian owned across from the Flamingo. After seeing how well Caesars was doing, Kerkorian decided that he wanted to own the casino, not the land.

In 1967, Kerkorian started construction on the International, a resort that shifted the paradigm of casinos in Las Vegas. Earlier hotels had been a cluster of mostly low-rise buildings with, in later years, towers attached (the Riviera, which was a high rise from day one, is an outlier). Architect Martin Stern, Jr., fresh off planning the Sands' expansion, sketched a monstrous high rise with 1,500 rooms in three wings, radiating in a Y-shape from a central shaft. It would feature fast service and a 2,000-seat showroom that would showcase artists who had not played Las Vegas before. The casino, showroom, and restaurants were, as in the Sands redesign, housed in a low, wide building that served as the tower's base. This still serves as the basic model for casino design to this day.

Hughes naturally took umbrage. He was the visionary, he was the one taking Las Vegas from sawdust to spacecraft. For the man who set air speed records to be upstaged by a mere grubstaker—this was humiliating.

Unable to buy or scare Kerkorian off, Hughes tried to starve him out. And the Sands was his weapon of choice.

On January 25, 1968, he announced that he was on the verge of reinventing the Sands, which would eclipse in every possible way Kerkorian's hotel.

The $150 million, 4,000-room addition would make the Sands—by far—the world's largest resort hotel. The International was poised to take that honor, but the New Sands, at 4,777 rooms, would be over triple its size. In a personally handwritten note disseminated by his staff, Hughes detailed the particulars. The expansion, which would be "a complete city within itself," would have a 24-hour shopping mall on one massive floor, and another floor with a range of family recreation like the world's largest bowling alley, a similarly sized billiards and pool facility, an ice skating rink, and rooms for chess, bridge, skeeball, and table tennis. A movie theater would be "equipped with projection equipment and sound equipment so modern it has not even been shown yet to the public in literature or trade publications." The bowling and pool tables would be similarly advanced. The resort would also have indoor and night-time golf facilities based on electronically calibrated shots—basically *Golden Tee*, twenty-some years early.

"I should not have devoted so much time to these novelties which will soon be commonplace," Hughes reassured his subjects, "but I wanted to make it clear that this is an ambitious undertaking—aimed at providing the most complete vacation and pleasure complex anywhere in the world.

"The resort, so carefully planned and magnificently designed, that any guest will simply have to make a supreme effort if he wants to be bored, whether he is a sophisticated VIP of Jet-Set type, or one of the children of a family spending their vacation with us."

All of this would be housed in multiple buildings, constructed from a corrosion-resistant steel alloy, which would enable it to rise as high as 50 stories, dwarfing its surroundings. It would be adjacent to the existing Sands and visually different.

"They are not the same architecture as the present buildings, but do not result in an unpleasant conflict," Hughes claimed.

With the Sands turning away thousands of people a month, and a survey indicating that the Sands brand was well known across the world, Hughes believed that the hotel, which would also include convention facilities, would easily fill up. It would utilize technology his team was already researching that would allow guests to check in electronically and use cards, rather than keys, to access their rooms.

"I maintain," Hughes concluded, "a hotel can be big and still keep the degree of service and luxurious treatment which has made Las Vegas famous. Anyway, this is the objective of all our careful planning."

Las Vegans were, of course, impressed, but soon began to ask what was in it for them. Contractor R. C. Johnson estimated that it would take 3,000 men to build such a project over a period of 18 months, bringing substantial paychecks to town. Johnson, who had been the contractor for the Sands tower, thought that as much as $75 million would be spent on labor.

Within a few days, Al Freeman reported that dozens of requests for comment, many of them from overseas, had come into his Sands office. The Clark County School District, in the process of requesting a bond issue to finance new school construction, began fretting that, should work on the Sands begin, it would not have sufficient space to accommodate the children of construction workers and hotel employees. School Superintendent James Mason estimated that the Sands project alone might translate into over 23,000 new students who would require 19 new schools.

By April, when Hughes was pushing for state approval to buy the Stardust and Castaways, he declared that he intended to also spend $400,000 modernizing the Desert Inn's rooms and $4 million on a new entertainment venue at the Frontier.

The Department of Justice ultimately rejected Hughes' purchase of the Stardust on antitrust grounds, though Hughes was so busy in the spring and summer of 1968 that he might not have been too bothered. First came a frenzied effort to halt the Atomic Energy Commission's 1.3 megaton nuclear test—code-named Boxcar—at the Nevada Test Site. Hughes offered to personally pay the costs of relocating all atomic testing to Alaska, and even tasked Maheu with delivering $1 million to President Lyndon Johnson as an inducement to stop the test. Then came an abortive attempt to buy the ABC television network.

In the end, the New Sands was to prove just as quixotic as Hughes' attempts to buy the Stardust, stop atomic testing, build a supersonic jetport, or buy a television network. Perhaps more so, since outside Hughes' handwritten announcement, no actual work on the $150 million project was ever done.

But even without moving a spade of dirt, the New Sands' true purpose might have been accomplished. The announcement stole the thunder of the International's February groundbreaking, making the black-tie affair, in which Nevada Senators Howard Cannon and Alan Bible joined Kerkorian in ceremonially turning earth after a fireworks show, sixth-page news. The Sands announcement also made it more difficult for Kerkorian to raise capital, although it didn't stop the International from continuing.

Hughes abandoned the New Sands by late 1968, setting his sights instead on buying the incomplete Landmark, a boondoggle that had languished, nearly complete but unopened, for years. The tower, almost as tall as the International, was catty-corner to Kerkorian's hotel. Hughes bought the Landmark in early 1969 (the Justice Department didn't object to Hughes buying an unopened casino with three dozen creditors), though its opening within days of the International's was a debacle.

The Sands, however, soldiered on.

***

As the Hughes empire solidified its hold on the Sands, there were fewer high rollers to be found, but money continued to flow through the casino at a respectable but not remarkable rate. Once the Hughes team had fastened its new controls atop the Sands casino, it seemed content. The Copa lost one of its longtime stars when, in December 1969, Dean Martin agreed to leave the Sands for the Riviera, where he received a large ownership share, the title of entertainment consultant, and a $200,000 per week salary. In a few years Sammy Davis, Jr. would depart for Caesars Palace, leaving the Copa without a single member of Sinatra's Clan to perform.

It was a new Las Vegas, one where Elvis Presley—practically laughed out of town after an uninspiring April 1956 stint at the New Frontier—

now reigned. While Governor Laxalt and the Chamber of Commerce were over the moon with the newfound respectability Hughes and others were bringing to Las Vegas, there were some dissenting voices.

As early as January 1968, journalist and commentator Bob Considine wrote with some misgivings about the changes in Las Vegas. He'd been away for four or five years, but found Las Vegas remarkably different. Previously, the second floor of a hotel was its top floor. Now, he was typing his "On the Line" syndicated column from the 18th floor of the Sands, and that wasn't the highest spot on the Strip.

It was a taller town, but a quieter one. "The jingle-jangle," Considine wrote, "seems much more muted than I remember it. Maybe they're using softer nickels in the slot machines." Whereas gambling once provided 80 percent of hotel income a few years back, Considine claimed it now only constituted half. That was an exaggeration (Strip casinos on average got more than 60 percent of their revenue from gaming well into the 1990s), but Considine was not wrong in saying that gambling was becoming less important for the Strip's new bosses. And, make no mistake, it was a new class of boss calling the shots in Las Vegas.

"I have yet to see a broken nose, a cauliflower ear, or hear a 'dese' or even a 'dem,'" Considine lamented. "Where did the Old Guard go? Back to Detroit? Cleveland? Miami? Where they went, they went away richer."

Las Vegas was now a great convention town, where guests were just as likely to go fishing on Lake Mead as gamble the night away. Much had been gained, to the delight of the Chamber of Commerce, but, Considine felt, much had been lost.

"I miss the days," he wrote, "when the place was filled with newsmen covering the big atomic bang ups of Yucca Flat....the all-night vigils in the often freezing desert...the first thread of dawn...the countdown by someone with the voice of God...the bracing of yourself...then the whole world, weird and shaking in scalding lightning and thunder."

That was the Las Vegas that Al Freeman had done as much as anyone to create—one where the detonation of a weapon of mass destruction was something to cherish, something to get nostalgic about over a decade later (above-ground tests ended in 1962, though underground testing continued for another three decades). And, as early as January 1968—scarcely three months after Cohen's right to Sinatra's mouth ended an era in Las Vegas, just a half-year after Hughes bought the Sands—it was gone, forever.

Considine was right in perceiving a shift in the class of casino managers; the Sands would get a new leader who, three years earlier, might not have been hired as a host. In May 1969, General Nigro was promoted to serve as Maheu's deputy. To replace Nigro at the Sands, Maheu hired Joseph Aspero, of Worcester, Massachusetts. Aspero, who had a law degree from Boston University, had served in the Massachusetts House of Representatives before being elected five times as a member of the Worcester County Commission.

Aspero had never worked in the hospitality industry in any capacity. Still, he thought that his move to Las Vegas, to run one of the city's most storied casinos, was an interesting challenge not that far out of his wheelhouse.

"I am still dealing with people and finances," he said, "which is what I have always done."

Casino executives had always come from diverse backgrounds, but it is hard to imagine what in Aspero's previous career had prepared him to manage the Sands. His biggest qualification seems to have been that his wife Lena and General Nigro's wife, Ann, were sisters. Nigro himself would leave the Hughes organization in early 1970 to head Del Webb's Nevada casinos, which at the time included the Mint, Sahara, and Thunderbird in Las Vegas and the Sahara Tahoe.

The post of Sands president had always been something of a figurehead. Freedman was a glorified greeter who, as years went on, was increasingly distant from decision making, and Entratter would never question Cohen's dominance of the casino or Doc Stacher's behind-the-scenes decision-making. But Jack Entratter and Carl Cohen, with their decades of experience, were hardly going to report to Aspero as subordinates, so their responsibilities evolved. Entratter was ostensibly in charge of entertainment for all Hughes resorts, and Cohen in charge of all casino gaming. Both continued to live at the Sands and retained their vice presidencies at the hotel but were far less involved.

In the summer of 1970, Las Vegas seemed to be settling into a routine. Hughes had bought six casinos, a television station, two small airports, and plenty of real estate, but didn't seem to be buying more. No visible progress had been made on the space-age supersonic terminal or the ambitious New Sands (nor would any progress be made). Bob Maheu was the Hughes organization's most visible representative, with Nigro taking a prominent role alongside him.

That all changed on November 25, the night before Thanksgiving. Just as suddenly as he had arrived, Howard Hughes left Las Vegas. And, despite the immense power Hughes held, no one outside his inner circle had any idea he was gone at first. Maheu was concerned that he had been kidnapped. He had become increasingly distant from Hughes over the preceding months, but had received no precise indication that he was on the outs with "the Man."

A week later, the *Las Vegas Sun* reported that Hughes had "vanished." With Hughes' departure came an immediate power shift in his Las Vegas operations. Chester Davis and Bill Gay, two Hughes executives who Howard had apparently empowered to speak for him, fired Maheu. They ensconced themselves on the top floor of the Sands' tower and began moving accountants into the Hughes casino cages to assume control of the money and files. Maheu counterattacked with a restraining order barring the Davis/Gay faction from the casinos, which was answered by a restraining order barring Maheu and his loyalists from the casinos.

At 1 a.m. on the morning of December 7, Nevada Governor Paul Laxalt was summoned to a Sands penthouse suite where he, Clark County District Attorney George Franklin, Jr., and Gaming Commission Chairman Frank Johnson were met by Bill Gay. Gay then produced a phone. On the other end was Howard Hughes, safe and sound in the Bahamas.

"I'm feeling fine," he assured Governor Laxalt, confirming that he did indeed sign the paperwork authorizing Maheu's ouster.

"What's all the fuss?" he jokingly asked the governor. "All I'm trying to do is fire a couple of guys and go on vacation."

While litigation between Hughes and Maheu would drag on for several years, it was now settled: Maheu was out.

When the dust settled, Davis and Gay had devised a series of interlocking corporate umbrellas that put Hughes' Nevada properties under the control of Sands, Inc. Hotel Properties, Inc., and Harolds Club, Inc. (Hughes had recently bought the storied Reno gambling hall). Although the Sands had its own shell company, Sands, Inc., it remained under the control of the Houston-based Hughes Tool Company. Carl Cohen became a vice president and director of Hotel Properties Inc., removing him further from the Sands.

The new management structure was anything but stable. In July 1971, Al Freeman denied reports of a mass exodus from the Sands, even as former FBI agent Richard Danner (who had run the agency's Miami field office and worked on Richard Nixon's 1968 campaign before moving to the Hughes organization, where he would be a conduit to the president) had taken over as general manager of the Sands. Though Bucky Harris was stepping down as casino manager to resume his role as credit manager, Freeman insisted that General Charles Baron, a longtime gambling figure who served as a casino greeter, had not quit or been forced out.

Indeed, through the turmoil of the Hughes years, elements of the old guard remained at the Sands, though some moved on. Sandy Waterman relocated to Caesars Palace where, in September 1970, he pulled a gun on an irate Frank Sinatra, who had soured on his agreement to perform at the resort and was angry at Waterman for, predictably, limiting his credit. Jack Entratter himself was rumored to be on the verge of leaving, maybe to buy a restaurant in Hollywood, maybe to focus full-time on talent management (he had personally managed Red Skelton for years), maybe to run another casino. Entratter's frustrations became an open secret. Losing Sinatra was, at worst, a mixed blessing. But the departures of Dean Martin and many others was unambiguously bad. Entratter had built the Sands on its entertainment. It was now losing on that front.

Working for Frank Costello and later Doc Stacher, Entratter had become accustomed to a large measure of autonomy in his business. Entratter understood that as long as he kept the Sands in the public eye and gamblers filled the casino to see his performers, he had relatively free rein to do as he pleased. He could feel he'd honestly earned the lavish apartment he'd built for himself. Indeed, no one could begrudge it to him, since, in the fifteen years he'd been in charge of the Copa Room, he was the greatest entertainment director in Las Vegas, perhaps in all the country. Entratter enjoyed exceptional privileges, but he delivered exceptional results.

Under Hughes, Entratter found his autonomy eroded, bit by bit. Selling out to the billionaire didn't make him sad—at the time of the sale he was the owner (on paper at least) of 12 percent of the hotel, and he got a corresponding share of the $15 million sale price. The nearly $2 million he received would, in the late 1960s, be enough to set him up for a comfortable retirement, with plenty left over for his grandchildren. He didn't have to work another day in his life.

But a man's work was his life (particularly a man like Entratter, who had been in show business since his teens), and Entratter wasn't happy sitting back while someone else ran the Copa, particularly since the entertainment empire he'd built up over the preceding 15 years was crumbling.

At the same time, even the accountants couldn't deny that business at the Sands was down. With five casinos, Hughes' people should have had entertainment locked up. Instead, they'd lost stars to Caesars Palace, which had taken the Sands' crown as show capital of Las Vegas, the Riviera, and other casinos. So, in February 1971, the Hughes machine agreed to return to Entratter his duties as chief Copa booker. He would be rubbing shoulders with performers once again. Still, some felt that it was just a matter of times before Entratter left.

But Jack Entratter never left the Sands. On Tuesday, March 9, 1971, he was stricken at the hotel by what was at first believed to be a minor stroke. He was taken to Sunrise Hospital, where his local physician, John Fiore, was soon supplemented by New York's William Hitzig and Martin Levy of Beverly Hills, who were flown in to attend to Entratter, who was now suffering from a cerebral hemorrhage and related complications. On Thursday, March 11, he died.

Variety lamented his death as severing one of the last links between the early days of Las Vegas and "its present corporate image," and lauded Entratter's generosity to anyone who could do the Sands a good turn. Entratter had made the Sands the top spot in Las Vegas for entertainers, and thus the top spot for the general public and gamblers.

Entratter's Las Vegas funeral brought the Sands' old guard out in force. Pallbearers included Carl Cohen, Charles Turner, and Al Freeman of the hotel as well as *Sun* publisher Hank Greenspun. The list of honorary pallbearers bridged Las Vegas power brokers like Parry Thomas and Harry Claiborne, Sands stalwarts (Charles Baron, Charles Kandel, and Bucky Harris), and entertainment stars such as Joey Bishop, Jerry Lewis, Don Adams, Sammy Davis, Jr., and Louis Prima. Dean Martin, though he was now a Riviera executive, was credited as an honorary pallbearer. Frank Sinatra was not. Following a memorial service as Temple Beth Sholom (where Entratter had been a board member and president), Entratter's body was returned to New York City where, after a Manhattan memorial service, it was interred alongside that of his late wife Dorothy in Knollwood Park.

Without Entratter, life at the Sands went on, uneasily. In January 1972, after a Los Angeles television station broadcast a report that Cohen was lining himself up to be the new owner of the Sands, the hotel called a press conference (to which only print media reporters were invited) in which Cohen and Richard Danner took turns issuing denials.

"I don't intend to buy the Sands or any hotel," Cohen insisted. "There are no plans at all to sell the Sands that I know of. And I plan to stay here."

"There have not been any plans, even remotely for the future, to sell any properties," Danner added. Indeed, Hughes was notorious for not selling anything he bought. "The man who owns them says, 'No dice.'"

When asked if The Man himself had in fact weighed in, Danner backtracked, saying that the Hughes Tool Company Board of Directors, speaking for Hughes himself, was behind the statement.

Cohen professed to be slightly embarrassed at the claims that he was unhappy at the Sands, but it was obvious that both Cohen and the Sands were losing ground. Once, the Sands had been on the cutting edge of Las Vegas entertainment. Now, the hotel grabbed headlines for hosting a party that honored the 55th anniversary of Jimmy Durante's show business career. It was a wonderful opportunity to pay tribute to the 79-year-old Durante, but hardly in tune with current musical tastes. In the age of the Osmonds, the Jackson Five, and Elton John, the Sands was two generations behind.

The Sands suffered another blow in August 1972 when Al Freeman died in his sleep, the victim of a heart attack. Freeman's health had been precarious since his wartime service (for which he had received five battle stars, a Legion of Merit, three clusters, and a Purple Heart). He was credited for his instrumental role in selling both the Sands and Las Vegas. He had chaired the Las Vegas Chamber of Commerce's promotion committee from 1958 to 1964 and was responsible for the rollout of national advertisements touting the city as a convention destination.

Red Skelton, Danny Thomas, Sonny King, and Sammy Davis, Jr. eulogized Freeman at his funeral, and he was credited for helping to put Sinatra's Clan (later known as the Rat Pack) together in the Copa. More than ever, it was clear that an era had ended. In his obituary, *Review-Journal* columnist Don Digilio fondly recalled Freeman's constant generosity to the press and even regular tourists, crediting him with doing more than he realized to improve others' lives. He couldn't help but contrast the current state of the Sands with its glory years.

"There is word out that the Sands Hotel is concerned about losing their big name stars," Digilio wrote. "Martin is gone. Sinatra quit them,

Sammy Davis is leaving, and a few other top flight entertainers are off to other hotels. The Sands Hotel shouldn't worry about that. They lost their biggest attraction Tuesday when they found Al Freeman dead in his apartment."

The last of the holdovers from the glory years, Carl Cohen, remained. He'd been rumored to be leaving the Sands for over a decade now, but he professed to be as happy as ever under the Hughes regime, though he was taking more time off to play golf and try to lose weight with Duke University's rice diet, an aggressive in-patient program designed to combat hypertension. But Freeman's death, when added to the mounting frustrations of life under Hughes, perhaps pushed Cohen to make a decision.

On January 4, 1973, Cohen announced that he was resigning his position with the Sands and the Hughes organization, effective immediately. He took pains to take the high road.

"We parted the best of friends," he explained to reporters, "and I plan to take a long rest before I get back into business."

"Is it true you and Danny Thomas are buying the Sands?"

"No."

"Are you retiring?"

"I regret leaving the Sands, but I feel the time is right for me to rest a while, and then I'll be back in business," Cohen responded. When asked what that business would be, he merely shrugged.

Cohen wasn't on the sidelines for long. Four months later, he was named senior vice president of the MGM Grand, a massive casino hotel Kirk Kerkorian, who had sold the International to Hilton Hotels, was building. Perhaps not so coincidentally, he would be joining Al Benedict and Bernie Rothkopf, two other Hughes refugees. Cohen would have the number two position in the resort, with much more autonomy than he'd had with Hughes. The behemoth opened that December, with 2,100 rooms, a massive casino, two showrooms, a host of restaurants, and, a familiar name as its opening headliner: Dean Martin.

Two decades in, the Sands was at a crossroads. The hotel had known success and sadness. It remained to be seen whether the Sands could reclaim its former glory.

The Sands was one of the first Las Vegas casinos to offer baccarat. Carl Cohen presides over the game here. Courtesy UNLV SCA.

In 1962, the Sands was primed for expansion, first with the Aqueduct building and then a tower. Courtesy UNLV SCA.

Presidential aspirant John F. Kennedy takes a moment during his 1960 visit to shake hands with Jack Entratter. Courtesy UNLV SCA.

Though he hired to an exacting standard of feminine beauty, Jack Entratter insisted that the Copa Girls be elegant, never tawdry. Courtesy UNLV SCA.

The 1962 opening of the Aqueduct building gave the Sands a posh set of suites intended to compete on quality against the large room expansions its rivals were bringing online. Courtesy UNLV SCA.

In 1965, the Sands added its own major expansion, enlarging its casino and public spaces, adding restaurants, and constructing a tower. The "Sands" letter on the famous marquee was also modernized. Courtesy UNLV SCA.

One of the reasons the Sands needed more rooms was to woo convention groups, like this meeting of GMAC executives in the second-floor Emerald Room, which before the property's 1965 expansion was its primary meeting space. Courtesy UNLV SCA.

By 1966, as seen in this rendering, the Sands had been dramatically expanded. Bigger changes, however, were just on the horizon. Courtesy UNLV SCA.

Reinvigorated for a new Vegas, the Sands ended the 1960s with a new look and new leadership. Courtesy UNLV SCA.

As the Sands' president for most of the 1970s, Richard Danner presided over the casino for much of the Hughes era. Courtesy UNLV SCA.

In the 1970s, the Sands, like other Las Vegas casinos, offered more opportunities to all employees. Courtesy UNLV SCA.

In 1981, the Sands' new owners, the Pratt Hotel Corporation, renovated the hotel's exterior, including the replacement of the classic marquee by a readerboard behemoth. Courtesy UNLV SCA.

After bringing the Comdex convention to Las Vegas in 1979, the Interface Group became increasing invested in Las Vegas; a decade later, the company would buy the Sands. Left to right: Irwin Chafetz, Ted Benard, Sheldon G. Adelson and Jordan Shapiro. Courtesy UNLV SCA.

A few months before its June 30, 1996 closure, the Sands was still standing proud. The competition from new resorts (like Treasure Island, seen at the far left), however, was too much for the 44-year-old resort. Courtesy UNLV SCA and On Point Products.

$\mathcal{D}$anke Schœn

After Jack Entratter's death, Howard Hughes tabbed a longtime friend to take the impresario's place as his Las Vegas entertainment maven. Walter Kane broke into show business as Fatty Arbuckle's vaudeville partner playing the Keith and Orpheum Circuit. As vaudeville declined, he shifted to theatrical management, becoming president of Harry Webber Inc. before joining Zeppo Marx's agency as a partner. In 1938, he founded his own talent agency.

Kane befriended Howard Hughes in the late 1920s and visited Las Vegas with the future billionaire through the 1960s. After Hughes assumed control of RKO Studios in 1948, he installed Kane as the talent director. It was whispered along the Hollywood grapevine that one of Kane's duties was to procure women for Hughes; whatever the reason, he remained a confidant. With Entratter gone, Kane's sway over the Hughes properties' showrooms was unquestioned. He even moved into Entratter's old suite at the Sands.

In a 1974 *Billboard* interview, Kane took credit for rebuilding the Sands' entertainment lineup following the departure of Sinatra. He stressed that one of his biggest priorities was to keep overhead low.

"My weekly entertainment nut for the Sands, Frontier, Desert Inn, and Landmark," he said, "is less than Caesars Palace," which was reportedly paying Frank Sinatra $240,000 a week and Johnny Carson $200,000, with Sammy Davis, Jr. a relative bargain at $175,000. Casinos charged their customers accordingly; a Sinatra ticket at the Circus Maximus could cost as much as $35, while no Sands show cost more than $15.

Kane developed a core of performers that he rotated through the Hughes casinos. At the Sands, his roster centered on Phyllis Diller, Bob

Newhart, Lena Horne, Diana Trask, and Rich Little, with its undeniable centerpiece a symbol of the new Las Vegas: Wayne Newton, who Kane signed to a multi-year, multimillion-dollar contact in February 1973. In that year, Newton starred in the Copa for nine weeks straight. But this wasn't enough for Kane, who became so close with Newton that the singer adopted him as his grandfather.

"Next year, we'll do 12 weeks," he told *Billboard*. "No one's ever done 12 straight weeks." And if that worked, it might be all Wayne, all the time; Kane mused about giving Newton a 40-week engagement.

Possibly more than Elvis Presley, Wayne Newton defined Las Vegas entertainment in the 1970s. Nothing could match Elvis's box office appeal, and no one—no one—could approach him in packing the Hilton's massive showroom during his semi-annual stints. The number of Elvis's consecutive sellouts is a matter of debate, but his dominance is unquestioned.

But nobody could fill the Copa room, or other Las Vegas showrooms, night after night, year after year, the way Wayne Newton could. No one—not even Elvis or Frank—could end each performance with a standing ovation. In the 1970s, Sinatra was the class of Las Vegas, Presley its heart, and Newton its soul.

Kane would remain in charge of Hughes entertainment until his 1983 death. Newton, Robert Goulet, and Debbie Reynolds were his standbys. Kane kept costs down, kept the showrooms filled, and if there wasn't the same buzz as there was when Dean Martin and Jerry Lewis were giving away thousands of dollars, well, maybe that was the price of progress.

***

After taking over from Bernie Rothkopf in the aftermath of Hughes' 1970 exit from Las Vegas, Richard Danner would remain at the helm of the Sands for the rest of the decade, bringing the casino its first stability at the top since its purchase by Hughes in 1967.

Danner brought with him from the Frontier Harry Goodheart, a casino veteran. Originally from Kansas City, Missouri, Goodheart had honed his trade at the Beverly Hills Club of Southgate, Kentucky. Like many others when the public turned against illicit gambling post-Kefauver he moved to Las Vegas, where he worked as a craps dealer, rising by the mid-1960s to the role of floorman. In January 1969, he was licensed as a casino executive at the Frontier. In March of that year, he was named the Frontier's casino manager, replacing the retiring Chester Simms.

Coming into the Sands, Goodheart had the benefit of a robust junket network that he had built up at the Frontier. Ranging across North America, Goodheart's connections enabled him to keep a steady stream of gamblers in the Sands casino—an important tool given the exodus of high rollers post-Hughes. He was also possibly the first casino executive to use a computer to better understand his customers. Goodheart himself didn't operate the machine, but he had his secretary maintain a database that could be deployed when he made his prospecting calls.

"Bob," he might start. "We haven't seen you since last August. I hope Martha is well. How's your boy doing in Florida? We'd love to have you back—we've got a bottle of Macallan waiting for you."

Bob, amazed that Goodheart had remembered so much about him, would soon be back. Ultimately, database marketing would become more sophisticated, but Goodheart grasped early on how computers could revolutionize customer relations for casinos.

That regime got a new name in 1972, after Hughes sold the Hughes Tool Company. His core enterprise since the 1920s, Hughes Tool had been the umbrella under which his casinos were organized. Everything left over after the sale of the tool division—mostly the casinos and real estate, with the odd television station and mining operation thrown in—was consolidated under the Summa Corporation. Though the name changed, little else did in Las Vegas.

Similarly, Hughes' April 1976 death did not much affect day-to-day operations at the Sands or any of his casinos. For the most part, the same executives remained in charge, the same policies in place. Though Hughes was the Summa Corporation's sole stockholder, he was neither a director nor an officer of the company. With 6,000 employees in Nevada, Hughes was theoretically the state's biggest boss. But he had long ago given up day-to-day control of his empire. In Las Vegas, a triumvirate of Bill Gay, Nadine Henley, and Chester Davis were in command, with a small staff of increasingly interchangeable executives below them.

Former pit boss Ed Walters, who had laughed along with Dean Martin in the dealer's lounge, left the property in 1969 when Martin became a part-owner of the Riviera. In 1976, he returned to the Sands.

When he came back, there was a new breed of customer.

"Used to be, 60 percent of the people in here were serious gamblers," he confided to a friend. "The other 40, seriously wealthy people. Where'd they all go?"

It was a rhetorical question. Walters knew that having to sign a counter check for their markers was like giving a vampire a garlic-and-silver-bullet bouquet.

"These TV people," Walters named the tourists who now filled the hotel. "They're not here to really gamble. They're here to see the entertainers they've seen on television, to see movie stars." Now, a guest was more likely to ask Walters where the men's room was than to talk about blackjack. And when they did gamble, they needed to be held by the hand.

"Excuse me, sir, do I put my money in the circle?" one of them asked, pointing at the blackjack layout. And if someone the tourists had seen on TV walked through the casino, God help them. When Cary Grant came to speak briefly to Walters, the star was mobbed by autograph-seekers who had abandoned their 21 games in mid-deal.

Back in the day, a gambler wouldn't have looked up if Jesus Christ himself had walked through the pit. The gambler didn't mind that movie stars frequented the Sands; in fact, it gave the casino additional luster. But he wasn't there to see movie stars. He was there to gamble. The TV people, not so much.

The Sands wasn't that different from the rest of Las Vegas. In the 1970s, the town began shifting its appeal. Of course, non-gamblers had been courted since at least the early 1950s, when the Desert Inn opened its golf course, and the shift toward conventions after 1955 had changed the very nature of Las Vegas casino resorts, allowing them to add many more hotel rooms that could now be kept steadily full during the middle of the week, leading to higher capital outlays that, in part, dictated the shift toward corporate ownership in the next decade.

Howard Hughes and Kirk Kerkorian both demonstrated the importance of capital in the new Las Vegas. Hughes, of course, simply opened his wallet and bought as many casinos as he could. Kerkorian, though, took a more strategic approach, using a combination of cash, debt, and equity to finance the construction of the International. Difficulties in the financial markets, rather than operational inefficiencies, forced the International and Flamingo's sale to Hilton Hotels. Kerkorian, after buying MGM Studios, returned to Las Vegas in 1973 with the original

MGM Grand (today, Bally's). With Carl Cohen, Bernie Rothkopf, and many other members of the old guard, the MGM Grand might have been the last stand of the city's first generation of casino managers, but its size dictated that it be financed and operated under new models.

This meant a much greater sensitivity to costs than before. Previously, casinos were owned by small pools of investors, some legitimate, some not. Unless the casino was hemorrhaging money, managers generally tolerated lax controls over both cash and complimentaries. They could afford to be generous because the casinos were bringing in more money than the owners could spend; these were men for whom a few thousand dollars a month, plus unlimited RFB privileges for themselves, constituted an earthly paradise. Why not let some cash bleed off to the employees to keep the casino running smoothly? There was no reason to sweat comping policies. With low costs, it made sense to grant freebies even to small-time players who had some promise to develop into bigger fish.

The new owners—mainstream lenders and stockholders—wanted more than middling dividends and comp privileges at the property— they might, in fact, never visit the property in the flesh. Rather, they demanded constantly increasing financial indicators that would lead to higher stock prices, increasing their own net worth. This meant that every dime had to be accounted for. That the casino ran well or did not run well, that customers were happy or not happy, was no longer the guiding imperative for managers: boosting shareholder value was.

Though the privately held Summa was not beholden to the market in the same way as publicly held companies, Hughes' managers nevertheless had been conditioned to keep an eagle eye on the bottom line. Having not walked a casino floor since, perhaps, the 1950s, Hughes was more concerned with dollars and cents and his own flights of fancy than delivering an optimal customer experience. With an audience of one, the top managers made decisions that would be sure to meet with their boss's approval, and this attitude rolled downhill. Walter Kane's focus on financial stability over the raw star power of his headliners wasn't due to personal cheapness: It was standard Hughes policy.

Despite these constraints, Danner and Goodheart were good executives who launched new programs. They focused, for example, on golf, co-sponsoring the U.S. National Senior Golf Open Championship. In December 1976, Goodheart hired Al Besselink, who had won the first Tournament of Champions at the Desert Inn in 1953, to serve as a casino host specializing in golf promotions. While the Sands did not have its own course, the Desert Inn, also under the Summa umbrella, did, and many decent gamblers also had a fondness for golf.

Goodheart in particular was widely praised. In both 1976 and 1977, *Review-Journal* columnist Don Digilio, in December columns touting "shopping lists" for various local figures, wished for the Summa Corporation "another casino manager like Harry Goodheart."

The Sands debuted keno in 1972, a sign of the casino's new appeal to more casual gamblers. Keno, which has perhaps the worst odds of any casino game, is a far cry from craps or baccarat, which have among the least damaging casino hold, and are favored by big gamblers. The game is played by selecting numbers from a list; the object is to correctly guess the numbers that will be drawn at random. Keno offsets its ruinous odds with the will-o'-the-wisp promise of a possible six-figure payout, appealing mostly to novice gamblers. As keno became popular, casino coffee shops started stocking keno slips, with keno runners (typically attractive young women) picking them up while players ate. Frank Sinatra dealing *chemin de fir* it was not.

Still, the Sands didn't totally abandon the high roller hunt. With lavish tower suites and several large Aqueduct suites, Goodheart and his hosts courted well-heeled gamblers who preferred the "shabby elegance" of the Sands to the more modern resorts. In 1976, they rented Hawaii's entire five-star Manua Kea Beach Hotel as a "thank you" for their biggest players. The 150 lucky high rollers who made the cut had credit lines of at least $25,000. But the all-expense-paid trip was more than a show of gratitude. The festivities started with a Saturday night luau at the Sands, and the plane departed for Hawaii Monday morning, plenty of time for them to gamble plenty of money. After five days in paradise, they returned to Las Vegas with another evening to kill before being flown home. All in, with hotel, chartered airfare, and associated expenses, the event cost the Sands a cool million. It generated, however, $3 million in gaming revenue. The Sands' competitors soon started offering their own "thank you" trips along similar lines.

The biggest high roller that Goodheart lured to the Sands was Adnan Khashoggi, an infamously wealthy Saudi Arabian businessman. An intermediary in international arms deals whose generous commissions funded an ostentatious lifestyle (12 homes, a private jet described as "a flying Las Vegas discothèque" and a $70 million yacht), Khashoggi was any casino host's wildest dream come to life: a man with means (he earned as much as nine figures for some of his brokering) and a commitment to spend extravagantly (he reportedly spent $250,000 a day simply to maintain his lifestyle).

Though Khashoggi lost $500,000 on his first trip to the Sands, he took a big enough liking to the casino that, in June 1974, it was rumored that he was looking to buy it. It wasn't an entirely outrageous scenario; by that point the up-and-coming businessman had already bought two California banks and dabbled in Arizona ranching, California restaurants, New Mexico trucking, and New York-based mutual funds. He ultimately invested heavily in Salt Lake City, but a foray into casino ownership would not have been entirely out of character, although it is doubtful that he would have submitted himself to a suitability investigation by Nevada gaming authorities. His play was big enough that he was given not only Suite 707, in which Ed Nigro had resided while he ruled Hughes' gaming empire, and Suite 720, where Jack Entratter once lived and where, in 1984, Ronald Reagan would stay, but the entire Aqueduct building. And, as high rollers went, he was good about paying his bills; he paid for all the incidentals charged to his account (though naturally the rooms themselves were gratis) and even paid in full a $1 million birthday party thrown for his daughter. This was a once-in-a-generation rainmaker.

The physical plant of the casino had little to impress the arms dealer, who among his residences boasted a 180,000-acre Kenyan ranch, a Manhattan penthouse created by knocking together 16 apartments, and a 5,000-acre seaside estate in Marbella, Spain, where he threw parties worthy of a king (his 50th birthday party lasted five days). Rather, it was probably the lengths to which Sands executives would go to keep Khashoggi contented. Roger Wagner, who later helmed several casinos, worked several stints at the Sands; in the late 1970s, as the head of Sands purchasing, he was instrumental in the high-stakes scavenger hunts that Khashoggi and his associates seemed to delight sending executives on.

In his first week in his new role, Wagner had to acquire a specific model of electric barber chair. Wagner was able to locate one in a Thousand Oaks, California warehouse, and was able to find an Angeleno with a pickup truck who was willing pick up the chair and drop it off at Los Angeles International Airport, where Khashoggi's famous jet was waiting. By six that night, the chair was installed in Khashoggi's suite.

Later that same week, Khashoggi, through his associate Bob Shaheen, demanded the largest Snapper lawnmower in existence. Wagner dutifully found the mower and, following Shaheen's instructions, had it crated up and marked for Nairobi, as it was meant for Khashoggi's Kenyan estate. A year later, however, the mower remained at the Sands, as Khashoggi apparently never bothered to have it shipped.

From the mid-1970s on, Khashoggi was consistently the Sands' biggest player. Not even a 1976 imbroglio in which American defense contractors were charged with funneling bribes to Middle Eastern political and military figures through Khashoggi cooled the Sands' affection for him. Richard Danner spiritedly fought a federal grand jury's order to turn over the hotel's records of transactions involving Khashoggi. The billionaire spent several months away from the United States to avoid his possible arrest, but he returned to Las Vegas with a vengeance, losing as uninhibitedly as before.

In early 1979, the management upgraded the Aqueduct building to accommodate their star. A garage housed his fleet of vehicles. A helicopter pad lay barely a football field from his suite's front door. At the Sands' expense, a dedicated phone system was installed. This system, with its own switchboard, was disassembled after each of Khashoggi's visits and reassembled at his return. It was worth every penny: Khashoggi lost $22 million that year at the Sands.

So while the bulk of the Sands' marketing efforts went to attracting smaller-limit players, the casino remained in the great whale hunt. And yet, as the casino got older and its competitors expanded (Caesars Palace's Fantasy Tower, which opened in 1979, was designed chiefly to cater to high-limit players), this became a more difficult game to play. Still, the Sands had a seat at the table.

***

The changes in the city and casino demanded some changes to how the Sands was promoted. After Al Freeman's death in August 1972, Richard Danner brought over Al Guzman from the Desert Inn to helm the Sands' publicity and advertising department. Guzman was a veteran PR man who had followed his service in the U.S. Army with a stint at the Hughes Aircraft Company's Radar Maintenance Division while moonlighting as an occasional sportswriter for the *Los Angeles Mirror*. He then moved to Las Vegas, initially working the sports beat for the

Sun before, in 1968, taking a job at the Desert Inn as the assistant director of public relations and advertising. In 1970, he was promoted to director.

Guzman's marketing philosophy was in many ways similar to Freeman's.

"Pretty girls sell," he argued. "Pretty guys don't sell. You need to do something to get people's attention. If you don't get their attention, you're dead. A pretty girl will get an editor's attention, then maybe he'll put you in his newspaper and you've got some free publicity."

Indeed, in Guzman's time, as in Freeman's, scantily clad women had a suspicious tendency to show up in press photos for which there was, strictly speaking, no logical reason for a scantily clad woman to be present. And Guzman was, the evidence suggests, a leg man.

A 1973 photo, for example, celebrating the opening of the 17th Annual U.S. National Senior Open Golf Championship doesn't feature a veteran duffer teeing off. Instead, it shows Hotel President Richard Danner and Vice President of Casino Operations Harry Goodheart wearing suits, flanked by professional golfer Vic Ghezzi, wearing a golf shirt, watching appreciatively while the leggy "hostess" Karen Brands holds a club, wearing shorts covering, perhaps, a quarter of her thighs. Another 1973 photo op, this one staged to mark the one-year anniversary of the Sands' keno program, featured comedian Bob Newhart playing a "human keno ticket" in the form of "Miss Sands '73" Kay Brown, on whose bare midriff was painted "an exact duplicate of a standard keno ticket." In August 1978, a photo accompanying a blurb about the Sands' renovation of 196 tower rooms and suites (which were, over a decade after the tower's construction, being given a "modified Louis XVI design") showcased a snapshot from the official announcement event. Vice President of Hotel Operations Rand Clark, Danner (holding a sledgehammer), and Goodheart, all wearing suits and hardhats, are joined by "greeter" Danielle Hansen, whose hardhat accessorizes a tank top and microscopically short shorts.

Guzman cultivated what he called "the art of getting free and favorable publicity." A stunt Guzman orchestrated for the Sundance casino in 1984 is emblematic of his approach. Las Vegas had gone nearly three months without rain—a record-breaking drought. In what would later be seen as a buffet of cultural insensitivities, Guzman "rounded up five pretty girls, put them in some scanty Indian maiden costumes, and had them do a raindance in front of the hotel," backing up Fremont

Street traffic for blocks. That a thunderstorm struck the next day helped make the resulting photographs "newsworthy," but Guzman insisted that the rain dance was effective in communicating that "people are having some good old-fashioned fun in Las Vegas."

In the 1980s, Guzman reflected that the new breed of Las Vegas PR executives didn't appreciate the value of stunts like the rain dance, and that they didn't try to cultivate members of the press, instead directing their secretaries to grind out press releases. This reflected, he thought, the less personal way that the business itself was run.

"They've lost the old touch," Guzman lamented, "which the old regimes held so high, and maybe some work run by the Mafia." Back then, employees felt they were part of an organization that wasn't all about profit and loss.

"In the old days, they just went by the overall picture. If they made money, it was great. They didn't give a damn if food and beverage was losing $100,000 a month, because at the end of the year they were going to make X amount of dollars. Now everything is controlled by accountants who are about as exciting as a dead rag."

Shortly after taking over, Guzman introduced a new slogan that replaced the original "Place in the Sun," which had served the hotel since its 1952 opening. "The Sands: Where the Fun Never Sets" highlighted the 24-hour action at the hotel and incorporated the late Freeman-era stylized sun of the Sands' logo.

The new slogan played up Guzman's belief that Las Vegas should be promoted, above all, as a fun place. Yet the reality was fun could be had, but somehow the Sands seemed less spontaneous than it had been a decade before.

***

The Sands was too small to operate with the economies of scale that the Hilton and MGM Grand enjoyed, plus it had lost much of its high-end play to Caesars Palace. Summa was itself not quite the picture of financial health in the late 1970s; the company's far-flung holdings, which included a slew of casinos, a television station, an airport, and large swaths of real estate, were not running profitably. In 1978, Summa sold the Landmark, which had never shown a profit.

Then the global economy slid into recession, and Summa's problems intensified. In addition, in early 1980, the company transferred over

12,000 acres of property in Las Vegas and Tucson to the Hughes estate so that it could be liquidated to pay the estate's sizeable death tax liability. Once a juggernaut, the Hughes empire was on the ropes. The Sands was further hamstrung by Richard Danner's health difficulties: In the summer of 1980, the casino president suffered a massive stroke from which he never fully recovered.

So it was not a tremendous surprise when, in October 1980, Summa's Chairman of the Board William Lummis announced that the company was selling the Sands.

The buyer was Inns of the Americas, a hospitality firm headed by Jack Pratt and his brothers Edward and William. The company was one of the world's largest Holiday Inn franchisees, with hotels in the United States, Central America, and the Caribbean. With 23 hotels already in its portfolio and another seven under construction, Inns of the Americas was on the upswing. The company had an eye on international expansion, having just contracted to operate La Quinta Motor Inns across Mexico.

While new to Nevada gaming, the Pratt brothers had every confidence that they would succeed. Inns was already a gaming operator, running a casino affiliated with its San Juan, Puerto Rico Condado Holiday Inn. The hotel business was all about filling rooms, and with their experience around the Western hemisphere, they had every confidence that under their watch the Sands would prosper.

All told, Howard Hughes and his successor corporation owned the Sands for about 14 years—from 1967 to early 1981—almost as long as the original group. The Hughes/Summa era seems to be one of consolidation. While managers made strides in improving the efficiency of operations, the resort lost much of its magic. Lummis admitted as much when he said that, in Pratt, the Sands would get "an owner that is committed to modernize and enlarge the property so that it will be able to maintain its prestigious image and competitive edge," suggesting that the Summa regime did not have the means to do so.

Jack Pratt believed that he could bring the storied Sands into a new era.

"The Sands has long been one of the jewels of the Strip," he said. "We will continue to operate the property as the Sands Hotel and Casino and have plans that will enlarge it and enhance its position of preeminence among the luxury hotels of Las Vegas."

Pratt promised a $40 million renovation and expansion, which would include an expanded casino and public space, more parking, and a second guest tower. Within a month, the investment was boosted to $50 million. It was now a three-phase plan, with a refurbishment of the façade and public areas followed by a 450-room tower expansion and, perhaps four years later, another expansion that would bring the hotel to 2,000 rooms.

To lead the Sands, the Pratts hired Neil Smyth, a veteran hotel executive and marketer who had spent the past 11 years working his way up the executive ladder at Caesars Palace, where he was currently senior vice president in charge of operations. The trilingual Smyth (he spoke English, Arabic, and Spanish), a graduate of the University of Pennsylvania's Wharton School of Business, was a hall-of-fame table tennis player who would continue winning championships into his 80s. He followed his military service with a stint as an internal auditor for Pan Am, after which he returned to Puerto Rico, where he had been stationed as a naval intelligence officer, to serve as an accountant for the San Juan International Hotel.

Smyth championed using the latest computer advances to improve casino financial management. He held a variety of leadership positions in hospitality accounting professional organizations and co-authored a revision of the collection of industry benchmarks known as the *Uniform System of Accounts for Hotels*. The soft-spoken Smyth wasn't one for theatrics, but he knew the hotel business as well as anyone.

Even before receiving their license for the Sands, the Pratts purchased the Brighton, a struggling, undersized casino in Atlantic City. They announced plans to rebrand the Brighton as the Sands, bringing some "pizazz and glamor" to the Jersey shore town. Likewise, the Puerto Rico casino was given the Sands name.

Though Smyth and the Pratts wooed Harry Goodheart, offering him a role as senior vice president overseeing all the company's growing casino operations, Goodheart begged off. Rather than take on the task of building an international casino brand, the casino veteran opted to move to the Desert Inn as a vice president, where he would work for the remaining 15 months on his contract before retiring to spend more time traveling with his wife and fishing.

"I haven't been able to go fishing in five years," he said.

In part because of the added due diligence Nevada Gaming Control Board investigators needed to pursue on Inns of the Americas' Puerto Rico casino, the official approval for the Pratts to be licensed and formally assume ownership was delayed until April 1, 1981. In recommending that the Gaming Commission grant Inns a license, Board Chairman Richard Bunker stipulated that the company must divest itself of small interests in two Panamanian casinos and that it agree to further investigation in Puerto Rico.

At the hearing, Jack Pratt made it clear that, if push came to shove, his company would sell the Sands, which was losing money hand over fist, rather than the profitable Condado Holiday Inn.

"The Sands today is losing huge sums of money—it's hemorrhaging," he said.

Smyth underscored his boss's point.

"The Sands lost money last year and it looks like it will lose money this year, too," he said. "It's difficult to try to work in an older property while everyone around us is modernizing." The plan was for the steady cash of the Puerto Rican casino to cover for lower income at the Sands, which in the best-case scenario promised to be a construction site for the next several years.

Licensed alongside Pratt, his brothers, Inns of the Americas' Latin American subsidiary president Luis Ponce, and Smyth were another pair of brothers, Burton and Richard Koffman of Binghamton, New York, who were to own 24.25 percent of the casino each. They were financing Inns' expansion plans and had agreed to also facilitate the acquisition of the casino that would become the Sands Atlantic City.

So, with a down payment of $25 million, an agreement to infuse $10 million in operating capital into the casino, and a monthly payment plan, Inns of the Americas officially became the Sands' new owners. At midnight on May 1, 1981, Summa Recreation Division Vice President Phil Hannifin turned over a ceremonial set of hotel keys to Smyth and Ed Pratt, executive vice president of Inns and the Sands' general manager. The Sands had its third set of owners. They inherited employees and department heads who were on the whole more experienced than their counterparts at other resorts. Although it was more than a decade after the end of the Sands' glory years, the hotel retained its reputation as a destination for good managers, rather than a stop along the road. This is why a casino manager like Harry Goodheart would move from the Frontier to the Sands, but not vice versa.

Smyth and the Pratt brothers immediately launched into the first phase of their modernization program, but economic headwinds made the $50 million expansion that had been promised in October unfeasible. Instead, the new owners spent $15 million to increase the size of the casino to 30,000 square feet, renovate the lobby, and add two new restaurants: the Mediterranean Room, a gourmet eatery, and the Sands deli, which served humbler fare. Other additions included the new Regency Bar and the Winners Circle Lounge.

The Sands didn't have a new tower to unveil, but that didn't mean that there couldn't be a gala opening. To launch the "new" Sands, the owners turned to Burt Peretsky, who in late 1981 replaced Al Guzman as director of marketing, advertising, and public relations. Peretsky had recently come to Las Vegas from Boston to work in a similar position at Del E. Webb's corporate offices, but burgeoning economic difficulties forced Del Webb to begin selling off their properties.

Sparing no expense, Peretsky and Ed Pratt hired Tommy Walker to stage the re-opening extravaganza. Walker had a reputation as "Mr. Spectacular," the man who could deliver an exceptional event. A dual place-kicker/drum major in his years at the University of Southern California, Walker turned down an offer to turn pro with the Washington Redskins to return to his alma mater as director of the marching band. In 1955, Walt Disney hired him to put together Disneyland's opening ceremonies. From there, he staged progressively more elaborate events; over his career, he directed galas at three Olympics and five world's fairs.

When Peretsky reached out to him, Walker was fresh off his biggest triumph to date: coordinating the special effects at Ronald Reagan's inaugural. To the strains of Aaron Copland's "Fanfare for the Common Man," red, white, and blue skyrockets and flashing lasers crossed the sky, giving Reagan's Morning in America a technicolor dawn.

On Friday, January 15, 1982, at 7 p.m., the Sands Hotel and Casino announced its rebirth with "Encore '82: The Sands Spectacular."

Peretsky and Walker planned a day/night event that would culminate in a black-tie ball featuring as many celebrities as Peretsky could fly in from Hollywood and, naturally, every high roller who still frequented the Sands.

But before that would come a signature Tommy Walker spectacular. What better way to etch the Sands into history than to have the hotel enshrined in the *Guinness Book of World Records*? Lacking the tens of millions of dollars it would take to make the Sands the largest hotel in the world, Walker decided on some relatively low-hanging fruit. High school students from around the Las Vegas Valley competed to see which school could blow up the most balloons, with the winners promised scholarships. After several days of exhaling, the Sands ended up with 300,000 balloons, which were deployed in a display that a Guinness fact-checker (flown out to Las Vegas courtesy of the Sands) verified was the largest simultaneous release of balloons in history.

To emcee the event, the Sands needed a figure who could simultaneously deliver star power, wow the audience, and provide a link back to the good old days. Sinatra, maintaining his grudge against the Sands long after Jack Entratter had passed away and Carl Cohen had moved on (and, indeed, Howard Hughes had died and his company had sold the resort), refused. Dean Martin was busy. So Peretsky turned to Sammy Davis, Jr.

There was one problem. Davis was currently under contract with Harrah's, who refused to let him perform for any other Nevada casino. But Peretsky found a loophole. If the Sands didn't pay Davis, he was free to perform.

"He'll never do it," Davis's agent to Peretsky.

"Can I just call him and ask?" Peretsky asked. The agent gave Peretsky Davis's phone number.

Peretsky called and outlined the Tommy Walker spectacular and the critical role that the emcee would play. But there was more than free publicity at stake. This was the Sands, the house Davis had practically built.

"Could you maybe do it...for old times' sake?" Peretsky asked. There was a long pause on the other end of the line.

"For old times' sake?" Davis finally answered. "I'll do it. For old times' sake."

The day before the event, Davis came to the Sands to run through rehearsals. As he walked through the casino, a crowd gathered. Davis, always a natural in front of an audience, spotted a dead blackjack table. He walked up and threw a hundred-dollar bill. "Money plays," announced the dealer, who replaced the bill with a single black chip. The dealer laid down the cards. Davis lost. The singer pulled out another hundred-dollar bill. Same results. He reached into his wallet a third time, and this time won. Although money was tight for him (Davis was on the edge of bankruptcy), the showman slid the chips to the dealer.

"A little something for you," he said, as the crowd applauded.

The Sands naturally put Davis up in its finest suite, which was promptly renamed the Sammy Davis, Jr. Suite. But Davis's tastes were unpretentious. For lunch, Peretsky offered to have the gourmet room opened especially for him, or to have room service send anything up to his suite.

"Do you guys have a Popeye's around here?" Davis asked. Yes, Peretsky replied.

"I'll have a three-piece box," Davis said. Peretsky sent a limo driver to Popeye's to retrieve the meal. Davis enjoyed his chicken sitting cross-legged on the suite's bed, watching cartoons.

The night of the gala, though, Davis was all business. He emceed the outdoor extravaganza from the top of the Sands' porte cochere and made, perhaps, the biggest entrance of his career, being flown into position on a helicopter in front of a mass of humanity along the blocked-off Las Vegas Strip.

Seven marching bands, one from each Las Vegas-area high school, set a parade-like atmosphere. Davis presided over the balloon release, a massive fireworks show staged by Grucci, the First Family of Fireworks. Set to a musical backdrop, a relative novelty then, the display climaxed with another helicopter swinging a blazing Sands logo in the evening sky.

From there, the party shifted inside. Davis fronted the Harry James Orchestra at the black-tie, invitation-only event.

Having weathered three decades, the Sands faced an uncertain future. Whether the reborn Sands would reclaim its place at the top of the Las Vegas pecking order, whether it would survive at all, remained to be seen.

While the Feeling's Good

The Pratts bet $100 million on a very specific market: Latin America. Even before it closed on the Sands sale, Inns of the Americas had 47 sales agents in Mexico City alone, with offices open in Panama and Venezuela and plans to operate as many as 40 hotels in Central and South America by 1985.

Jack Pratt was particularly bullish on Mexico.

"We think," he told the *Review-Journal* in late 1980, "that Mexico will become the Saudi Arabia of the Western Hemisphere, but with 70 million people and a high industrial base that Saudi Arabia does not have."

Further, Pratt wanted to do more than lure outrageously wealthy high rollers, as most casinos did when looking at Saudi Arabia. Instead, he would also target the upper middle class and middle class. With Inns' base of hotels and Neil Smyth's long history in the region, giving the Sands a Latin focus seemed like a can't-miss proposition.

But as the January relaunch approached, it was becoming clear that luck was not on the side of the Pratts. They had bought a casino during one of the worst years Las Vegas had yet seen. Concerns about organized crime connections led Nevada regulators to close the Aladdin for nearly three months. There was turmoil in the ranks of gaming regulators, though Gaming Commission chair Harry Reid was cleared of impropriety after allegations that he was "Mr. Cleanface," a regulator whom mobsters claimed they controlled in conversations caught on tape by federal investigators. But the Argent investigation (the inspiration for Martin Scorsese's film *Casino*) was deepening, grand juries across the country were conducting inquiries, and regulators were catching casinos in cahoots with alleged mobsters: The Dunes housed

14 reputed Colombo crime family members, and Tony Spilotro was seen having dinner at locals' favorite Sam's Town.

When they weren't dogged by allegations of mob influence, casinos struggled with cash flow. Downtown's Holiday International casino closed; it was losing $500,000 a month when the doors were shuttered. The Nevada Palace and Jolley Trolley, smaller casinos, also closed (though both reopened), and the Shenandoah Hotel was losing money and, due to licensing issues, unable to open its casino (it eventually evolved into the Bourbon Street hotel casino). The year's biggest calamity, however, was the November 21 MGM Grand fire, which claimed 87 lives and closed the newest resort in Las Vegas for seven months. A few weeks after the Sands' relaunch, a less deadly but no less publicized fire at the Las Vegas Hilton raised concerns about safety up and down the Strip.

Feeling the financial pressure, the Sands' new management made tough decisions. Adnan Khashoggi, at the time of the changeover, was still the Sands' biggest gambler. The high-powered dealmaker was at the height of his powers in the early 1980s. Dropping millions on each of his stays at the Sands, Khashoggi, a legendarily bad roulette player, had an understanding with Harry Goodheart that he would get a 30 percent discount on his losses—in other words, when he lost $1 million playing on credit in the casino, he would actually pay only $700,000 to satisfy his debt. Even with this generous allowance, Khashoggi could swing the casino from the red to the black. In 1979, he'd gone a long way toward making the Sands profitable enough that it paid its executives bonuses. Those financials went a long way toward convincing the Pratts to pay $85 million for the resort.

But with money tight, the Sands' new management thought that a 30 percent discount was a luxury they could not afford. So they informed Khashoggi that he would now receive a 10 percent discount. Khashoggi paid his marker, but he suddenly stopped returning hosts' phone calls, and was spotted at Caesars Palace not long after.

The loss of one gambler shouldn't be enough to doom a casino, but losing the nearly guaranteed income that came from putting up with Khashoggi's antics was a huge blow for a casino that didn't have much to fall back on.

***

The storied Copa started the 1980s about where it had been for the past decade. Wayne Newton, Alan King, Shecky Greene, Tony Bennett, Joan Rivers, Anthony Newley, Bobby Vinton, David Brenner, Debbie Reynolds, Doc Severinsen, and Neil Sedaka were the mainstays of the rotation that headlined the stage. Yet it was becoming more difficult to stage shows in the Copa. Following the MGM fire, regulators insisted that the Sands make seating reductions for safety reasons. In February 1981, public relations director Al Guzman announced that the Sands would be doing away with its dinner show. Switching to drinks-only allowed the Copa to increase its seating from 518 to 580, but the Copa was still the smallest showroom in the city with headline entertainers.

The casino business has never been a sentimental one. When the Pratts looked at how to best bring the Sands back into the black, the Copa—in its current form, at least—was expendable. Too small to compete with the massive showrooms at the Hilton or MGM Grand, too big to feature lower-priced lounge acts, the Copa was a relic.

So, in the early hours of June 25, 1981, the Copa's curtain came down for the last time. Glenn Campbell and Lonnie Schorr headlined the final show, which ended well after 2 a.m. The show started with host Gus Giuffre announcing, "Welcome to a wake." Comedian Norm Crosby gave a eulogy for the Copa filled with malapropisms.

"Even though this room is closing," he concluded, "the spirits of those acts who died on this stage will linger here forever."

Nevada governor Robert List read a proclamation declaring June 24 "Copa Room Day" across the Silver State and read telegrams from two former Copa stars.

"I have a lot of fond memories of the Copa Room and warmest wishes for everyone," Danny Thomas said.

"I wish you all the best," Frank Sinatra wired. "Save a piece of the floor for me."

This wasn't an unreasonable request. The floor of the Copa stage was being sawn into 4- by 6-inch pieces and given as souvenirs to select high rollers and a few preferred employees.

After being joined by Tanya Tucker for a few numbers, Campbell sang a special version of Nat King Cole's signature "Unforgettable" as a slideshow of famous Copa performers appeared on a screen: Danny Thomas, Red Skelton, Jimmy Durante, Judy Garland, Cole, Dean Martin, Joey Bishop, Sammy Davis, and Peter Lawford, along with later standouts like Wayne Newton, Sergio Franchi, Nipsey Russell, and Robert Goulet.

After the last guests departed, Copa staff retired to the lounge, where Jerry Tiffe sang classics made famous by Sinatra, Cole, and Louis Prima.

A few names associated with the Copa in the more recent past shared their sentiments on the showroom's closure.

"A lot of Las Vegas history was made on these boards," Wayne Newton said. "The Copa Room is the last cabaret left in Las Vegas and I for one will miss it."

Noting that he and Campbell had shared the stage for the final performance at the Desert Inn's showroom, Newton had a request.

"Hey, Glen, stay away from the Aladdin." Newton had just become a part-owner and performer at the resort.

Walter Kane, who had first brought Newton to the Copa and was still in charge of entertainment for Summa, reminisced about how he and Howard Hughes had been in attendance when Danny Thomas opened the room on December 15, 1952.

Teardown started almost as soon as Campbell walked offstage. The plan was to cut the Copa's total seating to 400. As part of the renovation, the Regency Lounge was demolished to make way for more casino space. This, along with space carved from the Copa, let the Sands enlarge its casino without much increasing the building's footprint.

The Copa would become a combined lounge/showroom that would feature lounge performers during the day and, twice nightly, a revue show. No more stars. A production revue, which eschewed high-priced headliners for a roster of easily replaceable and lower-priced performers, would be less costly than the "star" policy of the previous 29 years. It helped that the international visitors the Pratts banked on hosting would be more attuned to a flashy production show, with little dialogue but plenty of attractive dancers and special effects, than they would, say, the comic stylings of Shecky Greene. Revues were beginning to supplant headliners in Las Vegas venues; though production shows had been a part of Las Vegas from the 1950s, in the early 1980s they became increasingly prominent. The Desert Inn, which had long dueled with the Sands for bragging rights as the Strip's premier showplace, dropped out of the headliner game in 1980, running Broadway shows most of the year, with stars reserved for major holidays. Then the Frontier replaced Walter Kane's roster of stars with "Beyond Belief," a revue starring rising magicians Siegfried and Roy. The MGM Grand offered both the Jubilee revue in its Ziegfeld Room and headliners in the Celebrity Room; the Tropicana had a similar dual-showroom policy.

On December 29, 1981, the new Copa launched with a revue called "Top Secret." It would run at 9 p.m. and midnight, with lounge entertainment from the early afternoon up until 8 p.m. Originally, the Sands planned to add a late-night (or early-morning) showing, but audiences did not take to Top Secret.

"Critics said," entertainment writer Norm Clarke later quipped, "that this Sands' effort of the early '80s should have remained a secret."

The Sands was not alone in launching a revue: A week after "Top Secret" opened, the Sahara debuted "The West Was Never Wilder," a musical comedy featuring the Sahara Girls. Perhaps the market was oversaturated. Perhaps the show was just plain bad. Whatever the reason, Top Secret closed before reaching the two-month mark, failing hard enough that Sands president Neil Smyth announced that the Sands would be returning to its "big name" star policy.

To return the Copa Room to glory, the Sands turned to the man who had launched it back in 1952, Danny Thomas.

"I guess I'm one of the biggest cornballs in show business. I have a sentimental attachment to the idea of resurrecting the old days," the 70-year-old entertainer declared.

Sentiment aside, Thomas was a curious choice to debut the "new" Copa. In a January *Los Angeles Times* article, freelancer Bill O'Hallaren opined that Las Vegas was graying. He described watching tour bus passengers with an average age of 75 shuffling out with canes and walkers.

"Even Caesars, MGM, and the Hilton, the swankiest trio, seemed to have been taken over by the veterans of World War II and especially their auxiliaries. Almost everyone in town remembered Pearl Harbor," he wrote.

O'Hallaren was having some fun at the expense of Las Vegas, but the question cut deeply enough to prompt a *Review-Journal* editorial asking if the writer had a point. The Royal Americana had just closed, the third casino closure in three months. The editorial specifically called out the signing of Thomas, who, though "a fine man and a fine entertainer," probably didn't resonate with the younger, vibrant crowd that Las Vegas needed to court.

"Recent events," the editorial concluded, "inspire a nagging feeling that the vigor that gave Las Vegas its name and glitter is slipping away."

For his part, Thomas leaned into his age. His generation, he argued, could carry the Sands and Las Vegas back to prominence.

"Except for those who are already under contract to other hotels," he declared, "I intend to ask everyone who is still alive who ever played here to consider and then reconsider coming back to the Sands…. In addition to all the nostalgia, we intend to entertain—I'm not going to come out here and say, 'Good evening, I'm an old man, be kind to me.'"

Inns of the Americas entertainment director Phyllis Kaufman announced that the Sands would be reviving the Copa Girls. Jack Entratter's famed chorus line had been retired years earlier.

Sands PR director Burt Peretsky was charged with managing both the relaunch publicity campaign and the reopening's star attraction. Thomas had apparently developed a reputation as a bit of a curmudgeon. Peretsky made sure, before the big star's arrival, to have the casino filled with placards reading "WELCOME BACK DANNY!"

When Thomas's limousine arrived, Peretsky greeted the comedian and his wife personally.

"I want to go to my room," Thomas said gruffly, hardly a promising introduction.

Peretsky guided the couple to their room, being sure to steer them past the signs. The more Thomas saw, the brighter his smile got. For his entire stint at the Sands, he was, in Peretsky's words, "a puppy dog," despite his prickly reputation.

Opening March 17, Thomas was supported by singer Bunny Parker and the Copa Girls, who performed three numbers throughout the show. The return of "name" entertainers was sufficiently successful that it continued. The casino signed Steve Allen, Joel Gray, Anthony Newley, Sammy Shore, Marilyn McCoo, Sergio Franchi, Jim Bailey, and Rita Moreno.

At $14.95 per person, with two cocktails included, the Sands was offering an affordable night of entertainment. It might not have quite been Frank, Dean, and Sammy, but the Copa was again featuring name performers—a sign that, perhaps, the Sands wasn't so wrong to look to its past in trying to build its future.

***

The Copa's relaunch did not, in the end, improve the Sands' finances. The hotel had courted a small group of Mexican bettors who, among them, gambled about as much as Khashoggi had on his own. Then Mexico's economic problems became severe enough that the government devalued the peso twice. The $20 million in markers that Mexican high rollers owed the Sands was whittled down by nearly a half.

The Sands did enjoy some triumphs. In July 1982, the Nevada Gaming Commission approved the company's stake in Puerto Rico's Condado Holiday Inn. Having sent Gaming Control Board agents to investigate the popular vacation spot first-hand, the Commission concluded that Puerto Rico's controls were satisfactory and that Inns' involvement there posed no threat to Nevada gaming.

This approval marked the first time Nevada regulators had licensed a company that also owned casinos outside of the United States. Over the next several years Nevada operators pursued projects in Europe, Africa, and South America. And, in the 21st century, Las Vegas-based companies moved into Macau, which soon displaced the Mojave city as the world's gaming capital. Nevada's investment in international gaming might have evolved differently without the precedent the Sands set.

That same month, Jack Pratt announced that Inns of the Americas was changing its name to the Pratt Hotel Corporation, reflecting the company's commitment to managing major hotel and casino properties rather than mere inns.

The Sands hosted its biggest dignitary in years when, on October 28, 1982, President Ronald Reagan spent a night in suite 720 in the Aqueduct building. "Spent the night at the Sands in what was built to be the owner's apartment," Reagan noted in his diary. Perhaps he knew, but did not write down, that the suite had a lead-lined, bombproof room. Whether Jack Entratter had added this precaution due to fears of an atomic test gone wrong or a mob hit no one remembered.

Reagan arrived in Las Vegas at 4:30 and spoke at a campaign rally for Governor Bob List, Senator Chic Hecht, and the rest of that fall's Republican slate. Two Copa alums had prominent roles in the event: Robert Goulet sang the National Anthem and Wayne Newton, a longtime Reagan supporter, acted as emcee. Then, it was off to the Sands, where Reagan spent the rest of the evening. The resort rolled out the red carpet for the Gipper, including a lavish dinner catered in his suite, served on the casino's finest china, the service used in the Regency Room, emblazoned with the restaurant's logo, a mirrored pair of Rs.

Evidently, someone in the presidential entourage, or the commander-in-chief-himself, was under the impression that the plates were a monogrammed gift custom-made for the president's visit, a reasonable supposition as Reagan was constantly showered with tokens of appreciation. They were cleaned and taken when Reagan decamped.

The president liked the Sands enough that he returned on February 6, 1984—his 73rd birthday. Reagan started the day flying from Washington to Dixon, Illinois, where he had lunch and a birthday cake in his childhood home on Hennipen Avenue. From there, Reagan spoke at a pair of Illinois rallies before departing for Las Vegas, where he was greeted to a chorus of "Happy Birthday" upon disembarking from Air Force One. That evening, Reagan was again feted by the Sands. Pastry chef Benny Finale baked him a 700-pound birthday cake in the shape of the White House, complete with flag.

Perhaps because of the long day, or because of the emotional hangover of seeing, for the first time in years, his boyhood home, "another cake at the hotel," was all Reagan told his diary. The casino, however, took extraordinary security precautions, digging a six-foot trench behind the Aqueduct to foil would-be truck bombs (the previous October, 265 Marines had been killed by a truck bomb assault in Beirut), with dump trucks filled with dirt blocking ingress at key points.

Sands guests were more excited by the novelty of sharing a hotel with the president than they were bothered by the extra security. It helped that they each got cake. Reagan's team liked the Sands enough that it became their go-to hotel in Las Vegas, hosting First Lady Nancy Reagan on a 1984 solo trip.

Even while it was hosting the leader of the free world, the Sands was struggling to remain solvent. As it later came out, its owners did not make any significant payments to the Summa Corporation after July 1982. It was just a run of bad luck, Neil Smyth insisted, compounded by a jealous Mexican government.

"Mexico looks askance at the number of Las Vegas visitors from its own cities," he told *Variety* magazine shortly after Reagan's visit. "The state will not encourage visitors, will not help Las Vegas by taking money out of Mexico, when capital is needed to funnel back into Mexico."

Summa agreed to offer "financial relief" for the purchase payments. The deal with Summa would, Smyth hoped, buy him and the Pratts some time.

"Who knows?" he said. "We may get lucky in six months."

The odds, however, did not seem to be in Smyth's favor. The casino's continuing woes sparked a round of layoffs, with 250 employees let go in September. In December, the Sands got dragged into a dispute about the Nevada Rally, an off-road performance rally, which was in its fourth year. The Sands, which had been slated to sponsor the 1981 race, dropped out at the last minute. Race promoter John Angus blamed the cancellation on the casino's financial woes.

"They went broke," he told the *Review-Journal*. "Their doors are open now, but they're barely open."

Smyth answered a bit testily.

"You're still reaching the Sands and we're still answering the phones, aren't we?" he responded to a request for comment. The Sands backed out, he insisted, not because of financial problems, but because of a sanctioning squabble between Angus and the Sports Car Club of America.

The Sands barely made it into 1983 before Summa ratcheted up the pressure. In early January, the company's Frontier, Castaways, and Silver Slipper casinos announced that they would no longer cash Sands paychecks. Allowing local employees to cash their paychecks was a "convenience" that many Strip resorts customarily extended and refusing to honor a rival's checks was an unprecedented vote of no confidence. Summa spokesman Fred Lewis, however, insisted otherwise.

"We are in constructive negotiations with the Pratts," he said, "and this does not cast aspersions on the Pratts' ability to cash the checks. It's simply better if we don't have paper floating between the two hotels at this point in time. If the checks had gotten to the bank, the checks probably would have been good, but we considered it more prudent for our casinos not to cash the checks."

Of course, saying that the checks "probably" would have been cashed cast major aspersions on the ability of the Sands to pay them. And the Sands' management did not take this lying down.

"As former members of the Summa family," Smyth said in a statement, "our employees have always enjoyed a mutually beneficial relationship with all the Summa hotels, and particularly with our neighbor, the Castaways. It is unfortunate that they have been inconvenienced at a time when the Sands is working to the best of its ability to solve financial problems for our benefit and that of Summa Corp, our employees, and the community."

Lewis sniffed at Smyth's statement.

"Certainly, we don't intend to dignify it with any further comment," he said.

On April 5, Summa announced that, pending the requisite regulatory approvals, the company would be resuming control of the Sands, with no cash changing hands.

Summa senior vice president Phil Hannifin cast the takeover as an errand of mercy. "We feel the most important thing here is to keep people working," he told the press. Summa spokesman Fred Lewis amplified the humanitarian nature of the re-acquisition of the Sands.

"The corporation's feelings on it are more human than a corporation usually is," he said. "The feeling is they have troubles over there and it would do no one any good to go through foreclosure."

It's possible, though, that Summa was not acting only in the public good. Investigative reporter Ned Day revealed that his sources told him that Summa chairman Will Lummis was more than willing to turn his back on the Sands, letting the Pratts find a buyer in bankruptcy court. But, as Summa received reports that the hotel's upkeep was starting to slip, he decided to take it back, shutting it down while looking for a buyer.

Governor Richard Bryan was not about to see over a thousand Nevadans turned out of work and a major Strip resort closed on his watch. So, sources told Day, Bryan used "a combination of persuasion and arm-twisting" to convince Summa not to close the Sands. As one of the state's major employers, certainly the company had a social responsibility to the community; but should it neglect that responsibility, it might find state gaming regulators being "much less accommodating" in the future.

And so the Pratt era of the Sands ended. The two years that the Pratts, along with their partners Richard and Burton Koffman, owned the resort were a bold gamble doomed to fail by an unforeseen economic collapse. Focusing on wealthy international visitors in general was a wise strategy; three decades later, it would see major Strip operators through the worst of the Great Recession. But, like any gambler knows, sometimes the dice just run against you.

***

Summa wasn't too badly hurt by its failed sale of the Sands. In early 1981, when the nation's economic woes were at their worst, the company was relieved of its obligations toward the Sands and received a $25 million down payment. For more than a year, Summa collected monthly payments of approximately $1 million. Then, just as the economy was primed to improve, the company got the resort back.

There were a few minor delays due to paperwork, but the takeover of the Sands by Hughes Properties, Inc., flew through administrative approvals—no surprise, given the behind-the-scenes arm-twisting that had led to Summa taking the property back. Pratt would be liable for $2 million owed to vendors, all payroll expenses through the end of April, and $600,000 in taxes still due the state.

With little fanfare, Summa resumed control of the Sands on May 1, 1983. Neil Smyth stepped down as president, though he remained on site until August 1 helping to wrap up the Pratts' connections with the casino. Later that month, Smyth was back at Caesars World as executive vice president for Latin American Operations.

Summa named as the Sands' new president Phil Griffith, who retained his presidency of Reno's Harold's Club casino. Griffith planned to split his time between the two resorts, with Pat Cruzen, former vice president of hotel operations at Caesars Palace, overseeing the daily management of the resort.

Griffith built around him a team of top executives, including Terry Oliver as vice president of casino operations, Max Page as vice president of human resources, and Paul Manske as vice president of marketing. They repositioned the Sands for the mass-market Las Vegas of the mid-1980s, as coupon books migrated from Downtown grind joints to the Strip. Circus Circus led the way, offering breakfast, lunch, and dinner at its buffet (with 76 items to choose from) for a combined $7.97. Most rooms sold for under $30, and outside of Caesars Palace, the predominant price point for casino shows was $10 to $15. In the summer of 1983, the Sands offered a bargain for Angelenos. For $99, visitors from Los Angeles received round-trip airfare and transport to the hotel, a prime rib dinner, and $25 of "free" casino chips—$50 during the week. For all guests, the all-new Garden Buffet offered weekday lunch and weekend brunch for $2.99 and dinner seven nights a week for $3.99. If visitors to Las Vegas now wanted value, the Sands would give them value.

For New Year's 1983, the Sands brought back a voice from the past, as Robert Goulet took center stage in the Copa room. That signaled a look back to the past, but with Las Vegas evolving, headline entertainment at the Sands became too costly to maintain indefinitely.

Griffith's tenure at the Sands was short. In October 1984 he, along with three of his top executives, resigned from the Sands to take leadership and equity positions with Reno's Fitzgerald's Hotel and Casino. The departures were amicable. Summa elevated Pat Cruzen to the Sands' presidency to replace Griffith. Cruzen then put together his own team, with Pat Dibble coming over from Caesars Palace to run casino operations and Bob Vanucci, who had been at the Sands since 1982, taking charge of marketing.

The Sands forged ahead in the mid-1980s, suffering, along with others, a taxing 75-day strike by the Culinary Union in early 1984. At the Sands, much of that year and the following one was disrupted by safety retrofit work made necessary after the 1980 MGM Grand fire. With some buildings dating to 1952, the Sands needed an inordinate amount of work done, including adding sprinklers and voice announcement systems to all hotel rooms. With more work needed than all the other Summa properties, the Sands was the last to finish the work, which cost $7 million. The retrofitting was completed, perhaps, just in time. In February 1986, Thomas Edward Littleowl was arrested at the Sands on suspicion of arson, following a series of suspicious fires at the Sands, Dunes, and Flamingo Hilton. He was ultimately convicted and sentenced to ten years in prison. The new safety features may have stemmed tragedy, as none of the fires were deadly and their damage was restricted.

The Desert Inn remained Summa's elite property, with the Frontier as a reliable workhorse, but the Sands had a place as well. Maybe because of the reputation the hotel had earned in its earlier days, in 1984 Summa agreed to license the Sands name and logo to be used on an assortment of products, including clothing, luggage, and games. This move came as rival Caesars Palace was creating a global brand for itself, with everything from logoed bathrobes to a pair of signature fragrances, Caesars Man and Caesars Woman. Though the Sands never reached Caesars' level of brand saturation, the licensing agreement does show that Summa executives still saw value in the Sands name.

Like other casinos, the Sands added a sports book in 1985, and by the end of the year was touting its first Bowl Game Contest, in which the lucky bettor who came closest to picking the winners of all 15 major bowl games would receive a $10,000 prize. In the Copa, a new revue named "Outrageous" alternated with star performers like Chaka Khan. The revue staged three shows a night, taking its place along shows like the Tropicana's "Folies Bergere," MGM Grand's "Jubilee," the Stardust's "Lido de Paris," and more recent shows with staying power, like "Boylesque" at the Silver Slipper, "Legends in Concert" at the Imperial Palace, "An Evening at La Cage" at the Riviera, "City Lites" at the Flamingo Hilton, and "Playboy's Girls of Rock and Roll" at the Maxim.

By the end of 1986, Las Vegas had fully recovered from the recession and looked ahead. Steve Wynn had bought the Castaways and adjoining land across the Strip from the Sands and was planning to build a major new resort. Two casinos, the Dunes and the Landmark, were about to emerge from bankruptcy (the Dunes did but struggled; the Landmark never made it). And Manhattan developer Donald Trump, who had just bought 10 percent of casino operator Bally, was rumored to be interested in Las Vegas, either by consummating his purchase of Bally or by building something new. It was a city full of optimism.

Former MGM Grand owner Kirk Kerkorian, who had sold his Las Vegas and Reno casinos to Bally in 1986, was poised to re-enter the game. Under the terms of the sale, he had been barred from re-entering Nevada gaming, but in 1987, Bally waived the restriction in exchange for the uncontested right to use the "Grand" name on Steve Wynn's former Golden Nugget in Atlantic City, which was renamed Bally's Grand. In August of that year, Kerkorian made a play for the Dunes in bankruptcy court, but lost to Japanese billionaire Masao Nangaku, who bid nearly $158 million for the casino and its 163 acres of surrounding land. Nangaku bested both Kerkorian and Sheldon Adelson, whose Comdex trade show was a Las Vegas fixture.

Summa, seeking to focus on its real estate holdings, had made no secret of its desire to exit the gaming industry. Within days, Kerkorian had reached an agreement with Summa: For $167 million, he would acquire the Desert Inn, the Sands, and the 250 acres surrounding them. It was an astronomically better deal than the one he was trying to strike for the Dunes.

Kerkorian added the casinos to a portfolio that included film and television producer MGM/United Artists and MGM Grand Air, a newly formed airline geared toward business travelers. Fred Benninger, president of Kerkorian's MGM Grand Inc., said that both hotels would keep their names and that no plans for renovations or expansion had been decided on. Kerkorian brought in Phil Hannifin, currently the general manager of Fitzgerald's and the Nevada Club in Reno, to oversee the two properties; Hannifin was no stranger to them, having been in charge of Summa's casino division before leaving to work for Harrah's in 1984.

With the sale still pending, the Sands celebrated its 35th anniversary with a month of festivities, starting on November 13 with fireworks, 1950s music, a hula hoop contest, and food and drink sold for retro 1950s prices. The Checkmates and Freddie Bell headlined a dance in the Copa, which was decorated with photographs and memorabilia from the hotel's history. Bob Hope emceed a private party in the Grand Ballroom for special guests. But it was a look backwards.

In January 1988, Kerkorian breezed through the Nevada Gaming Commission's licensing, having not spoken a word at his Gaming Control Board hearing and not even being present before the Commission. MGM Grand Inc. formally took ownership of the two hotels on February 1. With 20,000 new rooms in various stages of construction in Las Vegas, most assumed that Kerkorian, who had twice built the world's largest hotel, would be making big moves. But Benninger merely said that, for now, no changes were planned.

Less than two weeks later, Kerkorian officially affixed his corporate name to the Sands, renaming the hotel the MGM Sands, combining the old sunburst logo with the MGM lion. But the MGM-Sands marriage was not a long one. In early March, it was rumored that Kerkorian was ready to part with his new hotel, scarcely a month after getting the keys. Indeed, on April 25, Kerkorian had announced that the MGM-Sands was no more. The Interface Group, helmed by Sheldon Adelson, had bought the Sands Hotel and Casino—and 60 acres of surrounding land—for $110 million.

The final chapter in the Sands' history was about to begin.

The Way You Look Tonight

In November 1988, Sheldon Adelson came to Las Vegas for Comdex, the computer expo so large that it needed eight locations throughout the city to house its 1.75 million square feet of exhibits and 100,000 attendees. Adelson had started the convention, whose name was a contraction of Computer Dealers Exposition, in 1979, when fewer than 4,000 computer suppliers and dealers met at the MGM Grand. By the mid-1980s, Comdex had grown into an institution, with three shows held annually. To accommodate his flagship Las Vegas show, Adelson built the West Hall of the Las Vegas Convention Center, donating the building to the Las Vegas Convention and Visitors Authority.

By 1988, Interface was producing several Vegas conventions, including the Cinetex film festival, which debuted that year. Adelson estimated that his company was responsible for 8 percent of Las Vegas convention traffic each year. The company also boasted a travel division, New England's largest tour operator, which tied into Adelson's plans to bring tour and junket groups from the region.

The Interface chairman and his associates had scrutinized the Sands over the previous months, and they had developed a plan. Adelson forecast a multi-stage expansion project, with the first phase including a 1,300-room tower, expanded casino, and new restaurants, as well as a large convention center. This was larger than the 1,000 new rooms Adelson had suggested in April, evidence of his growing bullishness.

"I like it more and more each time I'm here," Adelson explained. "It's a fabulous property and we have a lot of ideas."

The growth of Comdex was the driving factor in Adelson deciding to add a major convention center to the Sands. If he was able to replicate his success in building the West Hall (construction was completed in

71 days), he would only have to schedule two venues for Comdex's 1989 show.

Adelson and Interface, while they would own the Sands, would not be operating it. For that they turned to flamboyant veteran hotelier Henri Lewin. Having fled Nazi Germany as a teenager, Lewin was interred in both a concentration camp and Japanese POW camp before arriving in San Francisco in 1947. After rising to a leadership position at the San Francisco Hilton, Lewin moved to Las Vegas to oversee Hilton's Nevada operations, which included the Hilton and Flamingo Hilton in Las Vegas as well as the Reno Hilton. Lewin, who styled himself as "Mr. Hotel" and whose business cards read "Henri Lewin, Millionaire," had been one of the highest-profile leaders in Nevada gaming before his 1985 departure from Hilton. He left shortly after the company was denied a gaming license in New Jersey due to allegations about Hilton's associations with attorney Sidney Korshak and allegations that Lewin had acted improperly while running the San Francisco Hilton. So, a few months after the license denial, Lewin stepped down from Hilton to form Aristocrat Hotels, a management company. Adelson was banking on Lewin to revive the Sands. And Lewin did not lack confidence.

"Running a hotel is what I do best," Lewin said in an interview. "The Sands hasn't done well because it hasn't had good management. That will now change. I can give you the finest restaurant, but it is nothing without a good chef. One man makes a difference, and that's what I plan to do."

Lewin planned to transform the Sands into the first five-star hotel in Las Vegas. With characteristic modesty, he even took a shot at the game-changing resort then under construction across the street.

"I will tell Steve Wynn that if people have trouble finding his new hotel on the Strip," he told the *Review-Journal*, "then he has my permission to say it is right across from the Sands."

Lewin's confidence didn't prevent problems from arising during the licensing process. The applicants' hearing, originally scheduled for January, was pushed back while regulators evaluated "new information" that had emerged. Former Nevada governor Bob List, representing Interface and Aristocrat, said that the delay was merely a temporary setback, some "loose ends" that had yet to be tied up.

But things were not so easily resolved. In a February 8, 1989 session that stretched late into the night, Gaming Control Board members struggled to make a recommendation about the suitability of Interface and Aristocrat. Board members looked askance at the associations Irwin Chafetz, a 14.7 percent owner of Interface, allegedly had with the owner of a group of gay bars that may have been friendly with mobsters.

The allegations against Lewin were more serious. He had reportedly made unwanted sexual advances on a cocktail waitress in his office at the Hilton. Though he denied the charge, Lewin was involved in an out-of-court settlement. At 2:39 a.m., the hearing—now in its eleventh hour—ended with the Board unanimously recommending that Lewin be denied a gaming license. Gaming Control Board Chairman Bill Bible said that the board had serious doubts about Lewin's credibility. Adelson, who had earlier suggested he might cancel his purchase of the Sands if Lewin was denied a license, stood by the hotelier.

"I am still willing to bet my $100 million on Mr. Lewin," Adelson said.

Two weeks later, the Gaming Commission met to decide the fate of the Sands applicants. The Board had recommended against licensing Lewin and Paul Klapper of Aristocrat, although Lewin's son Larry and Ken Scholl were okayed to manage the Sands. The Board recommended Interface for licensing as owners, with the caveat that Chafetz receive a limited two-year license.

After a great deal of deliberation, Lewin was unanimously approved for his own two-year, limited license. The hospitality veteran was not to be involved with the direct operation of the resort and was forbidden from being involved in personnel matters below the level of department heads.

Adelson was now ready to take possession of the casino and begin a $150 million expansion project that would bring the hotel up to 2,000 rooms and add 45,000 square feet of casino space and a million-square-foot convention center that would be even bigger than the Las Vegas Convention Center. Lewin was front and center when Interface officially assumed control of the Sands in May, placing himself at the center of the new executive team and even singing a few bars of "I Can't Stop Loving You."

In his opening press conference, Lewin let slip a few more details about the upcoming changes to the Sands: The new hotel tower would be 42 stories, the showroom's size would be doubled, and a new culinary concept would be unveiled: 11 "mini-food outlets surrounding a theater in the round."

One of Adelson's first hires in Las Vegas was a familiar face. Attorney Shelley Berkley had practically grown up at the Sands; her father, George Levine, had moved the family across the country before taking a job as a waiter at the Sands' Garden Room. He eventually rose through the ranks to become the maître d' of the Copa Room, one of the most coveted jobs in town. In addition to spending time with her father at work and celebrating a series of family milestones there, Berkley worked her way through UNLV as a weekend brunch server. Now, she was back as the director of government and legal affairs. Her father was still working at the Copa.

Once more, a new owner was taking the Sands' helm. This time, it wasn't Mexican high rollers or the tried-and-true Summa management that would save the resort, but conventioneers. As skyscrapers were rising up and down the Strip, getting bigger seemed to be the only way the Sands could survive.

***

The first order of business, as far as new owner Sheldon Adelson was concerned, was to get the convention center up and running. This was the keystone to the new Sands that he foresaw, the engine that would power Henri Lewin's five-star aspirations.

Despite all the business Adelson had brought to Las Vegas in the decade since the first Comdex, not everyone in town welcomed him. While no one denied that Adelson's conventions filled rooms, they complained that convention visitors did not gamble. One set of numbers showed that gaming revenues fell by as much as one-third during Comdex.

Michael Gaughan, owner of the Gold Coast and Barbary Coast casinos, made a pointed comment when Adelson joined the owners club.

"He's going to find out how bad his conventions are for business."

Adelson, however, was convinced that more convention space was essential to Las Vegas. After all, how else would casinos fill the 12,000 rooms that were due to be built soon? The New Englander thought enough of Las Vegas and the Sands that, within a month of closing on the casino, he had shifted his permanent address to Nevada. He was eager to prove his worth to his new neighbors, promising to work with the Las Vegas Convention and Visitors Authority and other resort owners to keep rooms filled.

Hiring Lewin to oversee a hotel geared to conventions made sense since the Hilton had one of the most robust convention programs in town. Lewin's big personality asserted itself almost at once. As negotiations between the Culinary Union and other hotels broke down and a strike seemed imminent, he vowed that there would never be a strike at the Sands—before even discussing contracts with the union. He then renamed the Grand Ballroom—which had been hosting headline acts too big for the Copa—Henri's Celebrity Theater. The deli was reorganized to serve classic Lower East Side fare and renamed David Papchen's after his father. The Sands gift shop soon stocked Lewin's autobiography, displayed near a sign advising that the executive would be happy to autograph any copies.

Lewin was attentive to criticism, responding to an open letter published in the *Review-Journal* by entertainment columnist Don Usherson complaining about the layout of the Winners Circle Lounge by commissioning a redesign of that space. Lewin's magnanimity had that columnist, at least, eating out of his hand; Usherson posted favorable notices about Lewin's two entertainment coups, bringing in Sid and Marty Krofft's 100-puppet spectacular "Comedy Kings" to the Copa Room to replace the sputtering revue "Beach Blanket Babylon," and returning Broadway to the Strip by placing "Ain't Misbehavin'" in Henri's Celebrity Theater.

Whether taking out a quarter-page ad to personally welcome Steve Wynn's Mirage to the Strip (and to tout the Sands' expansion) or announcing to the media that, henceforth, all bread in the Regency Room would be served in monogrammed paper bags to ensure that they reached guests with the optimal moisture, Lewin proved adept at making news.

With construction on the convention center underway, Lewin's team tweaked the Sands' casino marketing, perhaps self-conscious about the charge that Adelson's conventions produced anemic gaming results. The "Never Ending Slot Tournament" was held every day, with contests competing for a grand prize that would allow them a free pull, with maximum coins in, on every slot machine in the Sands. Lewin promoted the new tournament with a "never-ending buffet.

The handwriting may have been on the wall when Lewin's press notices petered out in the fall of 1989. On January 30, 1990, Adelson fired Lewin, dismissing the Aristocrat Hotels team. No reason was given for the termination, but, coming two months after The Mirage's opening, some speculated that the Sands' numbers were disappointing. Lewin's replacement as president, Al Benedict, assumed his responsibilities that evening. Benedict, formerly of the MGM Grand, brought Morris Yeager to run the casino and Bernie Rothkopf to serve as executive vice president.

Benedict's team made only minor changes to Sands operations—the most famous of which might have been catering to locals by bringing back, after a seven-year absence, the weekend champagne brunch. Perhaps mindful of the example of his predecessor, or simply his inborn good sense, Benedict did not court the media as flamboyantly as Lewin.

But Benedict's regime lasted only until August, when Adelson confirmed reports that he would be changing managers again. He denied a local television station's report that his casino was about to declare bankruptcy and that the financing for its new tower had collapsed. Benedict agreed to stay on until his successor was in place, while the local media reported the talks were underway for Benedict to buy the Sands while Adelson retained control of the under-construction convention center.

Adelson announced that he was taking a more active role in the management of the Sands, taking over as chief executive officer and bringing in Steve Norton, who had spent more than 20 years managing casinos for Resorts International in the Bahamas and Atlantic City, as acting president and chief operating officer.

Norton had gotten to know Adelson's Interface partners while working with travel agencies and packagers in the Bahamas. When Donald Trump bought Resorts International and then sold the company to Merv Griffin (keeping the under-construction Taj Mahal for himself), Norton resigned. But Norton's contract, with a year remaining, prevented him for working in Atlantic City, or the states where he had helped riverboats become legal. So he headed west to Las Vegas.

"The Mirage had just opened, with four times our rooms and a volcano out front," Norton later recalled. "Our showroom was next to nothing, and we didn't have much outside of a good slot tournament. My goal when I got there was to reduce property costs, because we were running in the red," Norton said.

But the Sands' owner already had a plan. Denying reports that he was seeking a quick exit, Adelson revealed that trade show bookings for the convention center—whose first phase wouldn't open until November—

were already five to six times greater than his initial expectations. The trade show veteran was now planning two new towers to total 2,500 new rooms, and was seeking even more financing. As always, he was happy to demonstrate, with charts and graphs, why conventions were going to be the next big thing in Las Vegas, making Sunday through Thursday as profitable as the weekend. With as many as 30 trade shows slated for 1991 and another 50 possible in 1992, Adelson's bet on business travel was about to pay off.

***

Las Vegas casino operators had first flirted with the convention business in a major way after the disappointing summer of 1955. But, as the Sands Expo and Convention Center rose from the ground behind the Sands, alarm bells went off on the Strip. To date, casinos had treated meetings as a stopgap that kept hotels full when gamblers were scarce, and tended to work cooperatively, deferring to the Las Vegas Convention and Visitors Authority when it came to the big shows.

Now, Sheldon Adelson's new convention center threatened the status quo. The Las Vegas Convention Center existed to serve the casinos, and the convention business was seen as moderately profitable at best. A public-private partnership, the Convention Center contracted out a range of services, from providing flowers to maintenance. The Sands Expo Center planned to operate them in-house, with all profits flowing only to it.

The Convention Center's focus on room occupancy over convention hall profitability made sense, given that it was mostly funded by room taxes, and empty rooms didn't yield taxes. But the Sands was in business to make money for itself. So, some feared a new era of competition for mega-shows like Comdex that could upset everything the LVCVA had built over the previous three decades. Already, rival casinos were intimating that, in periods of heavy demand, they wouldn't make available blocks of rooms available to Sands convention-goers, which the new Expo Center would desperately need before its own room expansion came online.

Steve Norton even suggested something daring.

"What we're going to do here," he told the media in September, as the Expo Center was nearing completion, "is have the first Nevada operation where the catering department may be making more than the casino."

With a small casino and good margins on catering, it wasn't as crazy as it sounded.

The first phase of the Expo Center, with 576,000 square feet of space in three massive halls, opened just in time for Comdex 1990, whose 110,000 delegates filled up most of Las Vegas's 74,000 hotel rooms from November 12 to 16.

Adelson, exultant that it had taken only eight months to build the convention center, promised to add another 800,000 square feet to the complex within three years, making it the largest single-level convention facility in the United States.

Bringing the 170,000 Comdex delegates to Las Vegas was one thing; finding them rooms was another. With other casino owners not rolling out the red carpet for conventioneers, Adelson had a simple task for Norton.

"You know these guys—you get the rooms."

Norton began working the phones, offering a deal: Casinos could triple their typical mid-week room rate (usually around $50), cutting in the Sands for a 10 percent commission, which would cover the cost of bus transportation for Comdex delegates to all of the various exhibits, meetings, and banquets that would be held at the Hilton, Bally's, Caesars, and the Las Vegas Convention Center, along with the Sands Expo. The hotels would make money renting those spaces and catering functions, with Norton promising that their gourmet restaurants would be full of paying (not comp) customers all week.

"You might want to ask a few of your dealers to stay home that week," Norton concluded, "but you'll make plenty on the rooms and dining."

Booking attendees into Downtown hotels and even casinos well off the Strip, Norton was able to find rooms for everyone, with all major Strip properties, except Circus Circus, committing most of their rooms. The first day of the show, Circus Circus CEO Bill Bennett, hearing reports of hundreds of convention-goers at Circus Circus and Excalibur, called Norton.

"Can you send us some of those free buses?" he asked.

The experience opened eyes. Here was a way to turn loss leaders into profit centers. Though they were initially resistant, most of the Strip came around to Adelson's point of view and relying on business travelers to buoy profits became the "conventional" wisdom in Las Vegas.

The success of the Expo Center didn't lead to stability in the Sands' executive offices. Norton, who taken on the job as a consultant, continued to advise on riverboat legislation in three states. He departed in May 1991 ("before he could fire me," he later quipped) to serve as president of the Gold River casino in Laughlin before becoming president of Argosy Gaming, which operated five casinos in the Midwest and South.

Though Adelson took a larger role in planning the resort's expansion, he lured Phil Bryan from Reno's Peppermill Hotel to serve as the Sands' full-time president in January 1992. This was a new role expressly created for him. But Bryan lasted scarcely two months in the role before resigning. The longtime gaming executive professed to have had no disagreements with Adelson. Instead, he was leaving because of his growing commitment to his Buddhist faith. He would be leaving Las Vegas for a religious retreat in either Northern California or New York, after which he would pledge himself to environmental concerns.

Bryan's departure opened the door to speculation about the Sands' future. Former Harrah's executive Richard Goeglein was rumored to either be auditioning for Bryan's job or to be putting together a group that would buy the Sands from Adelson. Some thought that Adelson considered the casino resort itself a distraction and would welcome the chance to focus on the Expo Center, which would not be part of the sale. Months later, though, the Las Vegas Convention and Visitors Authority was exploring the opposite scenario, putting together a master plan that weighed the possibilities of buying the Sands Expo Center.

Nothing came of that idea, but ground hadn't been broken on the new hotel tower. Adelson admitted in November 1992 that money was not as easy to come by as it had been a few years earlier.

"The financing market for casinos is not good now," he explained. "If I could raise the money, I would build the tower. But lenders are concerned about overbuilding. They are watching MGM, Luxor, and Treasure Island." These megaresorts might expand the market—or they might glut it (soon, it was apparent that it was the former). Lenders were waiting to see how Las Vegas responded to these massive projects before financing anything new. Until then, it looked like a retheming and expansion of the casino for $15 million was the most that could be done.

So the Sands spent the next year in a holding pattern, although the growth of conventions in Las Vegas vindicated Adelson's faith in business travel. In the three years since he bought the Sands, annual convention revenues grew by almost 25 percent, from $1.5 billion to nearly $2 billion. By now, public opinion in Las Vegas had shifted; conventioneers might not gamble extravagantly, but they were, overall, good for business. "We are inclined to believe," a *Review-Journal* editorial said in October 1993, "that a Las Vegas which could bill itself as the 'convention capital of the world' would profit handsomely in the long run." So much so that the LVCVA should seriously consider Adelson's offer to double the size of his Expo Center before selling it to the convention authority for $150 million, instead of pursuing its own growth plan, which would take 15 years to reach fruition. Adelson promised to expand the Sands Expo in 14 months.

The LVCVA had not responded to Adelson's proposal when, in March 1994, he announced plans to expand the Sands Expo and Convention Center to 1.15 million square feet. By September, with the second phase nearing completion, Adelson came close to taking his offer to the LVCVA off the table.

"I don't think I want to sell it to them now," he said. "I'm making too much money." Demand was so high that he was charging up to three times more for convention space than the Convention Center. "I'm making millions of dollars of profit a year."

Business at the Expo Center was so good that, in February 1995, Adelson sold the Interface Group's 17 gaming trade shows to Tokyo's Softbank Corporation for $800 million. As part of the deal, Adelson bought out his erstwhile partners in the Sands, making him the sole owner. He had grown Comdex into a powerhouse—the previous November, it had welcomed nearly 200,000 visitors. Now, he looked to a new future at the Sands.

With Las Vegas growing to accommodate the now-opened Luxor, Treasure Island, and MGM Grand, banks were far more open to lending money for new projects. Then again, a man with $800 million in his pocket didn't have to worry quite as much about lenders. The long-awaited Sands expansion, it appeared, was now very close on the horizon.

***

Although the Expo Center got the most headlines, life went on for the rest of the Sands. The Copa Room continued to showcase the

Comedy Kings puppet show, although in early May 1990 there was a bit of a rebrand, as the show became "Playboy's Girls of Rock 'n' Roll with the Kroft Comedy Kings." The bunnies only lasted three months before the leaving the Copa; they were replaced by Melinda, the First Lady of Magic. This was in keeping with the rest of Las Vegas. When Playboy's rockers joined the Kroft marionettes, outside of Frank Sinatra at Bally's, Don Rickles at the Golden Nugget, Redd Foxx at the Hacienda, Diana Ross at Caesars Palace, and Wayne Newton at the Hilton, the kind of headline entertainment that had once defined the Sands was gone, with magicians, revues, and tribute artists now dominating Las Vegas. For the next several years, the Sands would alternate between revues in the Copa and headliners like Wayne Newton and Elayne Boosler in the Grand Ballroom, which reverted to its original name before being recast as the Celebrity Theater.

After selling Comdex and assuming sole control of the Sands, Sheldon Adelson mulled the possibilities. With $600 million, he was considering adding 2,500 rooms and a shopping center to the Sands and building a new 3,000-room resort next door or buying an existing property, either in Las Vegas or elsewhere, to serve as a "springboard" for future growth. To put together a comprehensive development plan, he turned not to Las Vegas, but Atlantic City, hiring William P. Weidner, Bradley H. Stone, and Robert G. Goldstein from the Sands Hotel and Casino in Atlantic City. The Sands, still owned by the Pratt Hotel Corporation, had long had no connection to the Las Vegas landmark, outside of licensing its name.

Weidner, who had been the president of Pratt Hotel, took that role with Las Vegas Sands, with Stone, the president of the Sands casino itself, stepping in as executive vice president, and Goldstein coming in as senior vice president. In explaining what had lured him from Atlantic City, Weidner said a great deal about the future of the Sands.

"That is arguably the best property in Las Vegas, a very exciting place," he said. "There are 60 acres right across the Strip from the Mirage and Treasure Island."

Little more needed to be said. It wasn't the Sands' long history that was its biggest attribute, or its casino, its rooms, or even its employees, but its real estate. Certainly, at this point the writing was on the wall.

The plan, as Weidner shared it, was to begin building a 3,000-room hotel tower on one side of the 1.4 million square foot Expo Center and, after its completion 18 months later, add a second one on the footprint of the currently functioning hotel. The resulting 6,000-room hotel would be the world's largest, wresting the title away from the 5,005-room MGM Grand. A 250,0000square-foot shopping center and huge parking garage were other components of the new Sands.

Las Vegas itself was changing. While in 1989 a revived Sands made some sense, the Sands was no longer competing with the Desert Inn, Frontier, and Riviera, but with megaresorts. The class of '93 had been successful enough to inspire a new generation: Monte Carlo, Bellagio, New York-New York, and the Stratosphere were already under construction. Casinos of the Sands' vintage, it was apparent, were living on borrowed time. The Bellagio had already claimed the Dunes. In November 1995, as Adelson's new team was planning for the future of the Sands, the LVCVA imploded the Landmark to make way for a parking lot.

While it seems obvious in retrospect that the Sands would have to close to make way for the massive resort complex Adelson foresaw, it wasn't a given. Adelson himself spent $20 million upgrading the Sands in what would be its final years. But in April 1996, concerns that the Sands would soon close—putting 1,200 employees, many of them who had been with the hotel for decades, out of work—began surfacing as the Culinary Union demanded aggressive action to save jobs.

And yet there wasn't much argument that the Sands' best days were behind it, particularly compared with its new cross-Strip neighbor, The Mirage. Its oldest hotel wings were 44 years old, relics in a city that prized newness over familiarity. The original Copa was long gone.

On May 16, 1996, it became official: The Sands was going to shut down on June 30, to make way for a $1.5 billion megaresort.

Shelley Berkley, by now a vice president, had perhaps the greatest emotional connection with the Sands among the executive team. She broke the news to Sands employees. Before each shift, she chaired an employee gathering in the Copa, sharing the closing date as well as plans to set up a career transition center to help employees find new jobs. Her father, still working as a maître d', was in the last group she addressed.

There was a sense of the inevitable.

Jim Chalker, who had been a bellman at the Sands for 25 years, took the news in stride.

"We've been expecting it," he said. "This baby's 44 years old, and time keeps marching on. This old girl's been wife, home and mother to me for a long time. Everybody who's been here a long time will shed some tears but we'll survive."

"It has very little to offer customers," casino shift manager Gary Saul told the *Review-Journal*. "The carpets are dirty. We only have 700 beat-up rooms. The only reason we get the business we do is the employees. The customers love the dealers. Everybody is on a first-name basis here."

In the end, Las Vegas wanted 6,000 brand new suites, 200,000 square feet of casino space, 150 shops, 30 restaurants, and more convention space (along with 10,000 new jobs) more than it wanted the old Sands. Regret over the Sands' demise was tempered by anticipation for what was to come.

True to the extended family that they were, most of the employees remained until the end. As the closing date neared, there was a sense that more than a casino was about to be lost—that a piece of old Las Vegas was disappearing forever.

"I miss most the camaraderie, the friends, the great times, the schmoozing. Now that's pretty much over," Don Rickles told the Associated Press.

"It was a very exciting time," former Copa Girl and current cocktail waitress Jeanie Gardner said of the resort's glory days. "It's a shame we'll never see anything like it again."

In the meantime, more details about the Sands' replacement trickled out. The 6,000-room resort would have a Venetian theme, complete with canals and gondolas.

On its last weekend, guests who had last been in the hotel decades earlier came to pay their respects. The last entertainers to perform in the Copa were the Viva Las Vegas afternoon revue and comedian John Pinette; the legendary venue went dark without any special ceremony.

Then it was the final day: Sunday, June 30. Maverick casino owner Bob Stupak, a rare breed in the new Las Vegas for being a true gambler, made the last craps roll. B.J. Mitchell of Seneca, Missouri, was dealt the final hand of blackjack; he drew 21 as did the dealer, who returned his $25 chip before restacking the cards for the final time. A push.

The casino closed on time at 6 p.m. As gaming regulators watched, workers began shutting down slot machines and ushering guests out the doors. With no fanfare, the doors were locked. Lubie Draskovich, the longest-serving employee, was given the honor of turning off the Sands marquee, which was no longer advertising the Copa, but thanking the world for 44 great years.

But many of the employees weren't ready to leave just yet. Without an official announcement, dozens of them gathered in the lounge, laughing, crying, sharing stories about the old times, exchanging phone numbers, saying goodbye. Shelley Berkley stayed for a bit; having practically grown up at the Sands, she had as much a claim to the hotel as anyone. But she knew she hadn't spent decades here sharing the good and bad days. And she had a future in the new, themed megaresort, while many of them didn't. This was a moment for family only. Out of respect, she left them alone.

Eventually, the last hugs were given, and it was time to go home. The Sands was no more.

***

Before it was demolished, the Sands enjoyed a brief but not quiet afterlife.

First, all remaining soaps, shampoos, and toiletries were donated to local charities. Many of the television sets were sent to UNLV. There were still a few special requests—one couple, who had honeymooned in the tower shortly after its opening 20 years before, called with a request that was forwarded to Shelley Berkley. They remembered their room number and said that in the years since their apparently memorable newlywed stay, they never forgot the painting of two kissing doves that hung over the bed. Could they please, please have it? Berkley had security take her up to the room where, against all odds, the painting still hung. She had it removed and sent to the couple.

After that, the auction houses of Butterfield & Butterfield and Rabin Brothers took over. On July 30, they started liquidating $3 million worth of hotel property—including slot machines, Copa chandeliers, and matchbooks—many, many matchbooks.

The auction emptied the buildings out, but they still had some use. The Sands had once been a coveted filming location, and after its closing it hosted one more film: Jerry Bruckheimer's big-budget action epic *Con Air*. The film, in which Nicolas Cage's Cameron Poe helps foil the hijacking of a prison transport plane by an all-star cast of criminals portrayed by John Malkovich, Danny Trejo, Ving Rhames, and others, filmed in Las Vegas for over a month starting in early September, with several action sequences involving the titular C-123 aircraft, buzzing helicopters, and a firetruck/motorcycle chase.

The Sands has a starring role in the film's climax, in which the plane crash lands in Las Vegas in a bizarre trajectory that took it from north of the Stratosphere to the Hard Rock Hotel to the Riviera (heading north), past the Boardwalk (where the plane's wheels touched down), onto Flamingo Boulevard, heading east past Battista's Italian Restaurant, through the Dunes' Oasis Casino sign (the casino itself had been demolished three years earlier), through a valet stand, and smack dab into the Sands' lobby entrance, the plane's nose coming to rest against a row of slot machines, one of which naturally lined up three sevens and paid out a flood of coins.

The crash, and its aftermath, offer one last brief look at the Sands before it came down, though there was some dramatic license. The pond, for example, that the plane plows through was added by the director to make the crash more visually striking, and was not part of the Sands' frontage at any point. Still, with its marquee lit and its neon signs aglow, it's possible to get a sense of the Sands in its last days.

Controlled Demolition, Inc., the same company that had brought down the Dunes and Landmark, demolished the Sands. The highest-profile part of the job was the implosion of the 1965 tower. The date was set for early in the morning of November 26.

At 2 a.m., a siren blared a warning, drawing cheers from a crowd that had waited in the cold for more than two hours. Then, a countdown, followed by a half-dozen syncopated explosions that lit up the tower's windows. Six seconds later, the structure crumbled to the ground, its rubble disappearing beneath the billowing smoke as the crowd applauded. It was 13 seconds from the first blast to the big crash.

Much of the Sands still remained (though it would be reduced to rubble in due time), but the implosion marked the symbolic death of the resort. Wisps of nostalgia blew through Las Vegas that night, but they were quickly driven away by the anticipation for the themed megaresort that was to come.

"It's sad to see it gone, but life goes on,' said Adelson, who had vacationed at the hotel in its glory days. "We're anxious to get on to the next level."

After more than four decades, the Sands had returned to sand.

EPILOGUE

That's Life

Sophia Loren drew the champagne bottle back, paused, then smashed it against the gondola's bow. A hundred doves, released from their cages, soared skyward. The Venetian was officially open.

It was May 3, 1999, nearly three years since the Sands had closed. With construction on the megaresort still ongoing, Sheldon Adelson held a "soft opening," meaning blue tape and hardhats were in evidence as the black-tie VIPs toasted the new resort. Over the previous weeks, 3,500 construction workers clocked ample overtime to get the canals, bridges, and hotel rooms of the Venetian in working order.

A scramble for occupancy permits meant that many of the 500 journalists invited to cover the opening had not been able to stay in their rooms the night before, but now the doors were open, just in time to host the hotel's first convention: 6,000 Blockbuster Video managers and franchisees.

Media accounts mentioned the most outstanding elements of the $1.5 billion resort. A few mentioned parenthetically that the new hotel was replacing the Sands, best remembered as the Rat Pack's haunt, with few other details of its 44-year history.

That history deserves more than a half-sentence.

Billy Wilkerson's connection to the Sands, which is almost completely forgotten, illustrates just how wide-open Las Vegas was in 1950. A restaurant and nightclub with a few gambling tables and no hotel attached? Why not? The evolution of LaRue into the Sands, with Jake Freedman emerging as the public owner, says a lot about how Doc Stacher and other invisible investors were approaching Las Vegas and how the Las Vegas power structure kept them at arm's length: Mack Kufferman, as anonymous as he tried to be, was just too close to Stacher. So Jake Freedman, a tried-and-true Texan by way of Odessa, was tabbed to be the casino's face. Stacher, of course, was actually calling most of the shots, along with a number of other hidden owners, each with a piece of the action.

The Sands, when it opened on December 15, 1952, combined Western hospitality (and a generous allotment of cushy jobs for influential locals and their relatives), underworld gambling savvy, and show business excitement. Thanks to the relentless press relating of Al Freeman, they jibed in the public mind. Only at the Sands could you lounge by the pool during the day, enjoy some of the country's finest entertainment at night, and gamble to your heart's content. Other Las Vegas resorts, particularly the Desert Inn, came close, but none of them did it quite as well as the Sands.

Most people think of the "Rat Pack era" when they think of the Sands, but the group of Sinatra, Martin, and Davis didn't truly come together until 1960 and Sinatra hated the term "Rat Pack," which didn't become widely used until the 1980s. True, the 14 years Sinatra spent at the resort were the Sands' real time in the spotlight. But the Sands didn't shut its doors when Sinatra stomped out. The resort's evolution under the Hughes regime into a mid-size, mid-market casino hotel demonstrates just how typical and unglamorous casinos would become. Gambling was no longer something lurid or shameful, and the people who offered it to you were just as upstanding as you.

When Sheldon Adelson bought the Sands in 1989, it was, by consensus, small, tired, and mostly of sentimental value. The opening of The Mirage that year ultimately shook away the last vestiges of the Las Vegas that the Sands had been built for. When your neighbor has a shiny new volcano, nostalgia just isn't enough. The New Vegas that emerged in the 1990s was no place for a mid-sized, mid-market casino hotel. Adelson might have taken the same approach that Harrah's did with the Holiday casino, or the Riviera and Circus Circus did, adding a tower here, an amenity there. Had he done that, though, the Sands would still be alive in name only. Already when he bought it, there was little of the original Sands left.

It was probably more respectful to the memory of the Sands to implode it. Las Vegas has never been a place for stasis. When the Sands stopped evolving, it died. Tearing it down just made it official.

So the Sands now remains alive in a way that, say, the Flamingo, doesn't. Say the word "Copa," and you are instantly transported back to a smoky night in the early 1960s, a drink in front of you, with Frank, maybe Sammy, maybe Dean, about to take the stage. No other classic Las Vegas hotel provokes such memories so easily—perhaps a testament to Al Freeman's publicity skills, perhaps a reminder that we will always look for a place in the sun.

Long after the tower had fallen, the dust had settled, and a new resort had risen to take its place, the Sands was fondly remembered as a place in the sun. Courtesy UNLV SCA.

Acknowledgments

Just like the original Sands, this book required the help of many people to see the light of day.

I'm fortunate in having picked a topic that is still within living memory, so I was able to speak with people who worked at or otherwise had knowledge of the Sands. Edward Walters, Roger Wagner, Lisa Medford, Burt Peretsky, Shelley Berkley, Steve Norton, and Michael Schutz all gave generously of their time. Getting to talk with them helped me see a much fuller picture of the Sands' history than would have been possible with only archival sources.

Further help came from research assistant Jasmin Bryant, Scott Deitche (who sent me some very informative troves of FBI files), and the entire staff of UNLV Special Collections and Archives, particularly Su Kim Chung, Stacey Fott, Aaron Mayes, and Peter Michel, who facilitated my access to important materials. A special thanks goes to Claytee White, Director of the Oral History Research Center, for maintaining and providing access to a wealth of interviews without which this book—and many others—would be incomplete. Lori Nelson-Kraft of the Las Vegas Convention and Visitors Association likewise helped with securing Las Vegas News Bureau photos.

My manuscript was immeasurably improved and supported by the copyediting of Cindy Beatty at Proof Positive Papers, the proofreading of James Fraleigh, and the indexing of Meg Daniel. Asya Blue provided an excellent cover that conveys the excitement of the era.

I'm also grateful to my friends, colleagues, and random people who have called me at work and who have listened to me ramble on about the Sands for the past year or so. And as always, the love and support of my family has meant everything to me.

Notes

Chapter 1   Fools Rush In

1   Big Dick Wilkerson: W. R. Wilkerson III. *The Man Who Invented Las Vegas* (Beverly Hills: Ciro's Books, 2000). 1, 13.

1   Wilkerson's gambling proclivities: Wilkerson, 1.

2   Wilkerson's move to Hollywood: Wilkerson, 3-4.

2   Wilkerson's divorces: "Fifth Spouse Divorces Publisher and Café Man." *Los Angeles Times*, March 8, 1949. 8.

2   Wilkerson discovers Lana Turner: "Writing the End to a True-to-Life Cinderella Story: Remembrance: The facts of Lana Turner's discovery at a soda fountain have changed through the years, but the legend remains." *Los Angeles Times*. July 1, 1995. Accessed at: http://articles.latimes.com/1995-07-01/entertainment/ca-19119_1_lana-turner

3   Irving Thalberg's poker games: B. James Gladstone. *The Man Who Seduced Hollywood* (Chicago: Chicago Review Press, 2013). 39.

3   Café Trocadero: "1934: The Strip's Style Setter." *Playground to the Stars*. Accessed at: http://www.playgroundtothestars.com/timeline/1934-billy-wilkerson/

3   Café Trocadero amateur hour, poker game: Mary McNamara. "A Night on the Strip." *Los Angeles Times*. December 15, 1996. Accessed at: http://articles.latimes.com/1996-12-15/magazine/tm-9152_1_night-life

3   Wilkerson sells Café Trocadero: Celia Rasmussen. "The Man Behind the Sunset Strip." *Los Angeles Times*. December 7, 1997. Accessed at: http://articles.latimes.com/1997/dec/07/local/me-61610/2

3   Ciro's and LaRue: "Hollywood institution." *Time*. July 3, 1944. 76-7.

4   Joseph Schenk's advice to Wilkerson: Gladstone, 82.

4   For a detailed treatment of the Wilkerson/Siegel relationship, see W. R. Wilkerson III. *The Man Who Invented Las Vegas* (Beverly Hills: Ciro's Books, 2000) and Larry Gragg. *Benjamin "Bugsy" Siegel: The Gangster, the Flamingo, and the Making of Modern Las Vegas* (Santa Barbara, California: Praeger, 2015).

4   Sale of LaRue: "8631 Sunset Blvd." J. H. Graham. Accessed at: https://jhgraham.com/2016/06/17/8631-sunset-blvd/

5   Las Vegas population: "Timeline." *Las Vegas Sun*. Accessed at: https://lasvegassun.com/history/timeline/

6   Wilkerson and Hahn buy the Kit Carson: Jack Cortez. "That's for Sure." *Fabulous Las Vegas*. September 30, 1950. 19.

6   Partners in LaRue: Jack Cortez. "That's for Sure." *Fabulous Las Vegas*.

December 23, 1950. 10.

6   Wilkerson's money problems: "Fifth Spouse Divorces Publisher and Café Man." *Los Angeles Times*. March 8, 1949. 8.

7   LaRue's opening: Jack Cortez. "That's for Sure." *Fabulous Las Vegas*. December 23, 1950. 10

7   Cocktail waitress uniforms: Jack Cortez. "That's for Sure." *Fabulous Las Vegas*. September 30, 1950. 19.

7   Atmosphere of LaRue: Jack Cortez. "That's for Sure." *Fabulous Las Vegas*. January 20, 1951. 9, 20.

8   Wilkerson sells LaRue: Jack Cortez. "That's for Sure." *Fabulous Las Vegas*. February 24, 1951. 25.

8   LaRue's new direction: Print advertisement. *Fabulous Las Vegas*. March 10, 1951. 28.

8   Further changes at LaRue: Jack Cortez. "That's for Sure." *Fabulous Las Vegas*. March 17, 1951. 33, and March 24, 1951, 24.

8   New maître 'd: Jack Cortez. "That's for Sure." *Fabulous Las Vegas*. April 14, 1951. 29,

9   Refrigerator for sale: Classified ad. *Las Vegas Review-Journal*. July 26, 1951.

9   Wilkerson stops gambling: Wilkerson, 116.

9   Nola Hahn's suicide: "Nola Hahn, Onetime Pal of Gamblers, Ends Life." *Los Angeles Times*. March 31, 1957. 2.

Chapter 2   Anyone With a Million Dollars

11   Mack Kufferman: "Kufferman Plans License Action." *Reno Gazette-Journal*. April 15, 1952. 5; *The Desert Sun*. March 31, 1950. 6, and November 6, 1952.

12   The Kefauver Committee background: "Special Committee on Organized Crime in Interstate Commerce." United States Senate. Accessed at: https://www.senate.gov/artandhistory/history/common/investigations/Kefauver.htm

12   The Kefauver Committee's findings: Estes Kefauver. *Crime in America*. Garden City, New York: Doubleday and Company, 1951. 12-16.

13   "As a case history...." Special Committee to Investigate Organized Crime in Interstate Commerce. *Third Interim Report*. Washington: United States Printing Office, 1950. 94.

13   Kufferman buys LaRue: "Tax Commission to Decide Fate of Project Here." *Las Vegas Review-Journal* January 29, 1952. 1.

13   "The man gambles..." Hearings Before the Special Committee to Investigate Organized Crime in Interstate Commerce. United States Senate. Part 10: Nevada—California. Washington: United States Printing Office, 1951. 23-4. Cited hereafter as "Hearings."

14   Doc Stacher's license denial: Hearings, 24-5.

14   Stacher's ties to Meyer Lansky: Carl Sifakis. *The Mafia Encyclopedia*. New York: Facts on File, 1987. 311, and Hank Messick. *Lansky*. New York: G.

P. Putnam's Sons, 1971. 71.

14   "The chairman of the board…" Hank Messick. *Lansky*. New York: G. P. Putnam's Sons, 1971. Inside cover.

14   "Go ahead…." Personal Communication. Michael Schutz. December 25, 2019.

14   "I'm the sole owner…" "Tax Commission to Decide Fate of Project Here." *Las Vegas Review-Journal.* January 29, 1952. 2.

15   Consideration of Kufferman's application: "Tax Commission Defers Action on LaRue Permit." *Las Vegas Review-Journal.* January 30, 1952. 3.

15   Kufferman's license denial: "Tax Commission Turns Down LaRue License." *Las Vegas Review-Journal.* April 9, 1952. 1.

15   Kufferman's more ambitious plans: "New Request to Be Made for LaRue's." *Las Vegas Review-Journal* April 13, 1952. 1.

15   "I'm the one…" :Kufferman to Appeal Planning Board Rule." *Las Vegas Review-Journal.* April 16, 1952. 3.

15   Cal Cory: "Beckley Takes UP Law Post." *Las Vegas Sun.* February 3, 1968. 3.

16   Real power elite: Interview with Edward Walters. January 9, 2018. Las Vegas, Nevada.

16   Jake Freedman's background: "Jake Freedman." Accessed at: https://www.geni.com/people/Jake-Freedman/6000000060438202821; "Domain Privee." Texas State Historical Association. Accessed at: https://tshaonline.org/handbook/online/articles/jgdom

17   Freedman's racing stable: "Nose Verdict Won by Singers Folly." *New York Times.* May 18, 1937. 31.

17   "Prince of the Houston gamblers:" "Domain Privee." Texas State Historical Association. Accessed at: https://tshaonline.org/handbook/online/articles/jgdom

17   "To say that…." Jack Cortez. "That's For Sure." *Fabulous Las Vegas.* December 13,1952. 9.

17   "Mr. Freedman is not home." "Domain Privee." Texas State Historical Association. Accessed at: https://tshaonline.org/handbook/online/articles/jgdom

18   "There's one man…." Jack Cortez. "That's For Sure." *Fabulous Las Vegas.* April 26 ,1952. 27.

18   "I own 13 corporations…." Jack Cortez. "That's For Sure." *Fabulous Las Vegas.* April 26 ,1952. 25.

18   Freedman's license application: "Delay Permit for Sands Hotel." *Las Vegas Review-Journal.* June 18, 1952. 1.

18   Harry Claiborne: Ed Koch and Jeff German. "Former U.S. Judge Claiborne Dies at 86." *Las Vegas Sun.* January 20, 2004.

19   Freedman's application deferred: "Tax Board Meetings Opened Up." *Las Vegas Review-Journal.* June 19, 1952. 1.

19   "We cant…." "Freedman Denied Gambling License for Sands Hotel." *Las Vegas Review-Journal.* August 6, 1952. 3; and "Freedman Denied

Permit. *Las Vegas Review-Journal*. August 6, 1952. 1.

19   Freedman buys out Kufferman: "Freedman Given 'Provisional' License." *Las Vegas Review-Journal*. September 11, 1952. 1.

19   Freedman's license conditions: "Freedman Given 'Provisional' License." *Las Vegas Review-Journal*. September 11, 1952. 1.

19   Ballard Barron: Larry Strawther. *Seal Beach: A Brief History*. Charleston, South Carolina: The History Press, 2014. Unpaginated.

19   Barron's parties: "Barron Home Is Scene of Party." *Las Vegas Review-Journal*. September 18, 1947. 18.

20   Freedman organizes Barron memorial fund: "Barron, Hotel Developer, Rites Scheduled Tuesday." *Las Vegas Review-Journal*. November 15, 1954. 3.

20   "I never got involved...." "Tax Commission Will Study Sands Permits Here Monday." *Las Vegas Review-Journal*. October 27, 1952.

20   Levinson's licensure: "Tax Body Backs Down On 'Net Worth' Clause." *Las Vegas Review-Journal*. December 2, 1952. 1.

20   Sid Wyman: "LV Gamblers Pay Homage to Sid Wyman at Dunes." *Las Vegas Review-Journal*. June 28, 1978. 1B.

20   Jack Entratter's background: "Jack Entratter of Las Vegas, 57." *New York Times*. March 12, 1971. 40; "Jack Entratter, 57, Top LV Showman." *Variety*. March 17, 1971.

20   Jack Entratter's association with Frank Costello: Jim Proser. *Mr. Copacabana: An American History by Night*. CreateSpace Independent Publishing, 2014.

Chapter 3   You and the Night and the Music

23   For a full consideration of McAllister's career and impact, see Chris Nichols. *The Leisure Architecture of Wayne McAllister*. Salt Lake City: Gibbs Smith, Publisher, 2007.

23   McAlister declines work on the Flamingo: Nichols, 134-5.

24   LaRue layout: Sands floorplan in Martin Stern Architectural Records, 1950-1990. MS-00382. Special Collections, University Libraries, University of Nevada, Las Vegas. Las Vegas, Nevada.

24   Sands sign: Nichols, 138.

25   Sands porte cochere: Nichols, 121.

25   Sands as Bermuda modern: "New $5,500,000 Hotel Opening in Las Vegas." *Las Vegas Examiner*. December 14, 1952. In Sands Hotel Collection, 1951-1980. 2000-12. Special Collections & Archives, University Libraries, University of Nevada, Las Vegas. Las Vegas, Nevada. Box 63.

25   Silver Queen mural: Nichols, 144.

25   Silver Queen bar description: Charles Spangler. "On the Hollywood Scene." *New York Telegraph*. December 20, 1952. In Sands Hotel Collection. Box 63.

25   Addition of the Copa: "Café LaRue" floorplan in Martin Stern Architectural Records, 1950-1990. Unboxed oversized materials.

25-6   "Brazilian Carnival" theme, Sands buildings: "New $5,500,000 Hotel Opening in Las Vegas." *Las Vegas Examiner.* December 14, 1952. In Sands Hotel Collection. Box 63.

26   El Rancho Vegas opening: David G. Schwartz. "The Columbus of Highway 91." *Vegas Seven.* November 8, 2012.

26   Opening press junket: Charles Spangler. "On the Hollywood Scene." *New York Telegraph.* December 20, 1952, and "The New Ziegfeld: The Story of Jack Entratter." In Sands Hotel Collection. Box 63, and Box 3, Folder 8.

28   Hiring of Matt Howard: "Matt Howard, Popular Las Vegan, Named Manager of Sands' Bar." *Las Vegas Review-Journal.* December 15, 1952. 19.

29   First Copa Girls hired: "First In Line." *Macon News.* November 22, 1952. In Sands Hotel Collection. Box 63.

29   Overtime work on Sands: Danton Walker. "Broadway." New York News. Undated, and Untitled item, *Hollywood Reporter.* December 12, 1952. In Sands Hotel Collection. Box 63.

29   Entratter turned down New Year's.... Frank Farrell. "4-Million Dollar Plunge." *New York World-Telegram.* November 18, 1952. In Sands Hotel Collection. Box 63.

29   Freedman's plans to add hotel capacity: Charles Evans. "Jakie's Colossal Casino Still Isn't Large Enough." *Houston Chronicle.* December 19, 1952. In Sands Hotel Collection. Box 63.

29    $75,000 of liquor stocked: "Matt Howard, Popular Las Vegan, Named Manager of Sands' Bar." *Las Vegas Review-Journal.* December 15, 1952. 19, and Charles Spangler. "On the Hollywood Scene." *New York Telegraph.* December 20, 1952.

29-30   Opening Copa lineup: Show listings. *Fabulous Las Vegas.* December 20, 1952. 32.

30   Opening night preparations: "The New Ziegfeld: The Story of Jack Entratter." In Sands Hotel Collection. Box 3, Folder 8.

30   Sands power outage: Hy Gardner. "Blackout from Storm Failed to Halt Gamblers." *Oakland Tribune.* December 25, 1952. In Sands Hotel Collection. Box 63.

30   "Miniature atomic blast" Jack Cortez. "That's For Sure." *Fabulous Las Vegas.* December 13, 1952. 29.

30   Thomas's illness and replacements: "Danny Thomas Ill So Big Names Take Over." *Los Angeles Herald Express.* December 18, 1952. In Sands Hotel Collection. Box 63.

30   Opening weeks' entertainment expenses: "Sands Spending 250G in First 10 Weeks." *Daily Variety.* December 10, 1952. In Sands Hotel Collection. Box 63.

31   Time capsule: "New Vegas Hotel Has Time Capsule." *Carson City Appeal.* December 18, 1952. In Sands Hotel Collection, 1951-1980. 2000-12. Special Collections & Archives, University Libraries, University of

Nevada, Las Vegas. Las Vegas, Nevada. Box 63.

31   "Just a bunch...." "Sands Hotel Drops $285,000 In Six Hours." *Pioche Record.* December 18, 1952. In Sands Hotel Collection. Box 63.

31-2   Reporting of opening losses: Earl Wilson. "Newest Las Vegas Hotel Gives Us $25 to Gamble." *San Jose Mercury Herald.* December 20, 1952. In Sands Hotel Collection. Box 63.

32   "It cost $5.5 million...." Earl Wilson. *Los Angeles News,* December 24, 1952. In Sands Hotel Collection. Box 63.

Chapter 4   On the Sunny Side of the Street

33   Seating at the Copa: Esper Esau. *Las Vegas' Golden Era: Memoirs 1954-1974.* Indianapolis: Dog Ear Publishing, 2016. 64-5.

33   Van Johnson Copa act: "The New Ziegfeld: The Story of Jack Entratter." In Sands Hotel Collection, 1951-1980. Box 3, Folder 8.

33-4   Johnson's past performances and act at the Sands: "Van Johnson to Sands at Vegas." *Billboard.* April 11, 1953. 13.

34   Sands employees wearing red socks: "The New Ziegfeld: The Story of Jack Entratter."

34   Tallulah Bankhead at the Sands: Alan Jarlson "On the Town." *Las Vegas Review-Journal.* February 4, 1953. 5.

34   "Entratter's going to fall...." "The New Ziegfeld: The Story of Jack Entratter."

34   "Tallulah Bankhead." *Variety.* May 27, 1953. 69.

35   "Bankhead was banknote...." "The New Ziegfeld: The Story of Jack Entratter."

35   Bankhead returns to the Sands: Erskine Johnson. "Hollywood." *Las Vegas Review-Journal.* February 25, 1954. 4.

35   Scale of Las Vegas entertainment: Aline Mosby. "Vegas Shows Are First In Cost, Talent, Size." *Las Vegas Review-Journal.* April 3, 1953. 1.

35   Las Vegas as talk of Broadway: Earl Wilson. *Las Vegas Review-Journal.* May 31, 1953. 9.

35   Sands $37,500 offer to Noel Coward: Earl Wilson. *Las Vegas Review-Journal.* November 24, 1954. 4.

35-6   "I'll be happy to sing...." "The New Ziegfeld: The Story of Jack Entratter."

36   Milton Berle retraction: Aline Mosby. "Vegas Shows Are First In Cost, Talent, Size." *Las Vegas Review-Journal.* April 3, 1953. 1.

36   "The Student Prince" at the Sands: "Tab Shows Fail to Make Vegas Grade." *Billboard.* December 19, 1953. 13.

36   "The Student Prince" revival: "Marie Wilson Set at Sands." *Billboard.* June 27, 1953. 13.

36   Billy Eckstine steps in: "Cancel Tab 'Prince' at Sands; Eckstine In." *Variety.* December 9, 1953.

37   Judy Lee John's Copa girl application process: "Interview with Judith Lee Johnson Jones." Claytee White, interviewer. Oral History Research Center at UNLV. 1-2.

37   For a complete discussion of not just Florenz Ziegfeld but the evolution of the chorus girl, see Derek and Julia Parker. *The Natural History of the Chorus Girl*. Indianapolis: Bobbs-Merrill, 1975.

38   Copa Girl statistics and description: "Copa girls are choicest, but difficult to choose." *Augusta Chronicle*. October 1, 1965.

38   Copa Girl working conditions and salary: Virginia James Papers, MS 523. Special Collections & Archives, University Libraries, University of Nevada, Las Vegas. Las Vegas, Nevada. Box 1, Folder 5.

39   Entratter's connection with the William Morris Agency: Virginia James Papers, Box 1, Folder 1.

39   Entratter's preferred Copa Girl, talent search: "The Man With 4,000 Girl Friends." In Sands Hotel Collection. Box 3, Folder 8.

39   "There don't seem...." And subsequent quotes from Entratter: "Copa girls are choicest, but difficult to choose."

40   Copa Girls encouraged to "decorate:" "Interview with Judith Lee Johnson Jones." 8.

40   Copa Girls discouraged from being seen in other casinos: "Interview with Corinne Entratter Sidney." Claytee White, interviewer. Oral History Research Center at UNLV. 8.

40   Johnson disappoints her "date:" "Interview with Judith Lee Johnson Jones." 16.

40   Copa Girls prohibited from hooking: "Interview with Corinne Entratter Sidney." 8.

41   "Naked in the steam room...." Interview with Ed Walters. Conducted by David G. Schwartz. January 9, 2019.

42   Sinatra's bad attitude at the Desert Inn: "Sands, Las Vegas." *Variety*. October 21, 1953. 64.

42   Sinatra's eclipse: Arnold Shaw. *Sinatra: Twentieth-Century Romantic*. New York: Holt, Rinehart, and Winston, 1968. 121-125.

43   Sinatra/Mortimer enmity: Earl Wilson. *Sinatra: An Unauthorized Biography*. New York: Macmillan Publishing Company, 1976. 69, 73.

43   Sinatra's immersion in Maggio role: Shaw, 174.

43   Sinatra's license application: "Pappas Seeks Interest in Tahoe Casino." *Las Vegas Review-Journal*. May 28, 1953. 3.

43   Sinatra hires Harry Claiborne: "To Press Sinatra Application in Hotel Here." *Las Vegas Review-Journal*. October 27, 1953. 3.

44   Dean Martin's share of the Sands: FBI file LV 57-511. 182.

44   Sinatra's announcement about possibly canceling Sands appearance: "Sinatra Wants to Act." *Variety*. September 23, 1953. 2.

44   Sinatra in Churchill Downs suite: Wilson, 137-8.

44-5   Sinatra's initial Sands engagement: Sands Hotel, "Las Vegas, Nev." *Billboard*. October 31, 1953. 12.

45   *Variety*, *Hollywood Reporter* reviews of Sinatra at the Sands: Alan Jarlson. "On the Town." *Las Vegas Review-Journal*. October 14, 1953. 5.

46   Sinatra's license hearing: "Sinatra Gets Gaming License and Tax

Rebuke." *Chicago Daily Tribune.* October 31, 1953. 3.

46   Sinatra's tax payment plan, license approval: "Sinatra's Sands Buy OK'd by Nev." *Variety.* November 4, 1953. 51.

Chapter 5   Nice Work if You Can Get It
48   "The deadly walk...." Ed Walters. Oral History Interview. Conducted by David G. Schwartz. January 9, 2019. 9.
48-50 Don Adams incident: Walters, 10.
50   Cohen's background: "Longtime Strip Exec Dies at 73." *Las Vegas Review-Journal.* December 28, 1986: 4.
50   Cohen associated with the Sands: *Fabulous Las Vegas.* December 26, 1952. 117.
50   Story about Cohen's split with Beldon Katleman: Stefan Andrews "Vegas casino manager Carl Cohen became a local folk hero after he knocked the caps off Frank Sinatra's front teeth." The Vintage News. https://www.thevintagenews.com/2017/02/07/las-vegas-casino-manager-carl-cohen-became-a-local-folk-hero-after-he-knocked-the-caps-off-frank-sinatras-front-teeth/
51   Hughes in Las Vegas in May 1953: *Fabulous Las Vegas.* December 26, 1953. 63.
51   Cohen's vacation and move to the Sands: *Fabulous Las Vegas.* December 26, 1953. 105.
51   Freedman's $2 million loan: *Fabulous Las Vegas.* December 26, 1953. 121.
51   Cohen's investment in the Sands: "Board Approves Gottlieb for Villa Venice." *Las Vegas Review-Journal.* December 22, 1953. 3.
51-2   Sands surveillance system: "Gambling Casino Sets Up TV to Keep an Eye on Cheaters." *Washington Post.* May 19, 1954. 3.
52   Al Freeman's background: "Sands Hotel Executive Dies." *Las Vegas Review-Journal.* August 29, 1972.
54-7   1954 TWA/Las Vegas promotion: Sands Hotel Public Relations Records, 1952-1977. MS-00417. Special Collections and Archives, University Libraries, University of Nevada, Las Vegas. Las Vegas, Nevada. Box 5.
57   Frank Sinatra's engagement beginning: *Fabulous Las Vegas.* November 6, 1954. 19.
57   Itinerary of press group: *Fabulous Las Vegas.* October 23, 1954, 22-3, 33.
58   Sir Russell Brock at the Sands: *Fabulous Las Vegas.* October 23, 1954. 35.
58   Sales managers at the Last Frontier: *Fabulous Las Vegas.* October 23, 1954. 17.
58   Press departure from Las Vegas: Sands Hotel Public Relations Records, Box 5.
58   Return of the "Quickie Vacation:" *Fabulous Las Vegas.* November 20, 1954. 17.
59   Antonio Morelli's early life: Antonio Morelli Papers, 1910s-1970s. MS-00558. Special Collections, University Libraries, University of Nevada, Las Vegas. Las Vegas, Nevada. Box 5.

59   Morelli's early career: "Antonio Morelli." *New York Times.* June 25, 1974. 27.

59   Olsen and Johnson's background: Roger Fristoe. "Spotlight on Olsen & Johnson – Friday, April 8th." TCM. Accessed at: http://www.tcm.com/this-month/article/92529%7C0/Olson-Johnson.html

59   "Oh! Whotta Nite" plans: "Olsen, Johnson Open 'Whotta Nite' Revue." *Billboard.* December 26, 1953, 49.

59   Performance of Carmen at Las Vegas High School: "Vegas Opera Empties Clubs." *Billboard.* November 14, 1953, 1,

60   "It's 117 degrees...." Helen Morelli. Oral History Interview. Jerry Masini, interviewer. UNLV Oral History Program, 1976. 1.

60   Las Vegas Community Chorus: Morelli Collection, Box 2, Folder 13.

60   Helen Morelli's open window: Morelli. 2.

61   Morelli's pride in Las Vegas: Morelli, 6.

61   "This is the only city...." Morelli Collection, Box 2, Folder 13.

61   "Birth of the Star-Spangled Banner:" Morelli Collection, Box 2, Folder 13.

61   The Morellis move to Las Vegas permanently: Morelli, 14.

61   Shirt-Sleeve Symphonies: Morelli, 10.

61   Billing of Antonio Morelli Orchestra: "Sands, Las Vegas." *Variety.* November 21, 1973. 73.

62   Shirt-Sleeve Symphonies: Morelli, 10.

Chapter 6   Please Be Kind
63-4   Proposed casinos: "Ask Licenses for Four More Strip Resort Hotels." *Las Vegas Sun.* August 19, 1953. 1.

64   The Fremont and other new casinos: "Groundbreaking Set for Five Million Dollar Fremont Hotel at Second and Fremont Streets." *Las Vegas Sun.* August 1, 1954. 3.

64   Moulin Rouge construction: "Planning Board Oks Rezoning for Resort Hotel on W. Bonanza." *Las Vegas Sun.* February 26, 1954. 1

64   Royal Nevada opening: "Traubel Gets $50,000 Offer." *New York Times.* April 11, 1955. 29.

64   Dancing Waters: "Dancing Waters to Dress New Las Vegas Spot." *Billboard.* April 23, 1955. 61.

65   Riviera opening: May Mann. "Going Hollywood." *Fabulous Las Vegas.* April 30, 1955. 11.

65   Royal Nevada licensing issues: "Tax Commission Tough on Strip Resort Applicants." *Las Vegas Sun.* February 27, 1954. 1.

65   Dunes licensing issues: "Defer Action on Dunes License." *Las Vegas Review-Journal.* March 31, 1955. 2.

66   Wally Cox saga: "Wally Cox Rehired." *New York Times.* July 20, 1955. 51.

66   New Frontier issues: "New Frontier Gets 2 Days for Cleanup." *Las Vegas Review-Journal.* July 12, 1955. 1.

67   Dunes entertainment: Advertisements. *Las Vegas Review Journal.* August

67   Merrill/Armstrong double bill: Robert Merrill. "To the Editor." *New York Times*. April 2, 2000. Section 2, page 4.

67   Dueling Dunes acquisition groups: "Negotiations for Dunes Sale Said Near End." *Las Vegas Review-Journal*. August 15, 1955. 1.

67   "Board to Study Sale of Dunes to Sands Group." *Las Vegas Review-Journal*. August 16, 1955. 1.

67   Final Dunes sales terms: "Dunes Hotel Leasing Awaits Tax Unit Okeh." *Las Vegas Review-Journal*. August 18, 1955. 1.

67-8   Revised Dunes construction price: "Angry Denial That Dunes Is Broke." *Las Vegas Review-Journal*. August 19, 1955. 1.

68   Acquisition rumors: "Report Talks Continuing on Royal Nevada Deal." *Las Vegas Review-Journal*. August 23, 1955. 1.

68   Gus Greenbaum's return: Jeff Burbank. "Gus Greenbaum, Las Vegas Casino Operator for the Mob, And His Wife Were Murdered 60 Years Ago This Week." The Mob Museum. December 8, 2018. Acccessed at: https://themobmuseum.org/blog/gus-greenbaum-las-vegas-casino-operator-mob-wife-murdered-60-years-ago-week/

68   Royal Nevada's closure: "Royal Nevada Hotel Leased in Las Vegas." *Los Angeles Times*. February 24, 1956. 15.

68   "The same inspired management...." Advertisement. *Las Vegas Review-Journal*. September 1, 1955. 8.

69   Sands to Dunes personnel moves: Les Devor. "Vegas Vagaries." *Las Vegas Review-Journal*. August 30, 1955. 5.

69   Levinson and Maier: Jack Cortez. "That's for Sure." *Fabulous Las Vegas*. September 17, 1955. 9.

69   Dunes reopening celebration: Aline Mosby. "More about the LA Dreams of a Las Vegas Bust." *Las Vegas Review-Journal*. September 15, 1955. 26.

70   Recession claims: Aline Mosby. "Another Crepe-Hanger Says Las Vegas Is Faltering Resort." *Las Vegas Review-Journal*. September 14, 1955. 11.

70   Reaction to reopening: Les Devor. "Vegas Vagaries." *Las Vegas Review-Journal*. September 15, 1955. 5.

70   Higher prices on the Strip: Aline Mosby. "More about the LA Dreams of a Las Vegas Bust."

70   October entertainment lineup: *Fabulous Las Vegas*. October 1, 1955. 23-5.

70   December entertainment lineup: *Fabulous Las Vegas*. December 10, 1955. 4, 58.

70   Chevalier and Horne engagements: *Fabulous Las Vegas*. December 31, 1955.

70   December pessimism about the Dunes: "Sands Relinquishes Lease with Dunes Today; Spa Up For Sale?" *Las Vegas Review-Journal*. February 1, 1956, 3.

70-1   Sands exits the Dunes: "Dunes Lease to Be Turned Back." *Las Vegas Review-Journal*. January 16, 1956. 1.

71   Cahlan's thoughts on the Dunes: A. E. Cahlan. "From Where I Sit." *Las*

Vegas Review-Journal. January 18, 1956. 4.

71   Miller/Riddle regime at Dunes: "Question Finances of Backers." *Las Vegas Review-Journal.* April 20, 1956. 3.

Chapter 7   If You Can Dream

80   Jane Russell charity event: Jack Cortez. "That's for Sure." *Fabulous Las Vegas.* August 27, 1955. 9.

81   *The Lone Wolf* filming: Sands Hotel Public Relations Records. Box 34, folder 16.

81   *See It Now* filming: Sands Hotel Public Relations Records. Box 35, folder 8.

81   Dorothy Kilgallen/Richard Kollmar radio show at the Sands: Larry Gragg. *Becoming America's Playground: Las Vegas in the 1950s.* Norman: University of Oklahoma Press, 2019. 46.

81-3   *See It Now* broadcast: Sands Hotel Public Relations Records. Box 35, folder 10.

83-85   *Meet Me in Las Vegas* negotiations and script: Sands Hotel Public Relations Records. Box 35, folder 1.

85   "Pasternak has ordered...." Sands Hotel Public Relations Records. Box 35, folder 1.

85-6   *Meet Me in Las Vegas* filming: Sands Hotel Public Relations Records. Box 35, folder 1.

86   *Meet Me in Las Vegas* cast: "Meet Me in Las Vegas (1956) Full Cast & Crew." IMDB. Accessed at: https://www.imdb.com/title/tt0049490/fullcredits?ref_=ttfc_ql_1

86-7   MGM promotional ideas: Sands Hotel Public Relations Records. Box 35, folder 1.

87   Freeman's promotional ideas: Sands Hotel Public Relations Records. Box 35, folder 1.

87   Milton Berle show: "Las Vegas to Get First Color Show." *New York Times.* February 13, 1956. 47.

87   *Meet Me in Las Vegas* debut screening at the El Portal: Philip K. Scheuer. "Gala Film Premiere Staged in Las Vegas." *Los Angeles Times.* February 22, 1956. 20.

87   *Meet Me in Las Vegas* New York debut: "Movie Premiere to Aid U.S. Team." *New York Times.* March 8, 1956. 23.

88   Broadway billboard Walter Winchell. "The Broadway Beat." *Washington Post.* February 26, 1956. J8.

88   *Meet Me in Las Vegas* reviews: Philp K. Scheuer. "Date with Cyd Charisse in Vegas Worth Keeping." *Los Angeles Times.* March 29, 1956. 32; Hedda Hopper. "Cyd's What a Star Should Be." *Los Angeles Times.* April 8, 1956. D1; May Tinee. "Here's Chance to Meet Stars in Las Vegas." *Chicago Daily Tribune.* April 25, 1956. B11; Bosley Crowther. "Screen: Las Vegas Visit." *New York Times.* March 14, 1956. 39.

88   "Here....": Gilbert Millstein. "Cloud on Las Vegas' Silver Lining." *New York Times.* March 18, 1956. 213.

89 $400 bet as serious action: *Interview with Ed Walters*. Table Games Management Oral History Project. Special Collections Oral History Research Center, University Libraries, University of Nevada, Las Vegas, 2016. 8.

90 Relationship between Sands personnel and the sheriff: *Interview with Ed Walters,* 13-15.

91-2 World premiere of *The Joker Is Wild*: Sands Hotel Public Relations Records. Box 34, folder 13.

93 Freedman's absence from 1957 Sands anniversary gala: Les Devor. "Vegas Vagaries." *Las Vegas Review-Journal.* December 17, 1957. 3.

93 Freedman's death: "Hotel, Gambling Figure Jake Freedman Dies." *Los Angeles Times.* January 20, 1958. 5.

93 Freedman's funeral: "Hundreds Attend Quiet Funeral Rites Held in LA for Sands' Jake Freedman." *Las Vegas Review-Journal.* January 22, 1958. 3.

93-4 "Ironically, Freedman will be buried...." "Jake Freedman Rite Set Tuesday in Los Angeles." *Las Vegas Review-Journal.* January 20, 1958. 1.

94 Sadie Freedman accepts UJA award: "Local UJA Drive Zooms Near Top Goal." *Las Vegas Review-Journal.* July 15, 1958. 3.

94 Gambling stopped at Sands: "Hundreds Attend Quiet Funeral Rites Held in LA for Sands' Jake Freedman."

Chapter 8 Something's Gotta Give
95 Archie Loveland: "New Post." *Las Vegas Review-Journal.* May 15, 1957. 6.

96 Entratter becomes Sands president: "Entratter to Top." *Las Vegas Review-Journal.* January 28, 1958. 3.

96 Chinese food in the Garden Room: Sands Hotel Public Relations Records. Box 1, Folder 5.

96-7 Convention bookings: *Sands Times,* 1958 in Sands Hotel Public Relations Collection.

97 Frank Sinatra and baccarat: Kitty Kelley. *His Way: The Unauthorized Biography of Frank Sinatra.* New York: Bantam, 1986. 232.

97 Baccarat advertisements: Display ad. *Las Vegas Review-Journal.* November 20, 1959. 4; Carlos Harrison. "Baccarat: A Peek Behind the Mystique." *Las Vegas Review-Journal.* March 13, 1983. 1D.

97 Judy Garland at the Sands: Les Devor. "Vegas Vagaries." *Las Vegas Review-Journal.* September 28, 1958. 16.

97 Garland's opening night: *Sands Times,* 1958.

98 Discussion with Ball/Arnaz about Sands television show: *Sands Times,* 1958.

98 "Guestward Ho!" summary: "Guestward Ho!" IMDB. Accessed at: https://www.imdb.com/title/tt0053505/companycredits?ref_=tt_dt_co

98-9 Entratter's car accident: "Sands Prexy to Face Charge on Accident." *Las Vegas Review-Journal.* August 29, 1960. 2; Joy Hamann. "N.Y. Industrialist Dies in Jack Entratter's Car." *Las Vegas Review-Journal.* August 28, 1960. 1.

99 Freeman's long absence: Sands Hotel Public Relations Records. Box 39.

Folder 8; Forrest Duke. "Visiting Fireman." *Las Vegas Review-Journal.* September 13, 1960. 5.

99   "I felt a definite...." "Witnesses Appear for Entratter." *Las Vegas Review-Journal.* September 26, 1960. 1, 2.

99   Washboard roads: Roy Wood. "The Physics of Washboard Roads." *Wired.* July 18, 2011. Accessed at: https://www.wired.com/2011/07/the-physics-of-washboard-roads/

100   Entratter released: Colin McKimlay. "Sands President Wins Court Hearing Battle." *Las Vegas Review-Journal.* October 4, 1960. 3.

100   "There was never...." "Entratter Tells His Side of It." *Las Vegas Review-Journal.* October 4, 1960. 3.

101   Dorothy Entratter's death: "Dorothy James Entratter." Find a Grave. Accessed at: https://www.findagrave.com/memorial/8259431/dorothy-entratter

101   Dorothy Entratter children's home: George Jacobs and William Stadiem. *Mr. S: My Life with Frank Sinatra.* New York: Harper Entertainment, 2003. 189.

101   Civil suits against Entratter: "LV Hotelman Sued over Auto Crash." *Las Vegas Review-Journal.* July 8, 1961. 3; "Jack Entratter Facing Lawsuit in Motor Death." *Las Vegas Review-Journal.* November 18, 1961. 1.

101   Civil case amended: "Jury Selection Begins in Entratter Lawsuit." *Las Vegas Review-Journal.* June 6, 1966. 1.

101   Civil case settled: "Entratter Civil Trial Settled Out of Court Here." *Las Vegas Review-Journal.* June 19, 1966. 2.

102   1931 request for black gambling operators: Las Vegas City Commission. *Minute Book, Volume 3.* 157.

103   Armstrong denied entry to the Flamingo: Robert Merrill. "Louis Armstrong: A Taste for Opera." *New York Times.* April 2, 2000. Section 2, Page 4.

103   Lena Horne at the Sands: Verena Dobnik. "Singer Lena Horne Dies." *Las Vegas Review-Journal.* May 9, 2010.

103   Sammy Davis, Jr. at the New Frontier: Katharine Best and Katharine Hillyer. *Las Vegas: Playtown USA.* New York: David McKay Company, 1955. 141.

103-4 Davis/White marriageSam Kashner. "The Color of Love." *Vanity Fair.* September 3, 2013. Accessed at: https://www.vanityfair.com/style/1999/03/sammy-davis-kim-novak-dating

104   "Nice concert...." Les Devor. "Vegas Vagaries." *Las Vegas Review-Journal.* June 1, 1958. 16.

105   James Gay's background: "Pioneering Civic Leader, Hotel Executive Gay Dies at 83." *Las Vegas Sun.* September 13, 1999.

105   Gay at the Sands: *Oral Interview of James A. Gay III.* Edited by Elizabeth Nelson Patrick. University of Nevada, Las Vegas. December, 1978. 3-4.

105   Gay at Freedman's funeral: "Hundreds Attend Quiet Funeral Rites Held in LA for Sands' Jake Freedman." *Las Vegas Review-Journal.*

January 22, 1958. 3.

105-6   Las Vegas integration efforts: James B. McMillan. *Fighting Back: A Life in the Struggle for Civil Rights*. Reno: University of Nevada Oral History Program, 1997. 82-3.

106   Gay refuses to cross picket line: *Oral Interview of James A. Gay III*, 13.

107   Decision to integrate: McMillan, 84.

107   Sands and integration: "Annual Ebony Fashion Show Will Be Held at Sands Hotel." *Las Vegas Review-Journal.* November 7, 1970. 3.

107   Sarann Knight Preddy's career: "Former Co-Owner of Moulin Rouge Fought for Civil Rights." *Las Vegas Review-Journal.* January 16, 2011.

107   Gambling stopping after MLK's assassination: "City Pays King Last Tribute." *Las Vegas Review-Journal.* April 8, 1968. 25.

108   "I've never seen...." *Oral Interview of James A. Gay III*, 9-10.

Chapter 9   Me and My Shadow

109   Entratter paying less: Sands Hotel Public Relations Record. Box 2, Folder 31.

109   Entratter's bookings: Sands Hotel Public Relations Records. Box 2, Folder 31.

110   Dhia Ja'afar's visit: *Sands Times*, 1958.

110   Konstantin Verhshinin's canceled visit: Sands Hotel Public Relations Records. Box 1, Folder 5.

110   Martin and Lewis at the Sands: Display Ad. *Las Vegas Review-Journal*, December 15, 1954. 12.

110   Martin and Lewis deal blackjack: "Comics 'Give Away' Hotel Money Here." *Las Vegas Review-Journal.* October 20, 1955. 15.

111   Sinatra's mushroom outrage: George Levine. *Oral History Interview*. Las Vegas. Southern Nevada Jewish Community Digital Heritage Project, 2014. 12-3.

111   Sinatra's other irritants: Gay Talese. "Frank Sinatra Has a Cold." *Esquire.* April, 1966.

112   Dean Martin buys the dealers a TV: Ed Walters interview, 2019.

113   Davis's gratitude to Sinatra: Anthony Summers and Robbyn Swan, *Sinatra: The Life*. New York: Alfred A. Knopf, 2005. 239.

113   Summers and Swan, 113-5.

113   Naming of the Rat Pack by Lauren Bacall: Summers and Swan, 228.

113   "Lucky you only have to..." Ed Walters interview, 2019.

114   Origins of *Ocean's 11*: Shawn Levy. *Rat Pack Confidential*. New York: New York: Anchor Books, 1998. 105-6.

114   Shooting at the Riviera: "Start Filming Sinatra Pix at Riviera Hotel on Mon." *Las Vegas Review-Journal.* January 17, 1960.

114   "Star lite...." Sands Collection. Box 1, Folder 5.

115   Shooting schedule: Levy, 108-9.

115   Conte/Cohen interaction: Walters oral history interview, 2019.

115   Benedict theft: Ken Hansen. "'Ocean's Eleven' Work Proves Dual

Performances Success." *Las Vegas Review-Journal.* February 5, 1960. 15.

116   Wide opening for *Ocean's 11*: "Odd Mark to 'Ocean's 11.'" *Chicago Defender.* September 17, 1960. 3.

117   Freeman's publicity efforts: Levy, 118.

117   *Ocean's 11* reviews: William Leonard. "'Ocean's 11' Funny But No Thriller." *Chicago Daily Tribune.* August 2, 1960. B12; Bosley Crowther. "'Ocean's 11': Sinatra Heads Flippant Team of Crime." *New York Times.* August 11, 1960. 19; Richard Griffith. "'Ocean's 11' Fails to Awe N.Y. Critics. *Los Angeles Times.* August 30, 1960. A9.

117   *Ocean's 11* box office: Joel Waldo Finler. *The Hollywood Story.* London: Wallflower Press, 2003. 358-9.

118   Kennedy's early visits to Las Vegas: David G. Schwartz. "JFK in Vegas.' *Vegas Seven.* July 2, 2013.

118   Kennedy's support for Democrats: Summers and Swan, 256-7.

118   Kennedy's Palm Springs itinerary: George Jacobs and William Stadiem. *Mr. S: My Life with Frank Sinatra.* New York: Harper Entertainment, 2003. 133-9.

118   Kennedy's onstage introduction: Summers and Swan, 263.

118   Sinatra's suite: Roger Wagner. Personal Communication. April 17, 2020.

118   Kennedy and Campbell at Sinatra's show: Summers and Swan, 263.

119     $1 million delivered to Kennedy: Levy, 110.

119   Mob's connections with Kennedy: Summers and Swan, 258-9.

119   Sinatra's support for Kennedy: Summers and Swan, 262.

119   Campbell/Giancana/Kennedy connection: "Reputed JFK Mistress Exner Dies." *Washington Post.* September 26, 1999.

119   "What did you say...." Summers and Swan, 263.

120   Sinatra asks Davis and Britt to delay their wedding: Jacobs and Stadiem, 146.

120   Sinatra produces inaugural gala: Summers and Swan, 276-80.

120   Kennedy/Sinatra break: Summers and Swan, 285-6.

121   Tensions between Sinatra and Sands staff: Sands Hotel Public Relations Records. Box 1, Folder 5.

122   "The notoriety...." Nevada Gaming Control Board, June 13, 1960. Cited in Farrell and Case, 31.

122   Sinatra fronting for Giancana at the Cal-Neva: Summers and Swan, 289.

122-3   Giancana's presence at the Cal-Neva: Edward A. Olsen. *My Careers as a Journalist in Oregon, Idaho, and Nevada; in Nevada Gaming Control; and at the University of Nevada.* Reno: Oral History Project, 1972. 372-3.

123   RFK's planned raid: R.T. King. *Hang Tough! Grant Sawyer: An Activist in the Governor's Mansion.* Reno: University of Nevada Oral History Program, 1993. 89-90.

123   Sinatra addresses Gaming Control Board concerns: Olsen, 374.

123-4   FBI surveils, loses Giancana: Olsen, 375-6.

124   Fight at the Cal-Neva: Jacobs and Stadiem, 202-3.

124   Giancana's Cal-Neva antics: Olsen, 376-9.

124   Attempts to interview Sinatra, others: Olsen, 382.

124-5 Initial Olsen/Sinatra conversation: Olsen, 390-2.

125-6 Second Olsen/Sinatra conversation: Olsen, 395-6.

127 "Why...." Olsen, 397.

127 Complaint against Sinatra: Olsen, 399.

127 Warner's ultimatum: Jacobs and Stadiem, 204.

127 Sawyer/Kennedy conversation: King, 94.

128 Sinatra exits Nevada gaming: Olsen, 404.

128 Giancana's reaction: Kelley, 326-7.

128 Sinatra sells Sands shares: "Sands Hotel Stock Sale by Sinatra Approved." *Christian Science Monitor*. October 24, 1963. 10.

129 Davis/Olsen chat: Olsen, 406-7.

Chapter 10   Gonna Build a Mountain

130 Early 1960s Las Vegas growth: Forrest Duke. *Las Vegas Review-Journal*. May 3, 1963. 1.

130 Hotels adding rooms: "Resort Hotel Begins Big Expansion Project." *Los Angeles Times*. August 11, 1963. 15.

130 Aqueduct suites built: "Las Vegas Really Growing Up." *Chicago Tribune*. March 10, 1963. H4.

131 Aqueduct amenities: "Plush Suites Opened." *Las Vegas Review-Journal*. April 28, 1963. 9.

131 Castaways: "New Luxury Resort." *Las Vegas Review-Journal*. May 19, 1963. 5.

131 Greene's project: "Strip Hotel Plans Told." *Las Vegas Review-Journal*. May 8, 1963. 1.

131 Hotels adding high rises: Tom Cameron. "Las Vegas Willing to Bet on 'Sure Thing'—Building." *Los Angeles Times*. April 2, 1963. L1.

131-2 Sands expansion: "Expanded Sands Hotel Opening Fete December." Sands Hotel Public Relations Records. Box 16, Folder 9.

132 New Sands facilities, conventions: *Sands Times*. December 1965. 18-23.

132 Dunes tower: Richard Joseph. "Las Vegas Now Bigger and Brassier Than Ever: Show Becoming More and More Elaborate." *Chicago Tribune*. January 31, 1965. F6.

132 Sands tower plans: George Lundgren. "High-Rise Hotels Dot Desert as Las Vegas Grows Upward." *Los Angeles Times*. June 6, 1965. M1.

132 Martin Stern background: "Martin Stern, Jr." The Sarno Awards for Lifetime Achievement in Casino Design. Accessed at: https://gaming.unlv.edu/sarnoawards/stern.html

133 Construction of tower: Martin Stern, Jr. Collection, Special Collections and Archives, University Libraries, University of Nevada, Las Vegas. Las Vegas, Nevada. Flat File 67a.

133 "All the warm...." "Expanded Sands Hotel Opening Fete December." Sands Hotel Public Relations Records. Box 16, Folder 9.

133 Tower dedication celebration: Telegram. Sands Hotel Public Relations Records. Box 16, Folder 9.

134-5   Stacher bugging: Memorandum dated October 29, 1962. FBI File of Carl Cohen.

135   "Put on some shorts...." Michael Schutz. Personal interview with author. 12/25/19.

135   Bugging Cohen's Beverly Hills apartment: Memorandum dated October 29, 1962. FBI File of Carl Cohen.

135   FBI Las Vegas wiretapping operation: Richard Harwood. "Las Vegas, 1961: A Federal Wiretapping Operation in Born." *Washington Post,* June 19, 1966.

136   Installation of devices in Cohen's Sands apartment: Teletype dated February 19, 1963. FBI File of Carl Cohen.

136   Cohen leaves Las Vegas: Teletypes dated March 26, 1963 and April 9, 1963. FBI File of Carl Cohen.

136   Overheard conversations: Microphone surveillance logs, May 3, 4, 1963. FBI File of Carl Cohen.

137   "We ordered...." Microphone surveillance log, May 12, 1963. FBI File of Carl Cohen.

137   Elson's extension request: Memorandum dated May 14, 1963. FBI File of Carl Cohen.

137   "A source in contact...." Memorandum dated May 14, 1963. FBI File of Carl Cohen.

137   Stacher's suspicions of being bugged: Michael Schutz. Personal interview with author. December 25, 2019.

138   Levinson discovers wiretap: Harwood.

138   Bugs found in Cohen's apartment: Memorandum (airtel) dated July 11, 1963. FBI File of Carl Cohen.

138   Additional bugs discovered: Harwood.

138   Lamb denies bugging: "Snooping Turned Up at Hotel." *Las Vegas Sun.* September 18, 1963.

138-9   Cohen files complaint: Civil complaint, Carl Cohen vs. Central Telephone Company. FBI File of Carl Cohen.

139   "I don't care...." and Elson's response: Memorandum (airtel) dated September 18, 1963. FBI File of Carl Cohen.

139   Central Telephone concerns: Memorandum (airtel) dated September 6, 1963. FBI File of Carl Cohen.

140   FBI bugging discontinued: Memorandum dated September 10, 1963. FBI File of Carl Cohen.

140   Laxalt's response: "Laxalt Rips Demos, Bobby's Wiretapping." *Las Vegas Review-Journal.* September 28, 1963, 1.

140   Evans' speculation: Memorandum dated September 9, 1963. FBI File of Carl Cohen.

140   Elson's advice: Memorandum (airtel) dated October 4, 1963. FBI File of Carl Cohen.

141   Cohen withdraws suit: "Wiretap Suit Here Dismissed." *Las Vegas Review-Journal.* October 12, 1963. 1.

141   "I embarrassed the phone company...." Memorandum dated October 23, 1963. FBI File of Carl Cohen.

141   "The reports we Republicans...." "Claims Gamblers Targets." *Las Vegas Sun*. October 31, 1963.

141-2   Levinson files suit, others join: Drew Pearson. "FBI Faces Six Million Dollar Suit Over Wire Tapping in Las Vegas." *Las Vegas Review-Journal*. February 9, 1966. 29; "Court Delays Wiretap Suit Involving FBI." *Las Vegas Review-Journal*. February 18, 1966. 3.

142   Central Telephone admits leasing: "Phone Firm Admits Leasing Vegas Wiretap Line." *Las Vegas Review-Journal*. September 9, 1966. 1.

142   Sawyer's response: Drew Pearson. "Sawyer Lauded for Standing up to FBI." *Las Vegas Review-Journal*. October 20, 1966. 58.

142   "Major embarrassment" "LV Skimming Case 'Demoralizes' Feds." *Las Vegas Review-Journal*. April 16, 1968. 3.

142   Trips away from the Sands: Memorandum dated October 30, 1964. FBI File of Carl Cohen.

142   Trips to visit Stacher prior to Stacher's deportation: Memorandum dated October 30, 1964. FBI File of Carl Cohen; "Doc Stacher Faces Gov't Fine, Term." *Las Vegas Review-Journal*. July 24, 1963. 1.

142-3   Sands and Stacher case: "U.S. Agents Follow Doc Stacher." *Las Vegas Review-Journal*. September 4, 1963. 2.

143   1962 Sands executive positions: Louella Parsons. "Liz, Burton Help Finance Filming of "Caretakers." *Las Vegas Review-Journal*. December 20, 1962.

Chapter 11   Ain't That a Kick in the Head

144-5   Hughes moves to Las Vegas: Omar Garrison. *Howard Hughes in Las Vegas*. New York: Lyle Stuart, 1970. 28-9, 3.

145   Greenspun's editorial: Hank Greenspun. "Where I Stand." *Las Vegas Sun*, December 2, 1966. 1.

145   Hoffa's involvement: Robert Maheu and Richard Hack. *Next to Hughes: Behind the Power and Tragic Downfall of Howard Hughes by His Closest Advisor*. New York: Harper/Collins, 1992. 158.

146   Morgan and Rosselli's involvement: Maheu and Hack, 161.

146   Sands sale rumors: Don Digilio. "There Has Been Talk about Selling the Sands." *Las Vegas Review-Journal*. March 14, 1967. 1.

147   Sands negotiations: Maheu and Hack. 169.

147   Sands sold: "Sands to Hughes." *Las Vegas Review-Journal*. July 23, 1967. 1.

147   Other Hughes purchases: David G. Schwartz. "Neon Ozymandias." *Vegas Seven*. November 4, 2016.

147   Ed Nigro hired: Earl Wilson. "Look at Car Park—Millionaire Henry Ford." *Las Vegas Review-Journal*. October 12, 1967. 21.

147   Nigro background: "Major General Edward H. Nigro." U.S. Air Force. Accessed   at: https://www.af.mil/About-Us/Biographies/Display/

Article/106080/major-general-edward-h-nigro/

147   Other Hughes Nevada hires: Maheu and Hack, 2, 179.

148   Executives continuing to live at the Sands: Roger Wagner. *No Work and All Play: Audacious Chronicles of a Casino Boss.* Denver: Outskirts Press, 2011.

148   Nigro's public activities: "Hughes Aide Reassures LV Negroes." *Las Vegas Review-Journal.* March 6, 1968. 14; "Hughes Nevada Operations Makes Scholarships Awards to Five Youths." *Las Vegas Review-Journal.* September 10, 1968. 23.

148   Hughes' impact with locals: "Hughes Action Exceeds Any in Nevada's History." *Las Vegas Review-Journal.* December 3, 1968. 41.

149   Sands credit procedures: Ed Walters. Oral History Interview. January 9, 2019.

150   Reaction to new Hughes procedures: Walters.

150   Warner distanced from Sinatra: Kelley, 325.

151   Sinatra/Farrow wedding: "Sinatra spent anxiously hopeful moments in Las Vegas." *Las Vegas Sun.* May 15, 1998.

151-2   Sinatra/Hughes tension: Kelley, 372.

152   Sammy steps in for Frank: "Frank Ill—Fans Settle for Davis." *Las Vegas Review-Journal.* September 5, 1967. 1.

152   Apollo astronauts at the Sands, 1966: Sands Hotel Public Relations Records. Box 21, Folder 1.

152-3   September 1967 astronaut visit: Sands Hotel Public Relations Records. Box 30, Folder 9.

153   Sinatra denied credit: FBI File of Frank Sinatra. Part 4c. Page 1.

153   "I'm going to break…." Summers and Swan, 311.

154   Sinatra's golf cart mishap: Jacobs and Stadiem, 240.

154   "I'm done…." Kelley, 372.

154   Sinatra's apology: Summers and Sawn, 331.

154-5   Cohen arrives in the Garden Room: Oral history interview with Steve Wynn. Las Vegas, Nevada. December 8, 2007. 9.

155   Cohen/Sinatra fight: Wynn, 9-10; Kelley, 373.

155-6   Sinatra leaves for Caesars Palace: Don Digilio. "Frank Sinatra Loses Teeth During Strip Hotel Brawl." *Las Vegas Review-Journal.* September 13, 1967. 1.

156   Reaction to Cohen's punch: "Frank Sinatra Loses Teeth During Strip Hotel Brawl."

156   Sinatra's initial denials: Murray Hertz. "Sinatra Flack Denied the Singer Was Punched." *Las Vegas Review-Journal.* September 14, 1967. 1.

156   Agent admits fight: "Sinatra's Dentist Says He Capped Two Teeth." "Sinatra's Fight Confirmed." *Las Vegas Review-Journal.* September 14, 1967. 1.

156   Sheriff's investigation and attorney general's statement: Don Digilio. "Sour Note Seen for Sinatra." *Las Vegas Review-Journal.* September 21, 1967. 1.

157   Theory that fight was staged: FBI File of Frank Sinatra. Part 4c. Page 1.

157   St. Jude's benefit: "Chairman Named for 'Nite of Stars' Benefit." *Las Vegas Review-Journal.* October 8, 1967. 30.

Chapter 12   Luck Be a Lady

158   Puzo's background: Mario Puzo. *Inside Las Vegas.* New York: Grosset and Dunlap, 1976. 111.

158   "What non-gamblers...." Puzo 1976, 110.

158   "No money in my...." Puzo 1976, 25-7.

159   "I was forty-five..." Mario Puzo. *The Godfather Papers and Other Confessions.* New York: G. Putnam's Sons, 1972. 34.

159   "I'm sorry...." Puzo 1972, 132.

159   "A few years ago...." Puzo 1972, 138.

159-60 Puzo and David Janssen at the Sands: Ed Walters. *Oral History Interview.* Las Vegas. Table Games Management Oral History Project. University of Nevada, Las Vegas, 2016. 36-7.

160   Carlo Gambino at the Sands: Walters, 12-3.

160-1   Cohen's refusal to let Puzo leave: Walters 2019 interview; Puzo 1972, 38-9.

161   "I needed the cash...." Puzo 1972, 40.

161   "a dedicated gambler...."Earl Wilson. "It Happened Last Night." *Las Vegas Review-Journal.* November 3, 1969. 11.

161   "But in my very worst...." Puzo 1976, 107-110.

161   "I hereby affirm...." Puzo 1976, 55.

161-2   "Sally Rags...." Puzo 1972, 141.

162   Hughes' aviation plans: Omar Garrison. *Howard Hughes in Las Vegas.* New York: Lyle Stuart, 1970. 131.

163-4   The New Sands: Colin McKinlay. "Hughes to Build Giant Hotel Here." *Las Vegas Review-Journal.* January 25, 1968. 1.

164   Johnson's estimates: "Hughes' Hotel Construction Would Employ 3,000 Men." *Las Vegas Review-Journal.* January 26, 1968. 12.

164   Requests to Freeman: Murray Hertz. "New Hotel for HH Stirs World's Interest." *Las Vegas Review-Journal.* January 30, 1968. 7.

164   School construction potentially impacted: "Bond Issue Up For LV Decision." *Las Vegas Review-Journal.* February 1, 1968. 1; Nedra Joyce. "Howard Hughes Projects Create Need for Schools." *Las Vegas Review-Journal.* February 13, 1968. 11.

164-5   Hughes efforts to stop Boxcar: David G. Schwartz. "Howard Hughes' Atomic Horror." *Vegas Seven.* November 7, 1916.

165   International groundbreaking: "Ground Broken for Huge Hotel." *Las Vegas Review-Journal.* February 11, 1968. 6.

165   Martin to the Riviera: Earl Wilson. "Dino to Become Riviera Prexy." *Las Vegas Review-Journal.* December 16, 1968. 1; "Dean Martin." Online Nevada Encyclopedia. Accessed at: http://www.onlinenevada.org/articles/dean-martin

166   Considine's unease with the new Vegas: Bob Considine. "Corporation

Types Hold Reins in Vegas." *Las Vegas Review-Journal.* January 21, 1968. 36.

167   Asperio hired: "Aspero New Manager of Sands Hotel." *Las Vegas Review-Journal.* May 11, 1969. 6.

167   Nigro leaves: "Gen. Nigro Named Top Del Webb Corp. Exec." *Las Vegas Review-Journal.* May 21, 1970. 3.

168   Hughes leaves Las Vegas: Maheu and Hack, 235-8.

168   New Hughes structure: "Gamers Approve Top Hughes Executives." *Las Vegas Review-Journal.* Nay 20, 1971. 1.

169   Sands rumors: John Hanna. "Purge Denied." *Las Vegas Review-Journal.* July 13, 1971. 1.

169   Sinatra/Waterman fracas: Don Digilio. "Sinatra Caper Keeps Strip Humming." *Las Vegas Review-Journal.* September 8, 1970. 1.

170   Entratter's death: Hank Greenspun. "Sands Show Producer Jack Entratter Dies." *Las Vegas Sun.* March 12, 1971. 1.

170   Variety obituary: "Jack Entratter, 57, Top LV Showman." *Variety.* March 17, 1971. 67.

170   Entratter funeral plans: "Sands Exec, Entratter, Dies Thursday in Hospital." *Las Vegas Review-Journal.* March 12, 1971. 1.

170-1   Cohen denies buying Sands: Nedra Joyce. "Sands Sale Denied." *Las Vegas Review-Journal.* January 7, 1972. 4.

171   Durante's party: Forrest Duke. "Sands: Jimmy Durante's 55th Anni Party." *Las Vegas Review-Journal.* April 2, 1972. 9.

171   Al Freeman's death: "Sands Hotel Executive Dies." *Las Vegas Sun.* August 29, 1972. 1.

171-2   "There is word…." Don Digilio. "Freeman Draws Another Crowd." *Las Vegas Review-Journal.* September 2, 1972. 17.

172   Cohen's remaining time at the Sands: Forrest Duke. "Jerry Van Dyke Directs Deedy & Bill Movie Here." *Las Vegas Review-Journal.* January 11, 1971. 5.

172   Cohen leaves the Sands: "Cohen Resigns Sands Position." *Las Vegas Review-Journal.* January 5, 1973. 12.

172   Cohen joins MGM: "MGM Grand Hotel's No. 2 Officer Named." *Las Vegas Review-Journal.* May 11, 1973. 3.

Chapter 13   Danke Schoen

180   Walker Kane's background: "Walter Kane." *UPI Archives.* May 28, 1983. Accessed at: https://www.upi.com/Archives/1983/05/28/Obituaries/5533422942400/; Burt A. Folkart. "Walter Kane, 82, Longtime Talent Agent for Howard Hughes." *Los Angeles Times.* May 28, 1983. A31.

180   Kane given Entratter's suite: Paul Anka. *My Way: An Autobiography.* New York: St. Martin's Press, 2013. 164.

180   "My weekly entertainment nut…" Eliot Tiegel. "Las Vegas Retains Its MOR Legacy." *Billboard.* December 26, 1974. 38-40.

181   Kane's signings: Tiegel; "Signs Long Contract." *Las Vegas Review-Journal.* February 19, 1973. 5.

181   Kane's closeness with Wayne Newton: Folkart.

181   "Next year...." Tiegel.

181-2   Harry Goodheart's background: Roger Wagner. *No Work and All Play: Audacious Chronicles of a Casino Boss.* Denver: Outskirts Press, 2011. 48. "Grand Jury Holds Night Skim Probe." *Las Vegas Review-Journal.* December 9, 1966. 2; "Commission Okays Golden Hotel Sale." *Las Vegas Review-Journal.* January 22.1969. 23; Dar Flanigan. "Hotel Tropicana Announces Several Recent Promotions." *Las Vegas Review-Journal.* March 30, 1969. 56.

182   Goodheart's player network: Wagner, 49.

182   Goodheart's use of a computer: Roger Wagner. Personal Communication. April 17, 2020.

182   Summa leadership: Robert Lindsay. "Small Staff Runs Hughes's Summa Corp." *New York Times.* April 7, 1976. 61.

183   Ed Walters' experiences returning to the Sands: Ed Walters. *Oral History Interview.* Las Vegas. Table Games Management Oral History Project. University of Nevada, Las Vegas, 2016. 23-5.

184   Co-sponsorship of U.S. National Senior Golf Open Championship: "Great Form." *Las Vegas Review-Journal.* September 21, 1973, 33.

185   Hiring of Al Beselink: "New Host." *Las Vegas Review-Journal.* December 14, 1976. 29.

185   Digilio praises Goodheart: Don Digilio. "Time to Shop for Christmas." *Las Vegas Review-Journal.* December 5, 1976. 17. Don Digilio. "Doing Some Early Shopping." *Las Vegas Review-Journal.* December 5, 1977. 19.

185   Sands keno debut: Forrest Duke. "Erroll 'Misty' Garner in Hilton Debut." *Las Vegas Review-Journal.* March 7, 1953. 7.

185   "Shabby elegance:" Wagner communication.

185   Mauna Kea event: Wagner, 121-2.

185-6   Adnan Khashoggi background: Michael Gillard. "Adnan Khashoggi Obituary." *The Guardian.* June 7, 2017. Accessed at: https://www.theguardian.com/world/2017/jun/07/adnan-khashoggi-obituary

186   Khashoggi rumored to buy Sands: Don Digilio. "Leavitt Will File for Congress." *Las Vegas Review-Journal.* June 9, 1974. 17. Roger Wagner. Personal Communication. April 17, 2020.

186   Khashoggi's diverse holdings: Frank N. Hakins. "Arab Oil (and Cattle, Truck) Magnate a Jet-Setter." *Las Vegas Review-Journal.* August 28, 1974. 25.

186   Khashoggi's accommodations and largesse: Roger Wagner. Personal Communication. April 17, 2020.

186   Khashoggi's global holdings: Stephen Kinzer. "Adnan Khashoggi, High-Living Saudi Arms Trader, Dies at 81." *New York Times.* June 6, 2007. Accessed at: https://www.nytimes.com/2017/06/06/world/middleeast/adnan-khashoggi-dead-saudi-arms-trader.html?_r=0

186-7 Khashoggi's unusual requests: Wagner, 168-70.

187 Danner fights record request: "Grand Jury Demands Sands Records." *Las Vegas Review-Journal.* May 25, 1976. 1.

187 Khashoggi at the Sands, 1979: Wagner, 170-1.

187-8 Al Guzman's background: Barbara Guzman, collector. *Oral History Interview with Al Guzman.* Las Vegas: Ralph Roske Oral History Project on Early Las Vegas. University of Nevada, Las Vegas, 2018. 1.

188 "Pretty girls sell…" Ned Day, "The Selling of Las Vegas," *Las Vegan Magazine* (August 1984). 79.

188 Guzman photo ops: "Great Form." *Las Vegas Review-Journal.* September 21, 1973, 33; Forrest Duke. "Erroll 'Misty' Garner in Hilton Debut." *Las Vegas Review-Journal.* March 7, 1953. 7: "Sands Renovation." *Las Vegas Review-Journal.* August 8, 1978. 8C.

188-9 Guzman's rain promotion: Ned Day, "The Selling of Las Vegas," *Las Vegan Magazine* (August 1984). 79.

189 "They've lost the old touch…." Guzman, 5.

189-90 Summa land transfer: Jeanne M. Hall. "Sands Hotel Sold for $85 Million." *Las Vegas Review-Journal.* October 29, 1980. 13.

190 Danner's health issues: Wagner, 174.

190 Inns of the Americas background: Jeanne M. Hall. "Sands Hotel Sold for $85 Million." *Las Vegas Review-Journal.* October 29, 1980. 13.

190 Inns existing casino operations: Jeanne M. Hall. "$50 Million Sands Refurbishing Told." *Las Vegas Review-Journal.* November 21, 1980. 3C.

190 Lummis and Pratt comments on sale: Jeanne M. Hall. "Sands Hotel Sold for $85 Million."

190-1 Promised renovation: Jeanne M. Hall. "$50 Million Sands Refurbishing Told."

191 Neil Smyth background: "Cornelius 'Neil' Smyth." *Las Vegas Review-Journal Obituaries.* Accessed at: https://obits.reviewjournal.com/obituaries/lvrj/obituary.aspx?n=cornelius-smyth-neil&pid=154543500&fhid=9487; "In Memoriam: Cornelius 'Neil' Smyth (1926-2011). Team USA Table Tennis. Accessed at: https://www.teamusa.org/USA-Table-Tennis/Features/2011/November/04/In-Memoriam-CORNELIUS-NEIL-SMYTH-1926-2011

191 Smyth as soft-spoken but knowledgeable: Burt Peretsky. Personal communication. March 19, 2020.

191 Pratts purchase Brighton, rename it: "N.J. Casino Seeks Glamorous Image." *Las Vegas Review-Journal.* May 15, 1981. 20.

191 Goodheart remains with Summa: "Exec to Stay with Summa." *Las Vegas Review-Journal.* March 6, 1981. 15.

191-2 Sands licensing hearing: Clyde Weiss. "Sands Sale Gets Tentative OK." *Las Vegas Review-Journal.* April 23, 1981. 20.

192 Koffman brothers' involvement: "N.J. Casino Seeks Glamorous Image." *Las Vegas Review-Journal.* May 15, 1981. 20.

192 Sands as destination for good managers: Peretsky.

192-3   New additions to Sands: "'Encore '82'" to Observe Big Reopening." *Las Vegas Review-Journal.* January 15, 1982. 7F.

193   Burt Peretsky hired: Peretsky.

193   Tommy Walker's background: Ted Thackery. "Tommy Walker, 63, Fireworks Magic Man, Dies." *Los Angeles Times.* October 22, 1986.

193   Encore '82: "'Encore '82'" to Observe Big Reopening." *Las Vegas Review-Journal.* January 15, 1982. 7F.

194-5   Details of Encore '82: Peretsky.

Chapter 14   While the Feeling's Good

196   Pratts' bet on Latin America: Jeanne M. Hall. "$50 Million Sands Refurbishing Told." *Las Vegas Review-Journal.* November 21, 1980. 3C.

196-7   Las Vegas troubles in 1980: Clyde Weiss. "Nevada Gaming Hits Rocky Road During Past Year." *Las Vegas Review-Journal.* January 4, 1981. 2B.

197   Khashoggi's big losses, departure: Burt Peretsky, Personal Communication; Roger Wagner. *No Work and All Play: Audacious Chronicles of a Casino Boss.* Denver: Outskirts Press, 2011. 168.

198   Copa eliminates dinner show: Tim Walter. "Sands Hotel in Las Vegas Axes Dinner Shows; Seating Boosted." *Billboard.* February 14, 1981. 30.

198-9   Copa closing: Pete Mikla. "Copa Room Closing Ends Era at Sands." *Las Vegas Review-Journal.* June 26, 1981. 4D.

199   New Copa: Walter.

199-200 Other showroom policies: "Ira David Sternberg. Vegas Hilton Into Productions; Move Prompted by Economics." *Billboard.* February 27, 1982. 32.

200   "Top Secret" announced: "Sands, Sahara Plan Revues for Showrooms." *Las Vegas Review-Journal.* December 11, 1981. 50.

200   "Top Secret" review: Norm Clarke. *Vegas Confidential: Sin City's Ace Insider 1,000 Naked Truths.* Las Vegas: Stephens Press, 2004. 175.

200   Sahara's revue: "Sands, Sahara Plan Revues for Showrooms." *Las Vegas Review-Journal.* December 11, 1981. 50.

200   Return to headliners: "Sands Will Return to Big Names." *Las Vegas Review-Journal.* March 2, 1982. 17.

200   "I guess I'm one...." "Sands Will Return to Big Names."

200   "Even Caesars....: Bill O'Hallaren. "The Graying of Las Vegas Glitter." *Los Angeles Times.* January 3, 1982. G2.

200-1   "Recent events...." "Las Vegas Visitor Gray Around Temples." *Las Vegas Review-Journal.* March 3, 1982. 10B.

201   "Except for those...." "Thomas Hopes to Spark Sands Revival." *Las Vegas Review-Journal.* March 5, 1982. 5D.

201   Revival of Copa Girls: "Vegas Sands Is Shifting Back to Names; Danny Thomas First." *Variety.* March 10, 1982. 189.

201   Peretsky's interactions with Thomas: Peretsky.

201   Thomas's show: Charles Supin. "Pacing Perfect in Thomas Debut." *Las Vegas Review-Journal.* March 21, 1982. 10D.

201   Copa line-up: "Sands Signs More Stars." *Las Vegas Review-Journal.* March 12, 1982. 11D.

202     $20 million in Mexican markers: Peretsky.

202   Nevada Gaming Commission approves Sands' Puerto Rico holdings: Clyde Weiss. "Inns of Americas Scores 'First' in Gaming Licensing." *Las Vegas Review-Journal.* July 11, 1982. 21.

202   Inns name change: "Inns of the Americas Expands with New Name." *Las Vegas Review-Journal.* July 27, 1982. 27.

202   "Spent the night...." Ronald Reagan. Presidential Diary. October 28, 1982. Accessed at: https://www.reaganfoundation.org/ronald-reagan/white-house-diaries/diary-entry-10281982/

202   Lead-lined room: Larry Werner. "The President Comes to Las Vegas." *Las Vegas Review-Journal.*

202-3   Disappearance of "RR" china: Wagner.

203   February 1984 return: Carol Cling. "Reagan Arrives in Vegas." *Las Vegas Review-Journal.* February 7, 1984. 1.

203   All guests getting cake: Larry Werner. "The President Comes to Las Vegas." *Las Vegas Review-Journal.* February 8, 1984. 11.

203   Nancy Reagan at the Sands: "First Lady Arrives." *Las Vegas Review-Journal.* June 20, 1984. 4.

203   Payments to Summa stop: Jeanne M. Hall. "Summa to Resume Control of the Troubled Sands." *Las Vegas Review-Journal.* April 6, 1983. 1.

203   "Mexico looks askance:" "Summa Oks Sands' Financial Relief; Mex. Markers Hurt." *Variety.* October 20, 1982. 326.

204   Summa financial relief: Wagner; "Summa Oks Sands' Financial Relief; Mex. Markers Hurt."

204   September 1982 layoffs: Peretsky; "Summa Retakes Helm of Sands." *Las Vegas Review-Journal.* April 6, 1983. 16.

204   Angus's remarks and rebuttal: Mike Henle. "Nevada Rally on Again, Scheduled Dec. 18-19." *Las Vegas Review-Journal.* December 10, 1982. 101.

204   Summa stops cashing Sands checks: "Sands Payroll Checks Shunned by Summa." *Las Vegas Review-Journal.* January 15, 1983. 4.

204-5   "As former members..." Clyde Weiss. "Check Cashing Dispute Disappoints Sands Hotel Boss." *Las Vegas Review-Journal.* January 85, 1983. 11.

205   "Certainly, we don't intend..." Clyde Weiss. "Check Cashing Dispute Disappoints Sands Hotel Boss."

205   Summa resumes ownership: Jeanne M. Hall. "Summa to Resume Control of the Troubled Sands." *Las Vegas Review-Journal.* April 6, 1983. 1; Wagner.

205   Bryan's behind the scenes influence: Ned Day. "The Sands Hotel Came Close to Closing Its Doors." *Las Vegas Review-Journal.* April 10, 1983. 27.

206   Details of changeover: "Sands Action Approved." *Las Vegas Review-*

Journal. April 22, 1983. 20.

206   Smyth leaves Sands: "Ex-Sands Exec Joins Caesars." *Las Vegas Review-Journal.* August 24, 1983. 2B.

206   Griffith takes over: "Sands Takeover Delayed." *Las Vegas Review-Journal.* April 13, 1983. 3.

206   Griffith's team: Carlos Harrison. "Shake-up Reported at Sands." *Las Vegas Review-Journal.* October 29, 1984. 1.

206   Bargain hunting on the Strip: Al Strachan. "Vegas Lures with Bargain Bonanza." *The Globe and Mail.* August 6, 1983. T1.

206   Garden buffet prices: Sands Advertisement. *Las Vegas Review-Journal.* September 30, 1984. 60.

207   Goulet returns: : Bill Willard. "Goulet, Trademark Return to the Copa." *Las Vegas Review-Journal.* January 1, 1984. 55.

207   Griffith team departs: Carlos Harrison. "Shake-up Reported at Sands." *Las Vegas Review-Journal.* October 29, 1984. 1.

207   Cruzen's team: "On the Move." *Las Vegas Review-Journal.* December 2, 1984. 122.

207   Sands retrofit efforts: Carol Cling. "Sands Completes Retrofit Work." *Las Vegas Review-Journal.* May 25, 1985. 14.

207   Sands arson: "Thomas Littleowl Pleaded Innocent Monday." *UPI.* April 28, 1986. https://www.upi.com/Archives/1986/04/28/Thomas-Littleowl-pleaded-innocent-Monday-to-setting-a-rash/6997515044800/

207   Littleowl's sentence: "Deadly Casino Fires Helped Rewrite Safety Standards." *Las Vegas Sun.* January 25, 2008. https://lasvegassun.com/news/2008/jan/25/las-vegas-fire-history/

207   Licensing agreement: "Logo Licensed." *Las Vegas Review-Journal.* September 24, 1984. 15.

207-8   Bowl Game contest: "1st Annual Sands Sports Book Bowl Game Contest." *Las Vegas Review-Journal.* December 13, 1985. 43.

208   "Outrageous" and competitors: Merry Lynn Starling. "Spotlight on Las Vegas." *The Rotarian.* May 1986. 28.

208   1986 optimism: "Growth Eyed for Gaming in Las Vegas." *Las Vegas Review-Journal.* January 4, 1987. 17.

208   Kerkorian re-enters Nevada gaming: Warren Bates. "Kerkorian Quietly Takes Reins of Desert Inn and Sands Hotels." *Las Vegas Review-Journal.* February 1, 1988. 9.

208   Nangaku wins Dunes bidding: Robert Macy. "Japanese Businessman Wins Bidding Battle." *AP.* August 4, 1987. https://apnews.com/7747bd70b087753a4bf9f4df21de3097

208   Summa looking to exit gaming: Jon Ralston. "Kerkorian Has Eye on Sands, Desert Inn." *Las Vegas Review-Journal.* September 8, 1987. 13.

208-9   Kerkorian buys Sands: Sergi Lalli. "Kerkorian Buys Sands and Desert Inn Hotels." *Las Vegas Review-Journal.* September 10, 1987. 1.

209   Hannifin brought on board: "Vice President Named for DI, Sands Hotels." *Las Vegas Review-Journal.* October 23, 1987. 23.

209 35th anniversary: Mike Weatherford. "Fireworks to Mark Sands' 35th Anniversary." *Las Vegas Review-Journal.* November 13, 1987. 29.

209 Kerkorian approved: "Gamers Approve Kerkorian License." *Las Vegas Review-Journal.* January 22, 1988. 12.

209 Kerkorian assumes control: Sergio Lalli. "Vegas Enters Gaming Supermarket Era." *Las Vegas Review-Journal.* January 17, 1988. 1; Warren Bates. "Kerkorian Quietly Takes Reins of Desert Inn and Sands Hotels." *Las Vegas Review-Journal.* February 1, 1988. 9.

209 Lion added to logo: "MGM Lion Reigns Over Old Sands Hotel Logo." *Las Vegas Review-Journal.* February 12, 1988. 27.

209 Rumors of sale: Don Usherson. "Some Interesting Grist Coming Out of Rumor Mill." *Las Vegas Review-Journal.* March 2, 1988. 18.

209 Interface buys: "Sands Sold to COMDEX Organizers." *Las Vegas Review-Journal.* April 25, 1988. 1.

Chapter 15   The Way You Look Tonight

210 Comdex history: Jim Bartimo. "Q&A: Sheldon G. Adelson." *InfoWorld.* September 17, 1984. 51.

210 Comdex in 1988: "Howard Stutz. "Interface Has Strong History with Las Vegas." *Las Vegas Review-Journal.* January 8, 1989. 19.

210-1 Plans for expansion: Howard Stutz. "COMDEX Organizer Has Big Plans for Rejuvenating Sands." *Las Vegas Review-Journal.* November 16, 1988. 22.

211 Henri Lewin's hiring and background: Howard Stutz. "Flamboyant Hotelier Plans to Take Over Reins of Sands." *Las Vegas Review-Journal.* January 8, 1989. 17.

211 Lewin's departure from Hilton: Fen Montaigne. "Hilton Nears Deal to Sell Casino Hotel." *Philadelphia Inquirer.* April 19, 1985. A1.

211 Lewin's comments: Howard Stutz. "Flamboyant Hotelier Plans to Take Over Reins of Sands."

211-2 Lewin's licensing difficulties: Howard Stutz. "Licensing of Sands Owners Put on Hold." *Las Vegas Review-Journal.* January 12, 1989. 17; Ed Vogel. "Gamers Mull Sale of Sands." *Las Vegas Review-Journal.* February 9, 1989. 1.

212 "I am still willing..." Howard Stutz. "Lewin Vows Fight for License After Control Board Rejection." *Las Vegas Review-Journal.* February 10, 1989. 1.

212 Board recommendations: "Gamers to Decide on Lewin License Appeal." *Las Vegas Review-Journal.* February 23, 1989. 51.

212 Commission license approvals: Howard Stutz. "Lewin Granted Limited License to Run Sands." *Las Vegas Review-Journal.* February 24, 1989. 1.

212 Lewin's Sands plans: Howard Stutz. "Lewin Sings Praises of Sands." *Las Vegas Review-Journal.* May 4, 1989. 1B.

213 Berkley returns: Shelley Berkley. Oral History Interview. May 12, 2020.

213 Skepticism about conventions: Howard Stutz. "Sands Owner Showing

Interest in New Convention Center Project." *Las Vegas Review-Journal.*
May 22, 1989. 11.

214   Lewin's high profile: Howard Stutz. "Lewin Vows No Strike at Sands."
Las Vegas Review-Journal. May 17, 1989. 20; Don Usherson. "Bally's
Signs Connie Francis, Latoya Jackson." *Las Vegas Review-Journal.* June
23, 1989. 2C; Elliot Krane. "Culinary Experts to Gather at Caesars for
Five-Day Competition." *Las Vegas Review-Journal.* July 21, 1989. 2E.

214   Lewin placates Usherson: Don Usherson. "Has Local Union Sacrificed
Five of Its Own?" *Las Vegas Review-Journal.* June 23, 1989. 53; Don
Usherson. "Krofft Puppets 'Comedy Kings' Coming to Sands' Copa."
Las Vegas Review-Journal. June 26, 1989. 14E; Don Usherson. "Neil
Diamond Rejects Aladdin's Big Bucks Offer." *Las Vegas Review-Journal.*
August 6, 1989. 51.

214   Lewin at the center of news: Display Ad. *Las Vegas Review-Journal.*
August 6, 1989. 22; Elliot Krane. "Former Caesars Palace Culinary
Executive Opens Gourmet Restaurant." *Las Vegas Review-Journal.*
August 18, 1989. 8E.

214   Tweaks to casino marketing: Elliot Krane. "Fine Cuisine, Wines to
Be Sampled at Annual Culinary Capers." *Las Vegas Review-Journal.*
September 15, 1989. 7D. Display Ad. *Las Vegas Review-Journal.*
December 29, 1989. 54.

215   Lewin's dismissal: Howard Stutz. "Lewin Fired as President of Sands
Hotel." *Las Vegas Review-Journal.* January 31, 1990. 1.

215   Champagne brunch: "Sands Hotel Entices Locals with a New Weekend
Champagne Brunch." *Las Vegas Review-Journal.* April 20, 1990. 12E.

215   Benedict's short tenure: Howard Stutz. "Sands Changes Confirmed." *Las
Vegas Review-Journal.* August 25, 1990. 40.

215   Benedict stays on: Phil Hevener. "Fan or Foe Has to Agree Dice Is Big
Money for Operations." *Las Vegas Sun.* April 26, 1990. 53.

215   Adelson takes more active role: Howard Stutz. "Adelson to Take Active
Role in Sands' Management." *Las Vegas Review-Journal.* August 28,
1990. 35.

215   Norton's background, thoughts on arrival: Steve Norton. Oral History
Interview. May 15, 2020.

215-6 Greater trade show bookings: Howard Stutz. "Sands Changes
Confirmed." *Las Vegas Review-Journal.* August 25, 1990. 40.

216   Adelson's use of charts and graphs: Berkley.

216   Trade show increases: Howard Stutz. "Adelson to Take Active Role in
Sands' Management."

216   Sands threat to status quo: Penny Levin. "Unconventional Warfare:
Sands Expo to Compete for Convention Mega-Dollars." *Las Vegas Sun.*
August 19, 1990. 8C.

216   "What we're going to do..." Phil Hevener. "Catering to a New Angle for
the Sands." *Las Vegas Sun.* September 23, 1990. 55.

217   Opening of Expo Center: Stacey Welling. "Sands Opens Huge

Convention Center." *Las Vegas Review-Journal.* November 10, 1990. 19.

217 Norton's efforts to fill rooms: Norton.

218 Norton departs: Norton.

218 Bryan hired: "Sands Names President." *Las Vegas Review-Journal.* January 14, 1992. 41

218 Bryan leaves: Dave Palermo. "Sands New Chief Quits." *Las Vegas Review-Journal.* April 2, 1992. 49.

218 Rumors of Sands sale: Phil Hevener. "Changes May Be in the Sands." *Las Vegas Sun.* June 7, 1992. 49.

218 Rumors of Expo Center sale: Jeff Burbank. "Sands Expo in Buyout Plan." *Las Vegas Review-Journal.* October 14, 1992. 1.

218 "The financing market..." Jeff Burbank. "Adelson's Plans Less Ambitious." *Las Vegas Review-Journal.* November 16, 1992. 1F.

218 $15 million retheming: Jeff Burbank. "Adelson's Plans Less Ambitious."

219 Increases in convention revenues: Marcia Pledger. "Officials Disagree Whether to Buy or Build." *Las Vegas Review-Journal.* October 3, 1993. 1.

219 "We are inclined..." "An Unconventional Idea." *Las Vegas Review-Journal.* October 6, 1993. 22.

219 Expo expansion plans: "Sands Expo Will Be Expanded." *Las Vegas Review-Journal.* March 1, 1994. 7D.

219 "I don't think..." Marcia Pledger. "Convention Business Booming." *Las Vegas Review-Journal.* September 18, 1994. 16E.

219 Comdex sale: Jeffrey Krasner. "Comdex Show Sold for $800 million." *Boston Herald.* February 14, 1995. 27.

220 Melinda replaces Comedy Kings: Michael Paskevich. "Nothing Lasts Forever in Las Vegas; It Just Seems Like It." *Las Vegas Review-Journal.* July 8, 1990. 1K.

220 Decrease of headliners across Las Vegas: Show listings. *Las Vegas Review-Journal.* May 4, 1990. 4E.

220 Potential growth plans: *What's On.* February 1-14, 1994. 29; John G. Edwards. "Sands Co-Owner to Buy Out Partners after Sale of Computer Trade Shows." *Las Vegas Review-Journal.* February 14, 1995. 2.

220-1 Weidner team hired, plans for future: "Sands Execs Shift Westward to Build Las Vegas." *Newark Star-Ledger.* November 22, 1995.

221 Resort building in 1995: Elliot S. Krane. "Construction Boom Continued in Vegas Area in '95." *Press of Atlantic City.* January 7, 1996. F2.

221 Rumors of Sands closure: Jeff German. "Drawing a Line at the Sands." *Las Vegas Sun.* April 13, 1996.

221 Berkley announces closure: Berkley; "Sands to Shut; New Resort Coming." *Las Vegas Sun.* May 16, 1996.

221-2 "We've been expecting..." Dave Palermo. 'Time Runs Out for Sands." *Las Vegas Review-Journal.* May 17, 1996. 1.

222 Scope of new resort: "Sands to Shut; New Resort Coming." *Las Vegas Sun.* May 16, 1996.

222 Reflections on closing: Robert Macy. "Famed Casino Runs out of Luck."

Akron Beacon-Journal. June 27, 1996. E1.

222   Venice theme: Gary Thompson. "An Era Ends with Sands Closing." *Las Vegas Sun.* June 28, 1996.

222   Stupak has last roll: John Katsilometes. "Tyson Revisits Lewis in New Podcast." *Las Vegas Sun.* January 19, 2016.

222   Details of last night: Glenn Puitt. "Sands Deals Final Hand." *Las Vegas Review-Journal.* July 1, 1996. 1.

223   Painting located for couple: Berkley.

223   Auction: Marian Green. "Memories of the Sands." *Las Vegas Review-Journal.* July 24, 1996. 1B.

223   *Con Air* filming: Karen Zekan. "Don't Panic—Smoking Plane Part of Movie." *Las Vegas Sun.* September 10, 1996.

224   Sands in *Con Air: Con Air,* directed by Simon West. 1997; Burbank, California: Touchstone Pictures.

224   Pond added for filming: Carol Cling. "Con Air." *Las Vegas Review-Journal.* November 10, 1996. 1J.

224   Demolition set: "Last Week in November to Witness Sands' Doom." *Las Vegas Review-Journal.* November 15, 1996. 37.

224   Demolition details: Cathy Scott. "Venetian-Style Hotel Set for Sands Site." *Las Vegas Sun.* November 26, 1996.

224   "It's sad to see..." "Las Vegas Landmark Reduced to Pile of Rubble." *Las Vegas Sun.* November 26, 1996.

Epilogue   That's Life

225   Venetian opening: Robert Macy. "Sophia Loren a Hit as New $1.5 billion Venice." *Las Vegas Sun.* May 3, 1999.

225   Overtime work: Tara Weingarten. "Venice, Vegas, Vici?" A Tycoon Challenges Steve." *Newsweek.* May 3, 1999. 56.

225   First convention: Gary Thompson. "Adelson Courts Controversy in Bid to Outstrip." *Las Vegas Sun.* May 4, 1999.

I ndex

Titles of operas, books, records, films, and TV shows, are in italic font. Page numbers with illustrations are in bold font.

About the Author

Dr. David G. Schwartz is a gaming historian, affiliate professor of history, and administrator at the University of Nevada, Las Vegas, who writes about gambling, video games, hospitality, and history, and only occasionally pines for his days as Mr. Peanut on the Atlantic City Boardwalk.

An Atlantic City native and former casino employee, Schwartz has written several books. His nonfiction writing has won multiple Nevada Press Association awards, and he was named the 2014 Trippies Las Vegas Person of the Year in recognition to his many contributions to the study of gambling and Las Vegas—and perhaps his tasty artisanal nut butters.

Schwartz received his bachelor's and master's degrees (anthropology and history) from the University of Pennsylvania and his Ph.D. in United States history from the University of California, Los Angeles. In addition to his current work as Associate Vice Provost for Faculty Affairs, he also teaches history at UNLV and speaks to a variety of groups on numerous topics, including "Seven Things You Should Know about Casinos" and "How Bugsy Blew It." He is also appreciated for his macaroons.

You can learn more about Schwartz's creative and professional work at dgschwartz.com.

Also by David G. Schwartz

Boardwalk Playground: The Making, Unmaking, and Remaking of Atlantic City

Grandissimo: The First Emperor of Las Vegas

Roll the Bones: The History of Gambling

Cutting the Wire: Gambling Prohibition and the Internet

Suburban Xanadu: The Casino Resort on the Las Vegas Strip and Beyond

As Editor

Tales from the Slot Floor: Casino Managers in Their Own Words

Tales from the Pit: Casino Table Games Managers in Their Own Words

Frontiers in Chance: Gambling Research Across the Disciplines

As Co-Editor

All In: The Spread of Gambling in Twentieth-Century United States

Gambling, Space, and Time: Shifting Boundaries and Cultures

Made in the USA
Middletown, DE
19 April 2021

37904767R00168